Michael G. Kenny

The Passion of
ANSEL BOURNE

Multiple Personality in American Culture

SMITHSONIAN INSTITUTION PRESS
Washington, D.C.   London

The paper in this book meets the guidelines for permanence
and durability of the Committee on Production Guidelines
for Book Longevity of the Council on Library Resources.

Letters in the William James Collection are quoted with
permission of the Houghton Library, Harvard University.
Other permissions are indicated in the Preface.

Library of Congress Cataloging in Publication Data
Kenny, Michael G., 1942-
The passion of Ansel Bourne.
(Smithsonian series in ethnographic inquiry; 5)
Bibliography: p. 217
Includes index.
1. Multiple personality—United States—History—Case
studies. 2. Multiple personality—Social aspects—United
States—Case studies. I. Title. II. Series.
RC569.5.M8K46 1986   616.85′236   86-60457
ISBN 0-87474-572-1
ISBN 0-87474-569-1 (pbk.)

British Library Cataloguing in Publication data is available.

Edited by Michelle K. Smith

Photo credits

Mary Reynolds, courtesy Crawford County Historical Society, Meadville,
Pennsylvania.

William James, courtesy Houghton Library, Harvard University.

Richard Hodgson, from M.A. DeWolfe Howe, *Semi-Centennial History of
the Tavern Club 1884-1934* (Cambridge, Mass.: Riverside Press, 1934).

Mrs. Piper, from Alta L. Piper, *The Life and Work of Mrs. Piper* (London:
Kegan Paul, Trench, Trubner, 1929).

Contents

"But I don't want to go among mad people,"
Alice remarked.
"Oh, you can't help that," said the Cat: "we're all mad here.
I'm mad. You're mad."
"How do you know I'm mad?" said Alice.
"You must be," said the Cat,
"or you wouldn't have come here."

Preface

IT IS DIFFICULT TO KNOW, when all is done, how a project began and what its sources were. Long ago, I suppose as an undergraduate, it occurred to me that the cross-cultural study of mental disorder could tell much about how the mind works. Later, with more exposure to anthropology, I realized how difficult such comparisons can be in practice. A dissatisfaction on my part with ethnocentric applications of Western psychological theories led to a spirited and continuing debate with more medically oriented researchers as to the relative adequacy of cultural/sociological versus bioreductionist explanations of apparently psychopathological conditions. My study of multiple personality brings the problem back home again.

In parallel with these developments I became interested in the philosophy of mind and the way in which supposed "psychological" states become registered in a public and hence culturally specific vocabulary. Here I owe a great deal to Professor Rodney Needham of Oxford University for showing me the path into this obscure area. Then there was William James, the philosophical problem of personal identity, and the issue of the phenomenology of self-experience. James was sensitive to the exotic permutations of personal consciousness and identity encountered in other cultures, and in apparently pathological conditions such as multiple personality. His largeness of spirit and own intriguing biography were in themselves an inspiration. Sacvan Bercovitch's study of the American "self" and its relation to Puritanism provided a then badly needed sense of the cultural continuities in my own society. Eugene Taylor's Lowell Lectures on the intellectual context of the "Boston School" of psychopathology were also quite valuable. Taylor (1983) has also taken note of James's 1896 Lowell Lectures on "exceptional mental states," a series distinguished by its characteristic eclecticism and broadminded use of comparative materials from a variety of cultures and times pertaining to such things as possession, witchcraft, and psychopathological conditions. Taylor has attempted to trace the background to

James's thinking on these matters and the sources he used in composing his lectures.

Edward Winter and William Watson attuned me to anthropology (also providing a dash of romanticism); Rodney Needham I have mentioned. Godfrey Lienhardt, also of Oxford, attempted to show (as William James had done in a different way) how exotic forms of experience may be communicated to members of a different cultural tradition. I would like to think that my own work is in the same spirit, even if the exoticism is of a more domestic variety.

With regard to the present work as such, my greatest debt is to the Harvard University Library system, specifically to the Widener, Houghton, and the Countway Medical. Mr. Richard Wolfe, Curator of Rare Books and Manuscripts at the latter, was extremely helpful in bringing to my attention materials related to two nineteenth-century cases of multiple personality ("Miss Beauchamp" and "B.C.A."); I quote this material with his permission. Jane Knowles, Archivist of Radcliffe College, was extremely helpful in bringing to my attention other aspects of the "Beauchamp" case. Mr. Richard Ilesevitch, Librarian of the Crawford County Historical Society in Meadville, Pennsylvania, put at my disposal letters and other memorabilia relating to another early case (Mary Reynolds); again, I quote with his permission and that of the Society. His assistant, Mrs. Stewart, showed me the town and sites related to the history of the Reynolds family. Ms. Christine Ruggere, then at the Library of the College of Physicians of Philadelphia, showed me more material relating to this case—which I cite with the permission of Mr. Thomas A. Horrocks, Curator of the Historical Collections of the College. Mr. Francis Dallett, Archivist of the University of Pennsylvania, provided material relating to Mary Reynolds's physician. Stanton Waterman, Louise Nichols, and Rose Downs Arnold provided valuable information pertaining to the Beauchamp case.

Dr. Arthur Kleinman of the Department of Anthropology at Harvard supplied me with a useful concept ("idiom of distress") that has proved applicable to the problem of multiple personality; I also thank him and Joan Kleinman for their hospitality. Lawrence Taylor, Susan Ward, Norman Buchignani, Laura Wolff, and Brenda Orser have read part of this book and made valuable criticisms and comments; John Whitworth arranged timely financial assistance. Naturally I owe a great deal to Daniel Goodwin and Felix Lowe of the Smithsonian

Institution Press whose interest and enthusiasm have helped to sustain mine; my editor, Michelle Smith, has been most helpful in pointing out stylistic obscurities and other gaffes. There are of course others whose support and friendship I gratefully acknowledge; I think particularly of Rita Wright, David and Louise Landy, Jane Niebling and Jeannie of the morale-boosting "Coffee Aroma" in Newburyport; also of Dan Bauer, Marilyn and Gary Gates, Noel and Iza Dyck, Gillian Feeley-Harnik, Eugene Bridwell, David Strug, Steve Sharp, and Gordon Bowden. Last and certainly not least are my old comrades William Arens and Ivan Karp (in the idiom of East African herding societies I would say that myself, Arens, and Karp were circumcised together, and therefore are brothers of a kind).

Finally, I would like to thank Simon Fraser University whose liberal sabbatical and leave policy made this possible.

Introduction

ONCE, IN AFRICA, I MET a man with four souls, only one of them his own. The others presented themselves as spirit-beings temporarily occupying his body; they spoke through him in succession, each with its own particular tone of voice and personal characteristics—the women in falsetto. He had encountered the supernatural at an early age, having been driven raving mad by spirit obsession. An oracle then instructed him how to enter into a more congenial and domesticated relationship with those who afflicted him, and this amounted to his cure.

The drama of possession is both puzzling and impressive, though I knew enough about anthropology and spirit-possessed states not be be overly taken aback by it. But a kind of philosophical bafflement remained upon which this book is based. How can it be, one asks, that a single physical persona seems to contain more than one distinct personality, each hermetically sealed off from the others? This contradicts our assumptions about the continuity and integrity of the individual and, when encountered, arouses sensations verging on the uncanny.

Possession has largely gone out of fashion in Western culture; yet we retain analogous states, certain psychiatric conditions that closely resemble it. I realized that what this African experienced is similar to the currently much discussed phenomenon of multiple personality, and so undertook an examination of the latter in order to understand in the light of comparative knowledge of other cultures how subjective experience comes to be shaped in the context of our own. So the quest began and what follows is its result. In the process I discovered that the relation between the study of multiple personality and that of possession states has been intimate and enduring. My inquiry—via investigation of a seemingly bizarre aberration—is into the nature of the creation of self-knowledge as a cultural process. As a result I was inevitably drawn into an examination of the history of the time in which the concept of multiple personality as we now understand it took form—into the fermenting nineteenth-century intellectual and social world that gave birth to contemporary medical psychology. In the end I found myself to be producing an account of nineteenth-century American social and intellectual history (more particularly that of New England) seen through the lives of certain individuals—among them cases of multiple personality still regarded as paradigmatic of the syndrome as a whole—who expressed in their very being some of their society's most salient symbolic oppositions and social contradictions: the institutional war between God and the Devil, between individualism and conformity, between conventional women's roles and the libertarian ethic of a new nation, between man as actor and woman as passive nurturer.

And multiple personality *is* an affair of contradictions, a given victim expressing radically incompatible tendencies through what appear to be quite separate personalities—at least one of which is seemingly unaware of the presence of its associates. Here again there is an analogy to be drawn with possession because, through their spirits, individuals may express the inadmissible, and in the process force others to think differently of them. Insofar as such stresses become reconciled, possession can achieve a kind of self-transcendence. The curative treatment of multiple personality aims at the same thing by different means: a fusion of warring tendencies, the creation of one unified person out of several fragmentary parodies of conventional social roles.

The anthropological literature on possession focuses upon the cosmological assumptions that give it meaning, on the way in which such extravagant behavior may alter personal circumstances, and on the therapeutic sociality of the possession cult. Possession may be seen as a political act—an implicit adaptive or manipulative strategy—and because of this the question of the degree to which such behavior is consciously motivated is something of a vexed one; there may be false prophets and true.[1] Of course the idiom of possession stresses the action of the spirits, not the intentions of the possessed: the possessed person is a victim, not an actor. Just so with multiple personality: it is a disease, a passively endured affliction demanding medical attention in the same way that possession demands oracular diagnosis and treatment. But here too there is the problem of intentionality and dissimulation, and the literature suggests that it is not one likely to go away easily. Multiple personality can also be a spectacular disorder and for that reason it has attracted a great deal of public interest and of late sparked a growth industry within the psychiatric profession that is reflected in an increased popularity of the disorder among patients. The question boils down in the end to a simple one: In what sense and to what degree is multiple personality genuine?

As with possession this is by no means easy to answer. The distinction between inner and outer worlds is a primary aspect of human experience, but culture has a say in where the boundary gets drawn. Though we deny the objective reality of the spirit world, possession is reinforced through whatever credence others are inclined to accord it and is real enough as a subjective fact. I will argue that multiple personality is a culturally specific metaphor, not a universally distributed mental disorder. Like possession it is a way of representing distress embedded in the circumstances of time, place, and culture; like possession it is reinforced by the willingness of others to accept its reality. I will not justify this claim now since its proof is one of the aims of this book as a whole. Here I merely point out that the disorder has discernible cultural origins both as a medical concept and as a mode of behavior. However, those who deploy the concept—and on the other side those who accept specialist word as to its validity—have little sense of its culturally unique qualities nor of its history within Western psychological thought; it is also one of my aims to restore this lost past, a process that in itself will greatly aid in reaching some kind of conclusion about the genuineness of the problem. We will enter a nineteenth-century world in which spiritism and determinist psychology offered rival explanations of a most unusual and conceptually subversive phenomenon.

It is curious that the most sensible things to have been said about multiple personality originate not with psychologists but with artists and literary critics. Like the anthropologist, their job is to deal in meanings—to explore through their treatment of character and theme the stresses and contradictions of a culture. For example, Jeremy Hawthorn's *Multiple Personality and the Disintegration of Literary Character* develops a model of personality formation that he hopes "will allow for the 'importation' of social contradictions into the individual as well as for their subsequent projection back into society."[2] I am in complete agreement with this, and in the pages to follow pursue the dialectical relationship between individual and society through my case studies.

But literary artists not only describe culture, they invent it. Among other things they render problems explicit that formerly may only have been sensed; they provide through their creative activity new means for the acquisition of self-knowledge. The popular literature on multiple personality itself seems to have this function, and it is interesting to note how frequently case studies have come to be presented to the public at large in novelistic form. Evidently there is a market to which this exotic problem has considerable appeal—perhaps because it speaks to contradictions that many experience in their own lives. Both doctors and patients have a tendency to wax rhapsodic when writing of their struggles and triumphs as though *this* malaise has its own distinctive beauty based on transcendence through suffering (though one critic justly observes that "from art's point of view clinical multiplicity is not very rewarding").[3] Contemporary therapists emphasize the treatability of multiple personality, but also the immense suffering on both sides that therapy often entails.

There is also a deeper cultural issue. Running through the literature on multiple personality are two mythological characters whose presence immediately evokes the Christian themes at issue here: Dr. Jekyll and Mr. Hyde. Such frequent reference to Robert Louis Stevenson's great parable reveals something important about multiple personality itself. Dr. Jekyll was a Victorian bourgeois—repressed, moralistic, philanthropic; Mr. Hyde, liberated through Jekyll's ingestion of a transformative drug, of course was his mirror image—vital, ferocious, egocentric. Together Jekyll and Hyde metaphorically represent the dynamic antinomies of a Christian culture divested of religion. What was formerly construed as a war within one soul between the cosmic forces of good and evil became in Stevenson's hands the war of a soul with itself, and here his fable perpetuates the literary tradition of nineteenth-century Romanticism. As Dr. Jekyll's drug became addictive, the good doctor was literally possessed by his antithesis, the tragedy of the story being that, even though the results horrified him, his undoing was the product of his own desire:

> The powers of Hyde seemed to have grown with the sickliness of Jekyll. And certainly the hate that now divided them was equal on each side. With Jekyll, it was a thing of vital instinct. He had now seen the full deformity of that creature that shared with him some of the phenomena of consciousness, and was co-heir with him to death: and beyond these links of community, which in themselves made the most poignant part of his distress, he thought of Hyde, for all his energy of life, as of something not only hellish but inorganic.

It would be difficult to call Sigmund Freud a Romantic, but in his own way he documented the same antinomies that so deeply concerned the Romantics and run as a theme through nineteenth-century literature into our times. It is far from accidental that Stevenson and Freud achieved comparable understandings of a soul divided, and that their period was the one that gave rise to the concept of multiple personality. The war between the Id and the Ego—which, anticipating Lévi-Strauss, Freud characterized as a struggle between Nature and Culture—is the conflict between Jekyll and Hyde translated into psychological language. As Freud put it, "we are 'lived' by unknown and uncontrollable forces," while a late-nineteenth-century case of multiple personality cried, "I am possessed by *something!*" (she knew not what, but her doctor would soon tell her).[4]

Psychologist and artist have a similar cultural role in that they document the tensions to which the people of a particular time are exposed; the difference between them is that one is represented as a scientist—objective, inductive, value free—a stance which, in the context of the study of multiple personality, I regard as merely ethnocentric. In fact, artist and psychologist are the creative fabricators of the metaphors through which we make sense of experience; as Victor Turner said, "metaphor is, in fact, metamorphic, transformative."[5] Subjective reality, since it contains little inherent testimony as to its own nature, inevitably seizes upon images drawn from the outside world. As one author on multiple personality writes, "there are few things left to which mental life has not so far been likened."[6]

But not just any metaphor will do; no matter how creative cultural innovators may be, they must use the material at their disposal. This is not creation *de novo*, but the reworking of old tradition under new circumstances. Nineteenth-century psychology and literary art gave us a revised sense of self—documented so richly by Karl Miller (1985)—constructed out of the venerable Christian dualisms that are manifest in multiple personality as symptoms. These dualisms, and an unconsciously dualistic mode of thought to which they give rise, comprise what Turner has called a "root paradigm": "Paradigms of this fundamental sort reach down to irreducible life stances of individuals, passing beneath conscious prehension to a fiduciary hold on what they sense to be axiomatic values, matters literally of life and death. Root paradigms emerge in life crises, whether of groups of individuals, whether institutionalized or compelled by unforeseen events. One cannot then escape their presence or their consequences."[7]

Most of my subjects *knew* themselves to be divided, sinful souls and like Jekyll, were tormented by their knowledge: the root paradigm that they expressed owes its existence, perhaps more than to any other source, to the *Confessions* of St. Augustine and, more proximately, to what Perry Miller has characterized as the Augustinian flavor of New England Puritan culture.[8] Augustine wrote that in his youth, "I became to myself an unfruitful land," a self-despising attitude that is a constant theme of Puritan autobiography.[9] Elsewhere Augustine contrasted the earthly and heavenly cities and made the dichotomy between them into an image of the soul divided. Sacvan Bercovitch in his superb *Puritan Origins of the American Self*, also documents the influence of Augustinian dualism on the Puritans and on American culture more generally, pointing out that the theme of self-versus-God became transformed into self as figure and reflection of American national identity.[10] The various personalities manifest in clinical multiplicity resemble nothing so much as internalizations of the Virtues and Vices of medieval Christian iconography; however, as we shall see, these are virtues and vices with a distinctly American flavor.

The Protestant soul has considerable schismatic potential— one rich in the symbolism of mental disorder. The self, the theologians reasoned, is to be denied because tainted by old

Adam's sin. Conversion—an essential requirement of the Puritan pietistic tradition—entailed recognition of one's utter worthlessness; again, the autobiographers consistently write of how they were granted a vision of God only in the moment of greatest despair and self-surrender. Paradoxically the self had to be lost so that it could be found—but some, I think, lost it permanently. As the eminent physician Benjamin Rush noted in 1812, overly great concentration on religious matters can predispose to madness.[11] Accordingly the title of my book is derived from the sufferings of a man—Ansel Bourne—who had the queer fortune to undergo a conversion widely regarded as miraculous, and later to encounter representatives of early modern psychology and through their agency to enter into the literature of multiple personality as a classic example of the syndrome. To this day the popular literature on this disorder is based on the theme of suffering and transfiguration, of a new self achieved through a Christlike passion pointing in the old Augustinian way to rebirth—to resurrection. Thus my choice of Bourne as a representative figure.

If this generic Puritan loathing of self were not in itself enough to generate a problem, the intellectual world of the late nineteenth century was also filled with profound unease about the nature, fate, and reality of the soul. Scientific materialism clashed with traditional religion; many uneasily sought a middle ground where they could retain elements of traditional belief while also accepting the findings of science. Nineteenth-century American society itself was undergoing profound structural change that deeply affected those who endured it.

Perhaps I should now briefly introduce my cast, indicating in doing so the period at issue here. First and perhaps foremost is one of the first fully described cases of multiple personality on record:

Mary Reynolds—1785–1854
Ansel Bourne—1826–ca. 1910
Lenora Piper—1859–1950
"Miss Beauchamp" (Clara Norton Fowler)—1876–ca.1960
"B.C.A." (Nellie Parsons Bean)—1864–1950

Mary Reynolds was a Pennsylvania farm girl; Ansel Bourne a Rhode Island itinerant preacher; Lenora Piper of Boston one of the most famous and credible Spiritualist mediums of the

nineteenth century; Miss Beauchamp and B.C.A., urban Massachusetts women at sea in a world of undefined possibilities.
The historical situations in which these persons found themselves were well suited for raising questions about the content
of the self: from 1811 when Mary Reynolds was first afflicted
to 1908 when the case of B.C.A. was published, the culture
underwent many changes; each of my subjects exhibited one or
another form of divided personality expressive of their time,
place, class, and intellectual culture.

The paradigms used to explain their fortunes have also
been various: eighteenth-century medical materialism, divine
intervention, possession by the spirits of the dead, the psychology of the unconscious. The persons who studied and reflected
on these cases are of equal importance to my story. Specialists
have an important role in the cultural creation of self-knowledge, though scarcely the only one. They are raised in the
milieu of a time, place, and class and like anyone else are drawn
more or less unknowingly behind changing circumstances; yet
they are in a position to articulate and change public perception through their power over knowledge via the media, professional journals, schools, universities, and popular culture at
large. Three such specialists—three friends, respectively a philosopher-psychologist, a neurologist, and a psychical
researcher—will frequently be encountered in the following
pages:

William James—1842–1910
Morton Prince—1848–1929
Richard Hodgson—1855–1905

They, no less than their subjects, were faced with the problem of the self as such—of a distinctly *American* self, a self
perfectible through striving—the inheritance of a rapidly
changing society still greatly influenced by its Puritan roots.
One of the consequences of this collective obsession was a
characteristic American phenomenon, a plethora of self-help
literature and self-help movements—of which I take the
popularly oriented literature on multiple personality to be a
latter-day expression. My colleagues Michael and Anita Fellman document this genre in their evocatively titled *Making
Sense of Self*.[12] Therapy, another American obsession, is an

attempt to *get* the self to make sense. In their different ways James, Prince, and Hodgson were trying to do just that.

The factors that I have mentioned thus far, coupled with the idiosyncrasies of individual situations, have considerable neurosis-generating potential—but how are the victims to express and conceive of the meaning of their unhappiness? Here I draw upon a concept originating in medical anthropology, that of the "idiom of distress."[13] Returning to the spirit-possessed African, one can readily see what this means. The disorder that he so very publicly advertised when he ran mad took a culturally specific form, as did its domestication into oracular possession. I do not know what precipitated his affliction, but the literature suggests that such episodes can be a response to a number of situational factors—overly high social demands, an unfortunate marriage, a marginal family position. Though the factors leading to distress may have certain common features across cultures, the mode in which the distress becomes manifest is local—hence the linguistic analogy of an idiom.

Possession precipitates search for a cure, sometimes entailing alteration of a total life-situation. Assuming a new self can have a certain strategic advantage; the creation of meta-personalities may overcome otherwise irreconcilable contradictions or situational doublebinds. Every society poses questions of identity and value that can lead to instability in the content of selfhood. Each society has its own points of stress at which such questions arise, but what counts as stressful is a function of what is locally defined as *of* value, and so is itself influenced by culture. Puritan neuroticism, for example, arose from a theology that defined the structure of the world—and of the self as its microcosm—in dichotomous terms requiring mediation through Christ. Perry Miller, taking note of their pietistic anguish, remarks that though "we may declare that Puritans universalized their own neurasthenia, they themselves believed that their fears and anxieties came from clear eyed perception of things as they are."[14]

In addition to such culturally specific sources of tension there are unavoidable transitions in any life in which the content of selfhood is in flux: becoming an adult, finding a place in the world, marriage, having children, facing death. Here society often provides rituals of the rite of passage type that define and clarify the nature of the situation; therapy has a ritual aspect insofar as it provides guidance for people in such situations. But since the self is a *social* construct—a system of shared ideas defining in advance what people are and should be— it is also subject to historical change. Such change can engender acute anxiety and the creativity associated with it. The establishment of an idiom of distress is also a social process which, like the concept of the self, should be seen in historical terms. I see "multiple personality" as such an idiom and seek to document its emergence and function. As will be seen, this idiom coexisted with others, supplanted them, was supplanted in turn, and now has returned for another round. The neurasthenia to which Miller refers was replaced by constructs based on the psychology of the unconscious, among them multiple personality; some modern theorists are inclined to believe that multiple personality was unjustly supplanted by the concept of schizophrenia and seek to revive the former.

An idiom of distress has a doubly significant role. It serves to articulate the inarticulate and bring the underlying problem— whether mental, physical, or both (and many societies make no clear distinction here)—into a public context where it can be dealt with by culturally appropriate means; it defines a problem and does so in terms expressive of current perceptions about the nature of the person in illness and health. But the idiom may also define the content of experience in advance of the fact, in effect creating the pattern of distress that the idiom specifies. "Split" or "multiple" personality, whatever its status as a mental disorder, has considerable metaphorical value as a gloss on the human predicament; this is why, both in the nineteenth century and at present, it attracts such public interest. The studies presented below are alive with metaphor and symbolism, to the degree that the boundaries between fantasy, art, dramatic performance, current social issues, and mental disorder become exceedingly indistinct.

I do not for a moment question the real distress of those who have become the reported cases of multiple personality— or the existence in some cases of a problem that must be considered genuinely pathological (especially now that some multiples have taken to criminal activity). But, as I have said, distress must be translated into culturally appropriate imagery for it to be subjectively comprehended and objectively dealt with. The metaphor of multiple personality is one means through which this can be accomplished; however, in a pluralistic society such as nineteenth-century America there tend to be contending and even mutually hostile alternatives.

The self can be seen as a collection of disharmonious "spirits" just as readily as of antagonistic personified psychological impulses. Robin Horton, for example, points out that West African soul beliefs have much in common with the quasi-personified entities of Freudian structural psychology.[15] My cases reflect a nineteenth-century equivocation about whether materialistic or spiritistic interpretations of strange psychic phenomena should be considered the more appropriate. William James, in his *Principles of Psychology*, noted that there are similarities between demonic possession, spirit-mediumship, multiple personality, and insane delusions; as did many of his time he asked himself why this should be so and what type of theory could best account for it; he found he could not discount the spirit hypothesis.[16] More recently, the contrasting possibilities of human nature are sought in the cerebral hemispheres: in the "left brain" or the "right brain," where respectively verbal analytical logic is held to be counterpoised to intuitive poetic synthesis—man opposed to woman. These things may be true—and investigation into the localization of psychic function is a legitimate and venerable area of study— but, again, there is a strong possibility that this too is an expression of old dichotomies translated into the idiom of a new age. Localization studies had much to do with establishing the credibility of the concept of multiple personality as such, but not much has subsequently come of the idea that alternate personalities haunt different parts of the brain. I think that what can at least be said is that every time has metaphors of mind appropriate to its own social needs and intellectual perceptions: its own ideas of just what has been split apart—since something certainly has.

If the current medical and popular literature on multiple personality is any guide, a process of conceptual redefinition is under way (discussed in the Conclusion) that is leading to a greater interest in this exotic syndrome and an increased readiness to accept it as a diagnosis by both the psychiatric profession and its clientele. Out of the great reservoir of silent misfortune, certain of the afflicted are coming to derive understanding of their inner contradictions from publicly well-known cases of multiple personality. Though it is statistically insignificant relative to other mental disorders, one recent paper speaks of a current "multiple personality epidemic." Certain patterns of representing distress have a fashionable quality. In the 1960s schizophrenia (with which multiple personality is often publicly confused) was much in vogue as a healing illness—the only sensible response to a mad society. Perhaps for a while multiple personality is to have its day once more.

Aberrant patterns of conduct such as multiple personality and schizophrenia *may* be symptomatic of an underlying medical disorder, but whether intentionally or not (and, as I have said, this can be a vexed question), they also carry a message even if no one intended to send it. The message reads: "*I* am this kind of person in this kind of situation; now what are *you* going to do about it?" (Multiple personality sends the message: "I am both this kind *and* that kind of person. Now what?") To the degree that a disorder—any disorder—follows a culturally prescribed pattern it must be construed as a symbolic display guided by prior assumptions on the basis of present need. Patients and doctors, for example, may come to be locked into a situation shaped by their mutual presuppositions about it, into an already formulated plot. The terms identifying states of disorder do not merely label reality—in some measure they create it.

Though its fortunes as a concept have fluctuated historically, multiple personality had a considerable formative role in the theoretical development of modern psychology. Given this, some remarks are in order about psychology itself, if for no other reason than that it is our implicit and explicit psychological theories that make multiple personality seem so peculiar. Here I draw upon Peter Berger's and Thomas Luckmann's observations on what they term "psychologies"—"theories about identity." In *The Social Construction of Reality* they point out that "theories about identity are always embedded in a more general interpretation of reality; they are 'built into' the symbolic universe. . . . If theories about identity are always embedded in the more comprehensive theories about reality, this must be understood in terms of the logic underlying the latter. . . . Put simply, psychology always presupposes cosmology."[17]

One can easily agree with this, and much anthropological work is currently going on into what have been termed "indigenous psychologies . . . the cultural views, theories, conjectures, classifications, assumptions and metaphors—together with notions embedded in social institutions—which bear on psychological topics. These psychologies are statements about the nature of the person and his relations with the world."[18]

Robin Horton, in his commentary on Myer Fortes's remarkable *Oedipus and Job in West African Religion,* proposes a cross-cultural investigation of what he calls "social psychologies"—ideas about the constitution and nature of the person as they relate to their practical social milieu, the context in which these ideas are applied in explaining human behavior and subjective experience. He suggests that such a study would involve "sketching the main organizational features of each society considered; showing how these features placed individual members in certain types of life-situation; showing how these types of life-situation gave salience to certain kinds of personal problems; and finally, accounting for the social psychology of the society in question as a response to these difficulties."[19]

The Western theory of multiple personality is an aspect of a "social psychology" in Horton's sense and I will explore this proposition through historically situated individual life-situations to which "psychological" knowledge has been applied. Multiple personality must be seen in terms of the logic that has drawn attention to it—in terms of the psychological assumptions that make it of interest.

But, on the other hand, the public at large has been drawn to multiple personality through the ability of specialists to enunciate the meaning of certain patterns of distress within the uniquely credible framework of positivistic science and through the singularly evocative power of the metaphor itself. Both disorder and the understanding of it therefore are aspects of a single cultural process. Berger and Luckmann suggest how it works: "If a psychology becomes socially established (that is, becomes generally recognized as an adequate interpretation of objective reality), it tends to realize itself forcefully in the phenomena it purports to explain."[20]

The point is that psychological theory, because it pertains to a largely ineffable inner life—to the definition of inner reality—is peculiarly well placed to inadvertently create the facts it is studying. Again the question boils down to a simple one: To what degree is multiple personality the product of a belief that it exists? This has been, and still is, much argued. My view is that, in the main, multiple personality is a socially created artifact, not the natural product of some deterministic psychological process. Once multiple personality became an object for psychological inquiry and entered into the literature as such, it attained the capacity to recycle back on reality, providing a new definition of the permutations of human nature—becoming by this means an idiom of distress that enhanced the metaphorical value it already had by virtue of its ability to map the tensions of the Protestant soul. I will document this as we proceed, but should now say something about the terms in which psychology has attempted to make sense out of multiple personality phenomena.

As I will show in the second chapter, the relevant psychological theories grew out of a combination of philosophy, evolutionary biology, and mesmerism. There are two central aspects to these theories—one static, one dynamic. The static concept is that of the "unconscious": the idea that beneath conscious awareness there exists a realm in which are stored memories, instincts, and perceptual processes that at least temporarily are out of reach of normal access. In its crudest formulation this realm became *The* Unconscious, a foreign nation within, a kind of psychic fifth column that has the capacity to affect consciousness only by indirect means such as the formation of neurotic symptoms. The dynamic process can be characterized as "dissociation" ("repression" being a variant thereof): that means by which material is consigned to the unconscious, or at least put out of sight, and kept there. Multiple personalities are "dissociated" to whatever degree they stand in isolation, as gauged by the degree to which they are mutually amnesic and have no knowledge or memory of their respective activities. It is only this amnesic separation, I might add, that makes multiple personality into a distinctive disorder at all; without amnesia the phenomenon would have to be subsumed under some other category or dissolved entirely.

A noted psychoanalyst, Henri Ellenberger, wrote of "the discovery of the unconscious," and documented the role of the concept of multiple personality in it.[21] This has proven an ambiguous discovery; with historical hindsight it is possible to speak, not of the "discovery" of the unconscious but of its *creation:* the creation of the unconscious as a cultural rather than a psychological fact. Modern dynamic psychology arose out of late-nineteenth-century intellectual dissatisfaction with physical interpretations of neurotic disorder. But also the times were changing. In this context the unconscious was a singularly appropriate device for the exploration of a world struggling to be born. "The unconscious" can serve as a metaphor for what is merely the ill-defined. Those who became the patients of the medical psychologists suffered from disorders to which they could not give words; their plight was a quest for meaning. The psychology of the unconscious allowed for the renegotiation of reality, and in this context should not be seen as science, but as science-fiction—a creative exploration of the gray area of an evolving culture. How this operated in practice in the therapy of multiple personality—and how neurotic distress reflected the tensions of the age—we shall see.

Late-nineteenth-century psychology contained a hidden agenda that emanated from issues of wider public concern, most particularly the position of women in the new urban industrial world. The contemporary study of multiple personality also has a hidden agenda that can be detected in the complex of issues to which the problem is connected. As in the nineteenth century, psychic dissociation leading to multiplicity is frequently attributed to trauma; however, now the focal point is childhood sexual abuse. The changes set afoot in the nineteenth century in the structure of the family and patterns of work are still running their course toward an uncertain future. The intense ambiguities currently found in relations between the sexes and in the attendant problems of sexual identity to which they give rise have spawned a series of interlinked concerns—sexual abuse, divorce, rape, drugs, abortion, pornography, homosexuality, prostitution, adolescent suicide. In short, multiple personality—though for many years superseded by other patterns of disorder—has again become part of a public issue, and in fact, through the case of "Sybil," has a significant role in generating the issue itself. It is interesting that, unlike the nineteenth-century norm, men are increasingly at risk of coming down with this disorder, and multiples are increasingly likely to contain stereotypic representatives of the sex opposite to the sex of the body they share. Another noteworthy feature of the modern scene is that, unlike the earlier cases where only a few personalities were found, now the average number reported seems to be at least ten; some cases are reported to have separate personalities or "personality fragments" (whatever this may mean) numbering in the hundreds. Perhaps this is the result of a radically fragmented society paralleled by a fragmented psychology; perhaps, as has been suggested, it merely is a function of covert competition between therapists. However this may be, it would appear that the protean metaphor of multiple personality is assuming new functions and articulating new problems.

Clearly there is much in the culture from which one would rather be dissociated; however, the concept of dissociation as it is used in psychology pertains not to this but to isolation of sections of the mind from one another. Dissociation is a rather complex idea that has been extended to cover the separation of virtually anything having "conscious" qualities from the normative consciousness we think ourselves to have when using the first person singular; as such, "dissociation" covers such things as unconscious problem solving, hypnotic amnesia, and —of course—multiple personality. Ernest Hilgard, proponent of "neodissociation theory" and much cited in the contemporary literature of multiple personality, states that "the dissociated systems can be identified as relatively coherent patterns of behavior with sufficient complexity to represent some degree of internal organization."[22]

In the case of multiplicity, the dissociated systems appear to be not only coherent but organized to such a degree as to be worthy of the term "personalities." As said, theory focuses upon the influence of trauma in generating this state of affairs; it is widely believed that dissociation leading to multiplicity frequently occurs in childhood as a response to intolerable stress, commonly abuse ("This isn't happening to *me*, but to someone *else!*"). Why this dissociation should lead to the formation of extra personalities rather than to some other avenue of escape is less than clear and will not worry me now; as presented in the literature the process seems quite magical. What is of immediate concern is the degree to which the various personalities are in fact separate from one another, and this brings me back to the crucial question of memory.

Since some of their phenomena are similar, hypnosis and the study of multiple personality have long been associated. Hypnosis can be used to produce states quite akin to multiple personality—articulated modes of action sealed from one another by an amnesic barrier. Furthermore, hypnosis has been the preeminent therapeutic strategy in dealing with multiple personality: the principal means for exploring the worlds of the separate personalities and ultimately for accomplishing their fusion. However, doubts have persistently been raised about the therapeutic use of hypnosis; if, it is reasoned, hypnosis can *create* phenomena like multiple personality then much care must be taken to ensure that, through giving license for still more florid behavior, its therapeutic use does not abet the problem it is supposed to solve. As William James warned, "one has to be on one's guard in this matter against confounding naturally double persons and persons who are simply temporarily endowed with the belief that they must play the part of being double."[23] And there is a running debate within psychology about the status of hypnosis itself—whether, for example, it should be construed as due to some sort of neurological process, or to "dissociation," or (a more seditious suggestion) to a covert negotiation of reality in the hypnotic situation.

Hilgard says that "despite all that is known about hypnotic amnesia, its mechanisms are elusive."[24] Though he also finds that "the unity of consciousness is an illusion," Hilgard's comment on amnesia and his general use of the concept of dissociation suggest a latent Cartesianism—an implicit belief in the centrality of the ego and its various psychic faculties such as memory. "Dissociation" implies dissociation *from* something. I do not wish to get involved in a discussion of the phenomenology of consciousness, and here only point out that "memory" is not a faculty—a psychic tool at the disposal of the ego—but an immanent aspect of all goal-directed activity that binds the task together in relation to its end. Precisely because of this immanent quality we are normally not aware of "remembering," and are only caught short when we *cannot* remember something. Memory is generally in relation to an activity, and hence to how an occasion is defined; for this reason memory is as much a social as a psychological fact.[25] The hypnotic situation is one in which strange experiences can be expected—hypnosis being by definition an altered state of consciousness. If memory of what occurs while under hypnosis is defined as impossible then there quite likely will be none: not because a record of what occurred is "dissociated" from consciousness, but since not situationally relevant it is not being *looked for.*

If hypnosis must be seen in social psychological terms, what then of multiple personality? If hypnosis can be used to bridge the gap between personalities, then can their separation have been any more real than hypnosis itself? When this question is coupled to the fact that, in many multiples, at least *one* personality claims to have continuous awareness of what the others are doing and memory for what they did—then it begins to seem that the question of memory is a red herring. Perhaps, so far as these cases go, both memory and amnesia should be seen as closely related to the social situations in which the various personalities are situated. Both as formal academic concepts and in our reflective commonsense understandings they should be seen as elements in a "psychology," a culturally specific way of defining the possibilities of human nature in terms of a theologically derived and morality-infested notion of the unitary ego—one of dubious cross-cultural relevance.

I HAVE ADVANCED A NUMBER OF CONCEPTS that will prove useful in the substantive chapters to follow. I have indicated the importance of factors abroad in the general culture of the American nineteenth century (The *American* Century, as Emerson called it). The influence of literature will prove uncommonly important in the understanding of my subjects— just as literature was important to them in attempting to understand themselves. I have also deployed anthropological concepts that will prove of analytical utility—"root paradigm," "idiom of distress," "indigenous psychology"—and have suggested that each of these concepts must be applied in its sociological context, in the living situations of real individuals and relative to the cognitive schemes that they apply to the interpretation of their experience.

What now remains is the task of breathing life into abstractions; before launching forth onto the changeable tides of nineteenth-century America, I briefly outline the chapters to follow in terms of the themes explored in this Introduction:

CHAPTER ONE

The subject of the first chapter is, appropriately, a study of one of the first cases of multiple personality on record, Mary Reynolds. This case clearly points out the difficulty of arriving at a firm opinion about the status of multiple personality as a mental disorder. There was no obvious psychological precedent upon which she could have modeled her strange behavior, and this would seem a prima facie argument for the independent existence of a natural psychological process leading to psychic dissociation in response to stress and to an articulation of alternate selves along lines established by the dissociation. However, I do not find the matter so straightforward, and I explore what happened to her through what is known of her religious and literary background; I show that cultural elements had a considerable influence on what she became, and indeed what she had to overcome to become it. In addition to published material I draw upon her unpublished and largely unknown letters, on an autobiographical memoir she left behind, on memories of her relatives, and on other historical material never before considered in regard to this case. In some wise Mary Reynolds knew what she was about.

CHAPTER TWO

The next chapter focuses on Ansel Bourne and I apply the reasoning of the previous chapter to him as well, particularly to the circumstances surrounding his miraculous conversion in 1857, three years after Mary Reynolds died. I show how a heritage of evangelical religion also influenced what befell him, the symbolism through which it occurred, and how Bourne's own life story contributed to it. In the interval between 1857 and the enigmatic appearance of an alter-self—A.J. Brown—in 1887, a great deal had changed in the intellectual world. The second part of the chapter outlines the growth of the concept of multiple personality in the mid to late nineteenth century, a development that led to the interest the specialists took in

Bourne and in the other benchmark cases of multiple personality, among which Mary Reyonds took her belated place. I show how, through an amalgam of empiricist philosophy, mesmerism, and evolutionary neuroanatomy, the concept of psychic dissociation and splitting became a central psychological theme, and how this development led to therapeutic practices based upon it. Bourne's encounter with the psychologists therefore is symptomatic of a general shift in the way the operations of the mind were conceived, one that led directly to contemporary dynamic psychology. Of particular interest is the increasing nineteenth-century recognition that social factors play an important role in psychological functioning, development, and the acquisition of self-knowledge.

CHAPTER THREE

Here I examine an important aspect of the multiple personality issue as it presented itself to the investigators of the 1890s: spiritism, in particular the hypothesis that certain normal and abnormal psychic phenomena closely resembling multiple personality (if not including it) are due to intrusion into the mind of external ethereal beings. The problem is outlined as it was then conceived, accompanied by a discussion of the folk religious movement called Spiritualism, which greatly affected late-nineteenth-century psychological research. Of greatest significance is the finding—by William James among others— that the apparent existence of the "spirits" is largely induced by social factors: by a predisposition to believe in them activated during ritual occasions such as the seance. This realization was part of the unfolding of a new sociocentric psychology—a "social psychology"—discussed at the end of chapter 2. I then deal with a specific case—that of Mrs. Piper, of her spirit "G.P.," and their mutual investigator, Richard Hodgson—which shows how this new social psychology was profitably applied to such apparently exotic phenomena. This study also evokes the cultural ambience surrounding psychological research in the 1890s when for many it was not implausible that the spirits are what they actually seemed to be and that various forms of psychopathology are due to their influence.

CHAPTER FOUR

This chapter reverts to multiple personality as such, to the cases known as "Miss Beauchamp" and "B.C.A." Here, because of Hodgson's influence and Miss Beauchamp's own knowledge of Spiritualism, spiritistic influences are still to be found; however, now the dominant theme is the materialistic idea of "multiple personality." Through Morton Prince's own writings on these cases, coupled with their heretofore unconsidered letters to him and what has been found out about their lives since their true identities came clear, it is possible to determine how and why these cases manifested themselves in the form of multiple personality. B.C.A., for example, left a revealing document—"My Life as a Dissociated Personality"— which Prince arranged to have published, and which shows how the distress B.C.A. was undergoing became convincingly translated into the idiom and symbolism of multiple personality. In her case (perhaps in that of Miss Beauchamp also) what she underwent was not the unveiling of a hidden dissociative neurosis but rather conversion to it. Conversion is only possible to something already halfway believed in. Moreover, I argue that the situation of women and the general cultural milieu of the time conspired to make multiple personality an acceptable interpretation of what B.C.A. and Miss Beauchamp experienced. It is shown, for example, that there were literary influences available that could easily have led to the view that much of life is hidden and possibly unconscious, and that women more than men have to hide their true selves. The approach here is much like that in chapter 3, though the phenomena were construed in a different light. It is shown that, like spiritistic visitation, multiple personality can be conjured into existence through mutual expectations and interaction based upon it.

CONCLUSION

The end of the previous chapter sets the stage for the Conclusion to the book. The findings about these case studies are applied to the contemporary state of affairs: to studies such as of "Eve," "Sybil," and their increasingly numerous kin (in these times we see the phenomenon of "multiplying personality"—first a few selves, then more and more in a race for a truly championship pathology). The theme of multiple personality has again aroused considerable literary interest and found a wide market in the mid to late twentieth century; in fact it is mainly through the literary genre of the popularized psychiatric case report that this presumptive "syndrome" has become so widely known and legitimated. The interaction between scientific and popular knowledge is always intriguing, no less so here. The literary genre is also worthy of consideration, and I

will make a few remarks on it as critic, thence concluding with
a reiteration of the path this work has traversed, what it has
accomplished, and what its theoretical implications are.

My subject may seem an exotic minor psychopathology.
Yet multiple personality casts light not just on the strange fates
of isolated individuals, but also on the inner workings of a
culture and a time. If selfhood becomes an explicitly problematical issue it is both important and illuminating to investigate
the cultural milieu out of which the problem arose: hence my
concern for the intersection of biography and the history of an
idea.

Freud held that the pathological illuminates the ordinary;
whatever the general truth of this proposition, it is true here. A
student of William James, George Herbert Mead, wrote that "a
multiple personality is in a certain sense normal."[26] By this he
meant that every self is a composite of social roles, some of
which may be mutually inconsistent. Therefore when we
encounter the phenomenon called "multiple personality" we
behold ourselves through the mirror of certain individuals facing acute identity problems in particular circumstances of culture, place, and time. The dichotomies that define the
contrasting possibilities of human existence live on, and take
the shape of the persons who have come to be called multiple
personalities. The nineteenth century had its Mary Reynoldses
and Ansel Bournes, the twentieth its Eves and Sybils. The old
metaphors retain their power to fascinate, mystify, and compel. The present work is a commentary on this power and an
attempt to demystify it.

BEYOND ALL THIS, HOWEVER, I WISH to evoke the atmosphere of
a time to which, as the present work developed, I acquired a
personal affinity. When it began I was living on Beacon Hill in
Boston, around the corner from where William James once
resided on Louisburg Square; I was only a few blocks from
Morton Prince's home and office on Beacon Street and from
Richard Hodgson's flat on Charles. Behind the activity of the
present I seemed to see the shadows of those who worked,
speculated, dreamed, and suffered here at the end of the last
century: Hodgson setting out for the offices of the Society for

Psychical Research, Miss Beauchamp making her anxious way to Prince's consulting room, Mrs. Piper giving sittings for the Back Bay gentry, Morton Prince discoursing to his clubmates on the wonders of the unconscious. I also came to have an affinity for the vitality and the intellectual purpose of that time, the sense that inquiry into the place of the mind in nature is of paramount human importance. It has refreshed me to occasionally drop back into what in some ways was a more sedate period, though of course one with its own problems and obsessions. This work is about other lives—and I admit to a taste for biography—but also it has been an important part of mine.

Through it I began to recapture the past of my own family and the national history to which it relates. When investigating Ansel Bourne and Mary Reynolds I also discovered Moses Kenny—the first known ancestor of my father's line; this first Kenny migrated from Massachusetts to Vermont in search of open land, and his bones lie in the family graveyard in Newfane, a short distance from where the foundation stones of his homestead can still be seen—the land that he and his family worked so hard to clear now given over to the trees which Vermont grows so much better than corn. One of his sons, Monis Kenny, a lawyer, was the first college-educated member of the family; his unusual first name was given to him in honor of a Sephardic immigrant, the Rabbi Judah Monis—first teacher of Hebrew at Harvard, converted to Congregational Christianity by no less than Increase Mather, Cotton's father. Then there was Moses's grandson and my great-grandfather, another Moses Kenny, who left Vermont for the less rocky lands of Michigan and there became a Free-Will Baptist preacher, part of the same religious tradition to which his contemporary, Ansel Bourne, belonged. Sacvan Bercovitch noted a tendency for Americans to relate their personal lives to an idealized history of their country, to embed one's very self in a national vision. It would appear that I have done the same.

Newburyport, Massachusetts
December 1985

CHAPTER ONE

Mary Reynolds: A Pioneer Case ⊚ of Multiple Personality ⊚

*Old things are put away; behold all things are
become new.*
—2 Corinthians 5:17

To record the history of multiple personality in America
one must go back to a time familiar yet strange, of revolutions
political, scientific, and industrial, of Thomas Jefferson and
Tom Paine, of the greatest diaspora the world has known—the
settling of North America—and of an extraordinarily potent
ideology matched to an unsettled New World. The idea of
liberty is both pregnant and ambiguous, infinitely adaptable
and profoundly unclear: Freedom from what; from all social
constraints, or merely from oppressive political systems? And
for what; for individual interest—the untrammeled expression
of personality—or somehow for the common good? These are
questions that render selfhood problematical and that in
America make freedom such a perennially unsettling issue.
Couple this libertarian ethic with the heritage of evangelical
Christianity—with its anxious soul-searching, its dualisms,
and its messianic fervor—and one senses the powerful
dynamic of the American vision quest. Consider its expressions: the great revivals, the Revolution, the utopias of the
1840s, the antislavery crusade, Manifest Destiny, women's
rights, world salvation—"the last best hope of earth." Consider also its correlates: the expansion of population, the beginnings of Catholic immigration, the new industries and
their demand for labor, the growth of cities, the Civil War, the
closing of the frontier. This then is the intellectual and

25

social context of the nineteenth-century American search for
self-identity, here seen through the lives of certain individuals
who have been called multiple personalities: the first is Mary
Reynolds, who incarnated the paradoxes of liberty.

———————◄•●•►———————

THE WESTERN ALLEGHENY FOOTHILLS are dissected into claustro-
phobic, isolated sections by deeply cut stream valleys, beyond
which are the open spaces of Ohio. A certain amount of history
occurred here. There were the wars against the French and
Indians; Washington passed through in that cause. With the
good eastern lands filled, new settlers naturally were attracted
westward, as were speculators seeing much profit in the fact;
one group of interested parties obtained the so-called Holland
Purchase around Meadville, Pennsylvania. As the eighteenth
century turned toward the nineteenth, the population was
expanding and the towns slowly attaining a degree of civility.
William Reynolds turned his attention this way; because he did
a doctor from the East came to hear a very peculiar tale and this
chapter came to be written.

The first detailed report of the medical phenomenon that
came to be called "multiple personality"—that of Mary
Reynolds—appeared in 1816 in the *Medical Repository* of
New York. Because this was, in the view of many, the prototypical case of multiple personality, it should be expected to
exhibit this "syndrome" in pure culture unaffected by advance
commitment to theory and therapeutic practice; in fact it
reveals the ambiguity that has affected this issue from the
beginning. This is how it was originally described:

> When I was employed, early in December, 1815, with several
> other gentlemen, in doing the duty of a visitor to the United
> States Military Academy at West Point, a very extraordinary
> case of *double consciousness*, in a woman, was related to me
> by one of the professors, Major Ellicot, who so worthily occu-
> pies the mathematical chair in that seminary, vouched for the
> correctness of the following narrative, the subject of which is
> related to him by blood, and, at this time, an inhabitant of one
> of the western counties of Pennsylvania.
>
> Miss R___ possessed naturally a very good constitution,
> and arrived to adult age without having it impaired by disease.
> She possessed an excellent capacity, and had enjoyed fair

opportunities to acquire knowledge. Besides the domestic arts and social attainments, she had improved her mind by reading and conversation, and was well versed in penmanship. Her memory was capacious, and stored with a copious stock of ideas.

Unexpectedly, and without any kind of forewarning, she fell into a profound sleep, which continued several hours beyond the ordinary term. On waking, she was discovered to have lost every trait of acquired knowledge. Her memory was *tabula rasa;* all vestiges, both of words and things, were obliterated and gone. It was found necessary for her to learn every thing again. She even acquired, by new efforts, the arts of spelling, reading, writing, and calculating, and gradually became acquainted with the persons and objects around, like a being for the first time brought into the world. In these exercises she made considerable proficiency.

But, after a few months, another fit of somnolency invaded her. On rousing from it, she found herself restored to the state she was before the first paroxysm; but was wholly ignorant of every event and occurrence that had befallen her afterwards. The former condition of her existence she now calls the *old* state, and the latter the *new* state; and she is as unconscious of her *double* character as two distinct persons are of their respective separate natures.

For example, in her old state she possesses all her original knowledge; in her new state only what she has acquired since. If a gentleman or lady be introduced to her in the *old* state, and *vice versa;* and so of all other matters. To know them satisfactorily, she must learn them in *both* states.

In the *old* state she possesses fine powers of penmanship; while, in the new she writes a poor and awkward hand, having not had time or means to become expert.

During four years and upwards, she has undergone periodical transition from one of these states to the other. The alternations are always consequent upon a long and sound sleep. Both the lady and her family are now capable of conducting the affair without embarrassment. By simply knowing whether she is in the *old* or the *new* state, they regulate the intercourse, and govern themselves accordingly.[1]

Thus, Mary Reynolds entered into medical history through a descriptive account influenced by the English philosopher, John Locke, whose fundamental idea was that the mind is like a blank slate (*tabula rasa*) upon which experience of the world impresses its record. What it all meant the writer did not attempt to guess, but that it was somehow significant he did not doubt. The constitution of the self, the anatomy of the soul, is a preoccupation as old as philosophical speculation. In the seventeenth century Locke himself pondered the issue, asking himself what it is that gives us a continuous sense of personal identity: his answer was—memory. Without memory there can be no personal self, merely a number of fleeting states without any integral connection to one another. Hence, when nature provided specimens such as Mary Reynolds, philosophical instruction was to be found in the fact. Here was a woman who had become a *tabula rasa* in *adulthood*, and obliged because of it to constitute a new self through reeducation. Once done, however, she periodically reverted to her old self. The two remained separate—and in so doing illuminated Locke's proposition—because one, the first, had no memory for the activities of the other.[2] It was indeed as though two souls inhabited the same body—precisely the diagnostic criterion for multiple personality.

The above account, though generally accurate, neglects to point out that the original self that Mary Reynolds lost was conventional, pious, and according to the second, really quite dull. The second self that she acquired was gay, irresponsible, and mischievous—everything the first was not. This oppositional quality of the respective personalities would prove another recurrent feature of this phenomenon.

Mary Reynolds was indeed a pioneer, and the trail she had inadvertently blazed was followed by others into the depths of the unconscious. In the 170 years or so since she first came to public notice, her case has been subject to differing interpretations reflective of the evolution of psychological theory in general: from eighteenth-century medical materialism, to late-nineteenth-century neurology, psychical research and occultism, to twentieth-century psychoanalysis and its descendants. I will sketch this evolutionary course in the next chapter and show something of Mary Reynolds's role in it. But the very fact that she has been made to serve so many theoretical gods leads to a sense of anachronism, a feeling that the real person has escaped our comprehension, that theory has overwhelmed the truth. Therefore we must return to her world and begin again.

Happily, because Mary and her relatives left letters and other memorabilia that have not been consulted before, it is possible to do so; these new sources, in combination with the published material and what is known of her family and general circumstances, lead to a more complex view of her case than was possible hitherto.

Mary's fate was closely intertwined with the political and religious history of her country. Hers was a family ready for the new land and its great republican experience. Her parents were William Reynolds and Lydia Thomas Reynolds of Birmingham, England, where Mary was born in 1785. By the time the Reynolds family emigrated to America there were seven other siblings ranging in age from twenty-five to nine. Mary was the second oldest and much attached to her senior brother John.

William Reynolds had been a grocer in Birmingham and was a Baptist; his wife was the daughter of Joshua Thomas, also a Baptist and author of a number of historical and theological works in Welsh, sufficient to earn him articles in the British *Dictionary of National Biography* and its Welsh equivalent; he was remembered as a great evangelist, as a "true Calvinist," and as a historian of the Baptist cause in Wales.[3] During the last part of their stay in Birmingham, William and his family attended the theologically Calvinist Cannon Street Baptist Church under the Rev. Samuel Pearce.[4] It was remembered that "with the coming of 'the seraphic' Pearce to Cannon Street Church in 1790, a new spirit of fervent evangelistic zeal stirred and quickened the Baptist community of Birmingham."[5] The picture that emerges of William's family and class is one of earnest evangelicals with numerous intellectual and cultural interests belying their relatively humble trades and spilling over into anti-establishment political opinions.[6] The latter, in combination with an unpopular dissenting stance in relation to the Church of England, precipitated the departure for America, for they ran afoul of the Birmingham anti-Jacobin "Church and King" riots of 1791, aimed primarily at the Unitarian clergyman and natural philosopher Joseph Priestley—discoverer of oxygen.

Priestley was sympathetic to the French Revolution (the American also) and an active propagandist for the rights of Dissenters, with consequences he remembered as follows: "On occasion of the celebration of the anniversary of the French

Revolution on July 17, 1791, a mob encouraged by some persons in power, first burned the meeting house in which I preached, then another meeting house in the town, and then my dwelling house, demolishing my library, apparatus, and, as far as they could, every thing belonging to me. They also burned, or much damaged, the houses of many Dissenters, chiefly my friends."[7]

Certain Baptists were a target of the mob, among them William Reynolds:

> Removed in regard to religious views as far as possible from all sympathy with Dr. Priestley, William Reynolds, his fellow townsman, was a personal friend and in sympathy with him in his views on state and church establishments. This made him . . . obnoxious to the royalists and upholders of the established church of England. His advocacy of republican liberty and liberty of conscience brought him to poverty. . . . He declared that as he could not in peace hold the views he did hold, and express them, too, in England, he would remove to America where he could have his rightful liberty in these matters.[8]

John Reynolds recorded his own childhood memories of the riots and of how the family was temporarily dispersed in 1794 prior to their emigration. He and Mary (now nine) were sent to their maternal grandfather, Joshua Thomas, in Leominster while their parents went on across the sea. It can be supposed that the two eldest Reynolds children were already close to one another because the other children were sent elsewhere. It is at Leominster that we have our first view of Mary— already a clever young person—in the form of a letter sent by Thomas to a daughter and son-in-law he would never see again:

> You are thinking of the children. But endeavor to commit them constantly to Him that is able to take care of them only alone. . . . The two that are here are very promising for usefulness in America. . . . John is diligent at his latin and figures, and seems to have a good head on both. Mary began to write about a month ago and comes on very well for her time. She spells and reads likewise, and is very promising at whatever she puts her hand to. Is ever ready at business in the house. . . . Mary's first writing book was but six sheets, and she has six leaves of it you to write. I think she improves very nice. The leaf she wrote today is inclosed instead of a letter (to

Lydia Reynolds, September 13, 1794; alas, Mary's writing lesson is lost).

Mary and John made the crossing in 1795 and rejoined their parents in Lansingburg, New York, where William had again started a grocery business. This speedily failed for want of capital, and in 1797 he took up an offer of unbroken wilderness land in western Pennsylvania on Cherrytree Creek near Oil Creek—in the 1850s the site of the first great American oil boom. There on Cherrytree Creek the grocer became a farmer; John Reynolds evocatively describes the difficulties they labored under and the improbability of their fate:

> A sudden transition from all the comforts incident to home, kind friends with whom to hold social intercourse, church blessings, with all the nameless privileges of refined civilization to the dismal unbroken forest that then covered Cherrytree, within which no man dwelt. Occasionally the Indian hunter visited it. There the nightly howl of the wolf, at times the scream of the panther, and the rattling terror of the snake. Here God in his wise providence, set the bounds of my father's habitation thenceforward.[9]

The female side of the family was exposed to conditions as yet unimagined and, for eighteenth-century English city people, probably unimaginable: "Woman had her full share in the privations and discomforts of life, as also in the labours incident to the beginning of a home in this desolate region. No wonder that on her first introduction to the log cabin in the forest, her heart sank within her; and when the child [Mary?] asked, 'Mother, is this home?' she replied by a gush of tears, unable otherwise to answer. All the sweet memories of friends far distant, of church associations, of the thousand nameless comforts of former home ties, would, in contrast make the present moment inexpressibly painful."[10]

This therefore was the strange New World to which Mary Reynolds was introduced at age twelve, a long way from Birmingham and, from the perspective of Cherrytree, even the city's nearest kin—Meadville, the Crawford County seat, some twenty-five miles to the west near the Ohio border between Pittsburgh and Lake Erie.[11] John Reynolds recalled that, alone on Cherrytree, he heard a wolf one Sabbath while reciting these lines from the evangelical poet, William Cowper:

But the sound of the church going bell
These valleys and rocks never heard.[12]

Cowper was obsessed with his sinful self and wrote powerful allegorical poems of lost and divided souls seeking unity
through Christ. The quoted poem, imaginary reflections of a
man stranded on a desert island, expresses what Mary's attitude would come to be toward Cherrytree where, on a later
Sabbath, she was struck blind:

I am monarch of all I survey,
My right there is none to dispute,
From the centre all round to the sea,
I am lord of the fowl and the brute.
O solitude! Where are thy charms
That sages have seen in thy face?
Better dwell in the midst of alarms,
Than reign in this horrible place.

Mary's original temperament seemed to match that of the
desolation in which she found herself:

Mary's natural disposition tended to be melancholy. Her spirits
were low. She never gave herself to mirth, but was uniformly
sedate and thoughtful. Was reserved, had no need of company,
but on the contrary avoided it—was very fond of reading; and
her favorite book was the Bible, to read and meditate on which
she was very fond of retiring to some secluded place, where
she would not be exposed to interruption. She was much
engaged in prayer and devotional exercises and was to all
human appearances, decidedly pious.[13]

Solitude, wilderness, piety, and poetry were the principal
elements in Mary's life at the time. It is known that she also
read Cowper and, if she had studied him carefully, would have
assimilated a disdain for self consistent with her evangelical
religious tradition, but also a sense that Nature contains the
self's salvation. On a spring Sunday in 1811 it all began. How to
interpret what happened as she was transformed? Here it is best
to use her own voice. In what follows I juxtapose outside
accounts of the several phases she passed through in the course
of her transformation with extracts from Mary's letters, which
show what she herself experienced while doing so. I will then
return to the symbolism they contain and the social circumstances that conditioned the whole affair.

When she had reached about eighteen years of age she became subject to occasional attacks of "fits." Of the exciting cause and precise character of these no reliable information can be attained. . . . One Sunday in 1811, when she was about nineteen years of age, she had an attack of unusual severity. She had taken a book and gone into the fields, at some distance from the house, that she might read in quiet. She was found lying in a state of utter insensibility. When she recovered her consciousness, she was blind and deaf, and continued in this state for five or six weeks. The sense of hearing returned suddenly and entirely; that of sight more gradually, but in the end perfectly.[14]

I once thought that I should never look upon my dear friends any more nor hear the sound of their voices again. What a gloomy thought that was to me. But oh my dear Brother how good the Lord as [sic] been to me even to the unworthiest of all his creatures. He might have left me to have spent a long life in darkness never more to behold the light of the sun. He would have been a just God still—while I was blind I often thought of those words of Sollomon [sic] where he says truly the light is sweet and how pleasant a thing it is for the eyes to behold the sun —it was a pleasing sight indeed to me the first time I saw it after 5 weeks of total darkness (to John Reynolds, June 17, 1812?).

A more remarkable dispensation of Providence, however, awaited her. A little before the expiration of twelve weeks, one morning, when she awoke, she appeared to have lost all recollection of every thing, in a manner, she ever knew. Her understanding, with an imperfect knowledge of speech, remained; but her father, mother, brothers, sisters, and neighbors, were altogether strangers to her. . . . She, however, presently began to regain various kinds of knowledge. She continued five weeks in this way, when suddenly she passed from this *second* state into her *first*. All consciousness of the five weeks just elapsed was totally gone, and her original consciousness was fully restored. . . . From the spring of 1811, the subject of this address has been in this wonderful condition, frequently changing from her *first* to her *second*, and from her *second* to her *first* state. More than three quarters of her time, she has been in her *second state*.[15]

Sometimes I fear that I shall lose my recollection altogether never to return again—but I am in the hand of a merciful God who is able to restore me to the former use of my reason. I have great need to be thankful that I have some intervals of recollection, a blessing which many of my fellow mortals are deprived of. . . . Oh if it were the Lords will once more to restore me to the full use of my reason how thankful I should be. But may I be enabled to say that it is the Lord. Let him do as seemeth to him good. My afflictions are great but not so great as I deserve (to John Reynolds, January 15, 1812).

In her natural state, she was quite destitute of the imaginative faculty; in her abnormal, or second state, her imagination was remarkably active & discovered itself, among other ways, in a disposition to write poetry, in writing which, though her poetical effusions were not of a high order, she was very ready. . . . In her natural state she was quiet, sedate, sober minded, tending to melancholy; in her abnormal she was cheerful, even immoderately gay and frolicksome in spirit, fond of fun & practical jokes, ardent in her friendships, strong in her dislikes, extravagantly fond of society.[16]

According to promise I now write a few lines to your Britanic Majesty to let you know that I am waiting very impatiently for the day to arrive when I shall once more sport in the Sunshine of pleasure and where the peacefull [sic] hours of contentment will glide smilingly away—he-he-he-he—then the spark which now is only glimmering in the socket will burst forth in all its brilliancy (to John Reynolds, November 21, 1813).

Knowing that you have a heart formed for sympathy I know you will sympathize with your disconsolate Mother—I have at last arrived among the Nocturnal Shades. This is truly the dominion of solitude, too dreary for the roam of a hoary Hermit or the cell of a gloomy Monk—the weary traveler when he enters, instead of expatiating with delight, looks round with horror and like a Mountain-Oak shattered by flaming bolt trembles at every blast that blows—this my dear child is the present abode of your Mother.

> Here Jupiter his sceptre sways
> And sternly o'er his subjects
>   gaze
> The sun withdraws his light
> His splendor here is seldom
>   seen
> A subtle cloud oft hangs
>   between
> Black as Egyptian Night

(to Eliza Haslet, December 18, 1816)

Mary's affliction had three phases: the first was hysterical blindness and deafness preceded by obscure "fits"; the second was transformation into a new and radically different state during sleep (and occasionally back again); the last was stabilization into her mature, or "third" state. Each phase reveals something about her, her culture, and the social background to what occurred. Her course toward viable adulthood, the process that William James would describe as "straightening out and unifying of the inner self," was accomplished circuitously, but accomplished it was.[17]

The three-phase sequence to what occurred is itself illuminating, resembling as it does a rite of passage, a type of ritual that publicly announces a change of role or status: separation from the community, an intermediate period in which "wild" or asocial attributes are sometimes assigned to the initiate, and a final reincorporation to society on a new basis. Illness separates—particularly so if it is construed as insanity, which by definition entails isolation of the victim from normal canons of social behavior. Mary's hysteria accomplished this nicely, while the manic qualities of her second state effectively functioned to keep her in an intermediate condition: normal enough to remain on the edges of society without incarceration, yet wild enough to allow the negotiation of a new role in life. With a new persona in hand she slowly settled into a normal and useful position within the community, one in some measure consistent with secret desires I believe her to have had all along.

The degree to which this transformation was the unconscious product of a causally explainable psychological process is an interesting question. She did not (I believe) simply invent her madness as a tactic to force others to think differently of her. If the observations of her relatives and the hand-wringing piety of her first-state letters are to be taken seriously, her distress was real enough. But this is not quite the same thing as saying that it was pathological. Rather, I see it as the result of a particularly acute contradiction between her desires and her circumstances and between these desires and a Christian ethic of female self-sacrifice; this formidable combination was at first translated into the traditional hysterical idiom of female distress. I say "hysterical" because there is no sign whatever in Mary's later life of any neurological disorder that might have conditioned her illness. Of course this is interpretation, but I hope to establish its plausibility; my own view is that her hysteria (and that of others like her) amounted to "time out" from a stressful and probably inherently contradictory situation. The next stage, the emergence of her second self, is more interesting, less conventional, and also more obscure; yet there are indications within Mary's general culture of where such an intriguing character could have come from. I now explore these issues, beginning with her original hysterical blindness and moving on to what took place on the supposed *tabula rasa* of her mind once its original occupant had temporarily been erased.

———————

PSYCHOGENIC BLINDNESS LASTING FIVE WEEKS is certainly extraordinary; but it should be remembered that Mary Reynolds was the daughter of a family of evangelical Baptists. Blindness is itself a powerful Christian symbol, and a prototype for it occurs in the Acts of the Apostles with the conversion of St. Paul who, on the way to Damascus, was struck down by a Lord he had denied. Mary, we have seen, was fond of reading— her favorite book being the Bible. One Sunday she had gone out to a favorite solitary spot to read and failed to return.

> And Saul arose from the earth; and when his eyes were opened, he saw no man; but they led him by the hand, and brought him into Damascus. And he was three days without sight, and neither did eat nor drink (Acts 9: 3-9).

There was much hysteria in Mary's religious milieu: much in her Protestant culture on which a transformational experience—however unusual—could have been modeled. For the pietistic evangelical wing of Anglo-American Protestantism, conversion signified union with Christ subjectively experienced as an inwash of overpowering grace accompanied by visions or other physical signs that leave the self radically transformed in their wake. The Baptist faith requires adult baptism, but considers such baptism to be legitimate only following a conscious conversion experience publicly attested to. One can scarcely be a fully accepted member of the community of the Baptist faithful *without* such an experience and such testimony.

However, Mary's conversion went in the wrong direction —for the new self of her second state, instead of being a reborn Christian pietist, was a pagan daughter of Nature. Nonetheless her relatives still found it natural to apply religious imagery to what had happened. Mary's nephew, borrowing the language of conversion to describe its opposite, said, "in one sense, 'old things had passed away, all things had become new' (if I may be allowed the use of a scripture phrase)." He believed that there was *something* supernatural about what had befallen her: "Now the phrenologists say my bump of superstition is very small, and certain I am, I have from my earliest childhood laughed at the idea of witches, ghosts, and hobgoblins. . . . I offer no solution other than—superintending Providence. And certainly Providential interference in her behalf, is . . . manifest in . . . many particulars. . . . Indeed, a particular interference, is manifest throughout her whole history.[18]

Mary's Protestant culture set up the conditions for this strange twist, and the frontier revivalistic milieu of western Pennsylvania may well have set up the conditions for the form it took. As was mentioned, Mary's father was a Calvinist Baptist. Once in Pennsylvania, the Reynolds family, faced with a local insufficiency of Baptists, gravitated to the also Calvinistic Presbyterians; in the early days William Reynolds served as lay preacher and was often host to traveling evangelists. Mary's Presbyterian clergyman nephew, with whom she spent her last years, attended out of natural affinity the college at Princeton, which supplied the frontier with many of its early missionary-evangelists and had once given its presidency to the great empiricist philosopher and Calvinist theologian Jonathan Edwards.

Since the first "Great Awakening" of the 1740s—which Edwards himself helped stimulate—other revivals rolled in waves through the settlements of British North America accompanied by extravagant mass scenes of fits, faintings, and ecstatic testifying, which some attributed to the spirit of the Lord, others to the influence of the Devil. Though Mary's sophisticated family were no frontier ecstatics, their Calvinistic theology emphasized the experience of conversion as the only subjective evidence of true sanctification. In this theological context they were exposed to the emotional outbursts characterizing much religion along the western pale of settlement.

"Countless revivals spread through the settlements [of western Pennsylvania] from the 1780s into the early nineteenth century, spurred on by preachers educated at the 'log colleges' or at Princeton."[19]

John Reynolds recalled that "during those years the great revival of religion which spread over a large part of the western country, extended through these northwestern counties of the state, attended, as elsewhere, by the phenomena of spasmodic bodily action."[20]

In one western revival around 1800, mass meetings were accompanied by the "falling exercise" in which great numbers of the devout—and less than devout—fell to the ground comatose. One young woman was reported to have been in that condition for three weeks. Persons affected in this manner were first observed to pay close attention to the preaching, after which "a twitching or yerking [*sic*] seizes them, and they fall to the ground helpless, and convulsed through their whole frame as if in the agonies of death."[21]

Now, it is difficult to say whether Mary Reynolds saw things such as this personally but I think it improbable that she did not; she must at least have known of them through hearsay or theological works on the subject. Since she was by her own lights a great (if not the greatest) sinner, she was also worthy of great suffering—and she got it, great religious travail being a specialized form of narcissism. Transformation into her second state took place not only during sleep, but also as a result of what might be called, to pervert a phrase, "conversion hysteria":

> Her body would become stiffened out and rigid so that there
> was no yielding of joints and muscles and all life seemed
> extinct. This was succeeded by nervous trembling, so violent as
> to shake the whole bed. . . . Then her mind would commence
> wandering. . . . Her agony was so great as to draw tears from its
> witnesses. In such cases strong plasters of mustard mixed with
> vinegar were applied to the soles of her feet and she was daily
> cupped on the temples which remedies brought relief and final
> recovery. When she recovered she was in her second state. All
> life and vivacity—fun and company.[22]

Mary, by her own account, was greatly influenced by preaching—such that, as her nephew testified, her doctor was obliged to prescribe abstinence from churchgoing: "She would go to Church, until expressly forbid by the Dr. as she generally was seized with trembling and flightiness as the result of the excitement which singing never failed to produce."[23]

Mary herself knew full well the dramatic effects a clergyman can have on his congregation and indulged her newly found skills at versifying in describing them: "I was very fond of going to meeting, and could repeat without any difficulty a great part of the discourse. My friends have said, that my remarks upon some parts of the subjects would be very just, but sometimes rather singular. I had at times some very airy flights of fancy."[24]

> Pray say Mr. Editor [she wrote], what will be best
> To strengthen the nerves of your friends in the West
> They've become so elastic, of such delicate texture
> It unstrings them to look at a Clergyman's gesture.
>
> Some nerves are excited, when the sins of the nation
> Are brought into context, it raises their passion
> The disease of the nerves must sure be contagious
> Else why would a Christian become so outrageous.[25]

All of this was of course very puzzling, and her family did the sensible thing: they called the doctor. Mary's case was not treated in terms of religion or left to stand as an inexplicable affliction, but was forcefully attacked by the orthodox medicine of the day—in the person of Dr. Daniel Bemus, the Meadville physician. Not being aware that he had a case of "multiple personality" on his hands, which for posterity would have made him famous as the describer of one of the most unusual psychopathologies known, he proceeded to deal with Mary Reynolds in terms of what he had learned from his own great teacher: Dr. Benjamin Rush, a signer of the Declaration of Independence, friend of Thomas Jefferson, active participant in Benjamin Franklin's American Philosophical Society, and diligent medical researcher into alcoholism, yellow fever, and —above all—mental illness.

Dr. Bemus was a product of the University of Pennsylvania in Philadelphia, a town noted for its doctors; the university archives show that in 1807 he was "assistant in surgery" to Rush.[26] Benjamin Rush in turn had received his medical training before the Revolution, in Scotland, then the major center

for medical education in the British Isles. While there he speculated about the origin of mental diseases and came to the conclusion that they are due to irritated cerebral blood vessels.
Back in Pennsylvania he applied these theories to his patients
and addressed systematically both the classification of mental
disorders and their treatment. The result was his *Inquiries
upon the Diseases of the Mind* (1812), which was much
reprinted and is the basis for his present standing as father of
American psychiatry; the American Psychiatric Association
incorporated Rush's profile in its logo. Though Rush's medical
theories were mechanistic, what he arrived at in practice was an
eclectic melange of physical and psychological methods of
treatment. Physical treatments, however, had pride of place
and, through Bemus, Mary Reynolds was their beneficiary.

She was treated consistently with what Rush advised for
mania and derangement in the memory. Disorder of the memory was obvious given the amnesia Mary's first state had for the
doings of her second; that Bemus also regarded her as manic
there can be little doubt, since her early second-state letters, as
the following extracts show, easily enough give that impression
even now.

> My dear old father had like to have illuminated the house a
> few minutes ago with his wig for it had almost caught fire he-
> he-he-he and Mother is gone to bed to keep her old man's back
> warm. She desires her best respects . . . but is very sick. I sup-
> pose she will soon give her last groan he-he-he-he. . . . I know
> you will all congratulate me on the restoration of my reason
> again—he-he-he-he (to Jane Kennedy, November 16, 1813).

> I am almost out of paitence [sic] knowing that you do not
> like those wincing pincing letters no better than myself. I have
> wrote you one that as [sic] some sense in it for I never liked so
> much teasing and affectation but I like those that are wrote by
> persons that are possessed of their reasoning powers he-he-he-
> he. I must now bid you good night and pleasant dreams. I am
> as ever your Britanic Majestys most humble cum tumble
>
> > Mary Reynolds
> > (to John Reynolds,
> > November 21, 1813)

Bemus decided that strong measures were called for. Rush
had advocated for memory disorders—bleeding, purges, low
diet, blisters, and issues; and for mania—first and foremost

bleeding, accompanied by low diet, blisters, cold water, and purging with calomel and other remedies: with the addition of cupping and mustard plasters Mary got the lot—and this, in her second state, irritated her exceedingly.[27] She had a particularly "great aversion" to bleeding, to which (of course) her first self meekly submitted. She retaliated in verse to the kind of medicine she was receiving:

> Calomel, Tartar and Gamboge
> He deals me out good measure
> Could I the dose to *him* infuse
> Would be to me a pleasure.

> Blisters and Drafts he makes me wear
> For days and nights together
> Oh! had I wings to take me where
> I could enjoy some pleasure.[28]

Mary's attitude toward her doctors reveals a significant feature of her second state in general: "ardent in her friendships, strong in her dislikes, cheerful and frolicksome in spirit." Such a spirit took poorly to restraint; thus the dominant theme of her new self was—*liberty!*

She referred to:

> Those tormenting Doctors who oftimes attempted to scale the walls and pull down the flag of Liberty and hoist the standard of their authority.

> Plague on the Doctors, for ever since I have been sick I cant put my head outside the door, but I am salluted [*sic*] with a whole broad side of grape shot. I think they had better let *me* alone and keep their artillary [*sic*] for a better purpose.

> The Doctor thinks he has a right
> To be obey'd forever
> But were I only out of sight
> I'd take my fill of pleasure

> I'd range the woods, the fields and plains
> And visit friends at leisure
> Would spare no labor and no pains
> Could I but have my pleasure

> My liberty I ever prize
> As an exalted treasure

But oh, the Doctor thus deprives
Me of my greatest pleasure.

To Church he says you must not go
For there is too much pressure
Wherein then I would like to know
Have I one real pleasure?

Mary's doctors were not richly endowed with psychologi-cal insight; this was not a psychological age. Yet Benjamin Rush was in his own way well aware of what might loosely be called the "unconscious"; he found, for example, that manics are often quite creative and likened the "new and wonderful tal-ents and operations of the mind" brought into the light by their disorder to "precious and splendid fossils the existence of which was unknown to the proprietors of the soil in which they were buried."[29] This was surely true in the case of Mary Reynolds; but if her new abilities were already part of the subterranean strata of the mind, the natural question arises of how they came to be deposited there. Here again it is possible to achieve a provisional understanding through the attitudes revealed in Mary's letters, reminiscences, and poetry.

Mary's cultural background is a singularly important ele-ment in her case: her literary heritage provided her with images of the hidden "natural" self and an attitude toward Nature in general that were incorporated within the symbolic content of her second state, a symbolism that allowed her to fuse life and art and to escape through doing so the rigid constraints of her girlhood. Already set off on a solitary course by the unusual conditions of her youth and the vicissitudes of her family's history, Mary articulated through literature a romantic vision of life incompatible with the actual conditions of a frontier farm and the religiosity of her milieu. For her a contrast between Nature and Culture, the wilderness and the sown, was a metaphoric expression of the contrast between spontaneity and convention; madness could itself be assimilated to the nat-ural, and as such possessed a rationality of its own. We have her own testimony in support of this; looking back on life at the time of her illness, Mary wrote: "I was rather romantick [sic] in my disposition, and took great delight in rambling about the woods, and at such times was fond of being alone."[30]

However, the romanticism on which she was raised was not yet the fully self-conscious Romanticism of the early nineteenth century, but of its eighteenth-century forebears—the poetry of Nature and Nature's God; the Gothic Romance with its castles, its mysteries, and its glooms; the imagery of transmigration of souls imported from oriental sources into European awareness: an embryonic fascination with the mystery and infinite possibilities of the self. Mary had, I think, much in common with Ann Radcliffe, author of *The Mysteries of Udolpho*, and the leading Gothic novelist. The heroines of Radcliffe's works (and her leading characters were always women) invariably found themselves in exotic romantic surroundings beset by men of dubious intentions. Though it can be suspected that Mary's evangelical family would scarcely have approved of such literature, it nonetheless had an enormous popularity at the end of the eighteenth century and the beginning of the nineteenth, particularly among women who apparently found through it—as Radcliffe herself did—some relief from the constraints of their surroundings.

Eighteenth-century English literature made landscape into the image of the soul and simultaneously, through scientific understanding of the natural world—Nature's Book of Knowledge—an image of the mind of God. It is known by Mary's own account that she read the Bible, the prose of Joseph Addison, the poetry of John Milton, James Thomson, and William Cowper. Later Romantics looked back to Milton's Lucifer—whom Milton made to say, "Myself am hell!"—as a prototypical divided soul striving for redemption; Lucifer, angel of light before his fall, answered to their tragic sense of primeval division and perhaps appealed to Mary for the same reason (it has been often pointed out that Lucifer is far more interesting than the Lord). However, her own verse particularly reflects Thomson's very influential poem, *The Seasons*—a meditation on the changing year interspersed with rhapsodic philosophical digressions. This is the poetry of sublime melancholy, not of depression and religious anguish: it evokes the darkness out of which revelation comes, of "vast embowering shades, twilight groves and visionary vales, weeping grottoes, and prophetic glooms."[31] Even Cowper, who had religious anguish to spare, found that he could attain a momentary sense of relief and reconciliation to self through communion with Nature. This is one message of his monumental poem, *The Task* (which Mary must also have read): "Oh for a lodge in some vast wilderness, some boundless contiguity of shade, where rumor of oppression and deceit, or unsuccessful or successful war might never reach me more!"—words originally composed in response to the revolt of the American colonies and therefore particularly apposite to Mary's perceptions, as again revealed by her letters, of the War of 1812 between her original and adopted homelands. Mary spoke of Nature in terms such as these:

> I have just been taking a lonely walk on the bank of the Creek, viewing the brilliancy of the Sun sinking behind the hill tinging the lofty trees with his golden rays while the feathered choir were hastening to seek within their mossy cells a silent and secure repose, and I can assure you I was delighted with my ramble tho alone. I can sometimes enjoy a solitary walk with a great deal of pleasure (to Lydia Calhoun, June 25, 1816).

In her second state Mary rambled over hill and dale, involving herself in adventures with the natural world which all would recall with wonder:

> Though she was extraordinarily fond of company, yet she was much more enamoured with nature's works, as exhibited in the forests, hills, vales, and water courses.[32]

She faced down a bear ("a big black hog," she called it), attempted to capture a rattlesnake with her hands, crossed crumbling ice floes on Oil Creek, and undertook—citing a humorous poem by Cowper as precedent ("John Gilpin's Ride")—a solo horseback journey to Meadville to see her brother. She rejected every form of discipline brought to bear on her—parental, medical, and religious: but then . . . she was mad. In this state she rejected convention and hypocrisy and thought only of the moment:

> [I] had no idea of the past or future, nothing but the present occupied my mind. In the first state of my disease, I had no idea of employing my time in anything that was useful, did nothing but ramble about, and never tired of walking through the fields. My mother one day thought she would try to rouse me a little. She told me that Paul said those who would not work must not eat. I told her it made no matter of difference

to me what Paul said, I was not going to work for Paul or any other person.[33]

It should be remembered that in any event these people were not acknowledged as *her* parents:

The guests that inhabit this part of the globe are some poor outcastes that jupiter found in the highways and dominions and they were so deform'd that he was ashamed of them and hurll'd them down among the nocturnal shades of Oil Creek a nest for poisonous reptiles and a kennel for ravenous beasts— he-he-he-he (to John Reynolds, November 21, 1813).

This new Mary came from "somewhere else" and saw *them* as "strangers and enemies, among whom she was by some remarkable, and unaccountable means, transplanted, though from what region or state of existence was a problem she would not solve." The concept of transmigration served this perception well. It is interesting that case reports of multiple personality often, and even to this day, involve the imagery of possession by alien spirits. As will be seen, Miss Beauchamp's alter-self, the vivacious Sally, would also claim to have come from "somewhere else"; even Morton Prince did not venture to fully explain her presence nor, when she had departed, where it was she had gone.

At the time of Mary Reynolds's "possession," oriental philosophy was becoming known in Europe. Several numbers of Joseph Addison's and Richard Steele's *Spectator* contain orientalist vignettes patterned on stories in *The Arabian Nights* based upon the notion of the transmigration of souls (for example, numbers 343 and 578).[34] Two of these are preceded by a verse of Dryden's:

All things are but alter'd; nothing dies;
And here and there th' unbody'd spirit flies,
By time, or force, or sickness dispossess'd,
And lodges, where it lights, in man or beast.

We will see below that Mary believed herself to have had quite an active series of past lives, which soured her considerably on immediate marital prospects in western Pennsylvania.

The eighteenth-century artistic imagination also had a fascination with light.[35] Gloom was associated with melancholic profundity, a condition in which the distinction between subject and object becomes blurred and finally lost; the clear light of day, on the other hand, creates distinctions, emphasizes differences. Mary systematically contrasted "the Sunshine of pleasure" with "the nocturnal shades, the dominion of solitude, the cell of a gloomy Monk." Her illness began in the ultimate of glooms—the dark night of the soul, from which she emerged to quote Ecclesiastes: "truly the light is sweet and how pleasant a thing it is for the eyes to behold the sun."[36] Henceforth she used this contrastive symbolism to express the totality of her fate. She, in her second state, referred to Cherrytree as "The Nocturnal Shades," and continued to do so for some years afterward. Meadville, on the other hand, was the Sun of her heart's desire. She also equated her two selves to the places that were their spiritual homes: the first state, Cherrytree, piety and solitude; the second state, Meadville, secular poetry and conviviality. The first Mary was of the shadows, the second —like Lucifer—a creature of light and devilment. Of Cherrytree she wrote:

> I have scarce seen the sun since I have been an inhabitant of this gloomy region. The heavens wear a continual gloom and Natures Book of Knowledge which with you [in Meadville] is all fair and instructive is here one vast unmeaning Blank (to Eliza Haslet, November 18, 1816).

And of Meadville:

> I am waiting very impatiently for the day to arrive when I shall once more sport in the Sunshine of pleasure and where the peacefull [sic] hours of contentment will glide smilingly away. When I advance towards the enchanting plain the glittering prospect will so attract my sight as to cause new life and beauty to flow from every increasing beam—and where the very horizon will seem to widen and expand itself on every side while the sun will arise in his magnificent splendor and shine forth in all his meridian strength (to John Reynolds, November 21, 1813).

Yet there was an ambivalence in her attitudes. She regaled in the natural world and had a new natural self to match it. The out of doors, even the hills of Cherrytree, was her chosen home, and here she found a welcome vision in the poetry of Thomson. The gloom, the "nocturnal shades," had their own appeal.

Mary, wherever she was and whoever she was at the time, seems to have always had a literary paradigm at her disposal through which she structured and rendered her experience emotionally meaningful. When at one point she believed herself to be leaving Cherrytree for Meadville permanently she wrote a long verse, mirroring Thomson, in which she looked with some nostalgia on her old world, though with much greater anticipation of the world to come.

Welcome, ye shades! Ye bowery thickets hail!	Farewel ye lonely shades farewel
Ye lofty pines! Ye venerable oaks!	No more ye, my footsteps shall greet
Ye ashes wild, resounding o'er the steep!	To Meadville I'm going to dwell
Delicious is your shelter to the soul.	And leave your nocturnal retreat.
—Thomson	—Mary Reynolds

Mary was, it would seem, saying farewell to childhood:

Farewel to these woods, and these dales,
Ye mountains, ye rocks, and ye hills
In your shades, I have oftimes regal'd.
And drank at your murmuring rills.

And welcoming the future in Meadville:

There I'll range, oe'r the glittering plains:
While the hours slide sweetly away
New life and vigor, again
And sport in the sunshine of day."[37]

It was not yet to be. Mary did indeed go to Meadville for a time, but only so that she could be near her doctors. It was one of Rush's more apt recommendations that the patient be separated from his or her family so that the doctor could function without distraction.[38] In Meadville, however, her new-found freedom appeared to have received much encouragement. By the time of Mary's breakdown, her brother—apparently liking Cherrytree no better than she did—had left the farm and was living with the family of the Meadville physician Dr. Thomas Kennedy; Dr. Kennedy died in 1813 and was succeeded by Dr. Daniel Bemus. John Reynolds was attracted to Kennedy's widow, Jane, and by April 1813 Mary in her second state was regarding their eventual marriage as an already accomplished fact—addressing Jane Kennedy as "My Dear Brother's Wife" (to Jane Kennedy, April 16, 1813). When Mary was stricken the Kennedy household provided her with refuge while she was under Dr. Bemus's care; in fact, Mary *first* saw Meadville while in her second state. And if this Mary were a romancer given to "airy flights of fancy," Mrs. Kennedy and another boarder in her house, a Miss Dewey, were a receptive audience. Mrs. Kennedy was remembered as being "ever bright and cheerful. . . . Among other accomplishments, she possessed a remarkable talent for improvisation of stories. . . . While busy at the spinning wheel the children, forgetful of outdoor play, would gather around to listen to her wonderful and every varying tales of romance."[39]

Miss Dewey too was "a young lady of very lively disposition." Mary's most extravagant second-state letters are addressed to John Reynolds or Mrs. Kennedy—who evidently gave her rein for such performances. However, her outbursts seem to me more expressive of a kind of stage madness than the genuine article, and while with the Kennedys she appears to have been competent enough in a practical way. Miss Dewey commented in a footnote to one of Mary's letters: "I am not under the necessity of overseeing Mary for she is much the most capable of instructing me and I have given myself up wholly to her direction. Dr. Bemus is her overseer, she is mine . . . and Mr. Reynolds is superintendent of the whole" (to Jane Kennedy, April 16, 1813).

Mary was in the course of a transformation from submissive girlhood toward active, responsible adulthood. She would no longer be a pietistic recluse. Nothing could be plainer than the symbolism she chose to express her defiance, but it is not clear what set this process in train. One could say, as did William James when writing of religious conversion, that such an event requires a long unconscious process of gestation which, when it finally emerges, surprises the convert as much as anyone else. Though this may be true it does not satisfactorily explain the onset of Mary's "fits" nor her dramatic breakdown later; it merely begs the question. I suspect that there were objective situational factors at work that conditioned both the timing of her outbursts and the form they took. The pressures bearing upon Mary at the time of her blindness and transformative sleep can be seen, and others can be inferred. Her attitude toward Cherrytree is known and easily comprehensible. Her past experience in England, her longing for a social life on its civilized model, her sense of the crudity of country life, her attachment to a now absent brother, the democratic ethic of her father and her new land, all have a bearing on what happened. But another factor emerges through her letters while she was under the care of Dr. Bemus: marriage.

Contrary to a view that would have her younger, eighteen or so, Mary was twenty-six in 1811; and though the average age of marriage was relatively high in those times, there must have been rising expectations, perhaps subjectively shared, that she be found a husband. The consequences of not doing so were serious, given the scarcity of other employments for women. There were also medical considerations. Benjamin Rush, among other things, was a dedicated family man who considered frustrated sexuality to be dangerous, noting that, "single persons are more predisposed to madness than married people": "Celibacy [he wrote] . . . is a pleasant breakfast, a tolerable dinner, but a very bad supper. The last comparison will appear to be an appropriate one, when we consider further, that the supper is not only of a bad quality, but eaten alone. No wonder it is sometimes a predisposing cause of madness."[40]

Dr. Bemus shared these opinions and Mary absorbed them herself along with other accepted medical wisdom. Bemus appeared to have decided that marriage would cure what ailed her (I wonder if he believed that what she really needed was male discipline). In her letters of this time Mary writes of her suitors as "matrimonial pills" and even enlisted the aid of her doctor in finding a suitable one:

> Please to tell the Doctor that I had the offer of a matrimonial pill since I came home but would not except [sic] of it for it was an old man. He as [sic] had two wives. The first he lived with seven years and had none [children?]. I told him that I had lived these three hundred and 38 years and have had six husbands and no children. He blessed me and told me that he should like to have me himselfe [sic]. But I told him that I would not like him for a matrimonial pill he-he-he-he-he (to Jane Kennedy, November 16, 1813).

If we take Mary's second self at her word, she was first born in 1475 and had transmigrated into new bodies periodically since. No wonder a woman of such experience balked at marriage to a rustic ignoramus. Mary's unusual past and still more unusual present had the interesting side effect of driving these "matrimonial pills" away:

> I have had the offer of another matrimonial pill since you left us but he was a second *James Hamilton* [identity unknown]. The courtship went on very well till the time drew nigh for the ceremony to be perform'd. Then the deceitfull [sic] dog began to relinquish and said he would wait until I [her second state] went to sleep to know what my mind would be *then* [as her first state]. Tell the Doctor I intend to wait for the one he is to get me and I shall depend upon his judgment. I expect he will take his surgical instrument and probe him to the bottom of his heart to see if he is sound. Tell the Doctor that is the only way I think we can find out the dogs (to John Reynolds, November 21, 1813).

The doctor seems to have been unsuccessful in finding a permanent remedy, but he did at least manage a temporary alleviation of symptoms. Benjamin Rush was well aware of the sensation created by the labors of Franz Anton Mesmer in late-eighteenth-century Paris; Benjamin Franklin himself had participated in an investigation into the credibility of Mesmer's claims to be able to deploy the forces of "animal magnetism" in the cause of healing. These claims were in general judged harshly, but Rush perceived that there is nonetheless something of interest in them.[41] Dr. Bemus certainly knew of these things as well. Through an experiment of his (nature undisclosed but probably mesmeric) Mary's second self was put to sleep and the first restored. The second Mary knew that this was coming and appeared to have been an accomplice in allowing it. Perhaps the time had come when she recognized she could stay in Meadville no longer:

> I have bad news to tell you i.e. I am going to make my exit and Mary Reynolds [the first state] is coming to supply my place, and a poor drowsy substitute I think she'll be and if I had my will I would shut the door against her, but I presume they will all be very well pleased with the change for she will come without bringing any April fools with her (to Jane Kennedy, April 16, 1813).

And so she went back to Cherrytree, but this did not entail submission to authority for, once there, her second state reawakened:

> Oh Mrs Kennedy, Mrs Kennedy, how great was my astonishment when I opened my eyes this morning and found myself among the nocturnal shades of Oil Creek transmagrated [sic] from the heights of happiness down to the deepest abyss (November 16, 1813).

At this point an interesting question arises, seen also in other cases of multiple personality, of the degree to which the various personalities in question are indeed separate. I have suggested that the second Mary knew the first was coming back, and in effect allowed it. On at least one occasion and probably more, the second Mary intruded into the first's domain. John Reynolds asked the second Mary to explain where it was she got all the paper for the letters she was writing him, and received this answer:

> Well Sir in the first place you must know that I do not allways [sic] carry a *dumb Tunge* about me. It will speak sometimes, so that by what I can understand it spoke to answer my purpose when I arrived in Franklyn [another local town]. . . . It told me I should want paper when I changed to my second state. . . . I can assure you when I awoke and found myself transmigrated among these nocturnal shades, where nought but a sullen silence and a Deathlike inactivity slumbers, it afforded me inexpressible satisfaction to find I had pen ink and paper to amuse me and help to pass away a friendly intercourse with some enlightened part of the world (to John Reynolds, January 8, 1815).

So, the second Mary could appropriate the "tunge" of the first when it suited her needs. The former seems to have been claiming a degree of continuous awareness superior to the transitory awareness of her puritanical sister. Occasionally her first state still put in an appearance, and in such a way that it is apparent the second Mary associated her with everything weak —even normal sickness.

> Mary Reynolds is quite sick [she wrote]. She is not able to sit up today. She has the nervous headache. It was sick headache at first. The Doctor is attending her (to Lydia Craighead, June 3, 1815).

The mental disturbance which at times characterized the earlier portions of her second state grew fainter, and at length totally disappeared, leaving her permanently altered in character. This dates from about the year 1829, when she had reached her thirty-sixth year. In this state she lived the remainder of her life, a period of twenty-five years. During this quarter of a century no one could have discovered in her anything out of the ordinary way, except that she manifested an unusual degree of nervousness and restlessness; yet not enough to excite remark. It is to be borne in mind that she was still in this her abnormal state all the rest of her life, without memory although not without knowledge of her true self. The change from a gay, hysterical, mischievous woman, fond of jests and subject to absurd beliefs or delusive convictions, to one retaining the joyousness and love of society, but sobered down to levels of practical usefullness, was gradual. The most of the twenty-five years which followed was as different from her melancholy, morbid self as from the hilarious condition of the early years of the second state. Some of her family spoke of it as her third state.[42]

I presume my friend has heard how I have been employing my time this summer. In about two weeks I shall be liberated from my little charge, though still intend to continue the sabbath school while at home, and it may be that I shall engage for another quarter. Do not know of any better way to employ my time in this unenlightened part of the globe. Time would hang very heavy, if it were not for my school, for we have no society here. Nothing new, one dull round of sameness. In my school I have no time to be gloomy, plenty to occupy both body and mind. After school I take a ramble through the woods and fields, have two sisters which live within a quarter of a mile of us, run over there and chat an hour, romp with the children, then come home (to Lydia Calhoun, July 22, 1822).

The new Mary did not observe the old as an utter *stranger* but as a part of herself with which she refused to identify. As time went by her second state became increasingly dominant. She may not have liked where she was, but her "hysteria" receded with an increasing commitment to an active role in the world as it is. There was not much for a single woman to do in the country, so she adopted one of the few options available to her and became a teacher. It appears that she spent some twenty years at this calling before finally getting her wish to return to Meadville.

> I am among the Nocturnal Shades of Sugar Creek about ten miles from home. Have been here about seven weeks. I have engaged in a school here for six months. Have twenty scholars, sometimes twenty three. You may depend I have a good round family. They keep my mind and time pretty well occupied and help to pass away the dull hours of betweenity. . . . Sometimes when I think about Meadville I feel all in the figgits (to Lydia Calhoun, April 12, 1819).

While teaching in the country, the topic of marriage came up once more, though now in a very different light; Mary had concluded her teaching chores, taken her ramble through woods and fields, and gone home to her brothers:

> I chat to them a while and plague them about getting married. Sometimes I believe they are ready to wish me back to Meadville, and at last to put an end to the subject of matrimony. They will set me to read to them, till at length they go off one by one to bed and leave me alone. . . . I feel quite content though I had rather live in Meadville. . . . I am determined not to be forgotten, for while there are paper mills in the country, I will write (to Lydia Calhoun, July 22, 1822).

When this was written Mary was thirty-seven years old. She had achieved something of her dream of freedom and finally would also get her wish to reside in Meadville where she spent her remaining years as housekeeper with the family of her clergyman nephew. She never married, but so far as her chatty and good-natured letters reveal, was happy enough with the life of the town and her adopted household. When, around 1836, she wrote a memoir of her experiences at the behest of her nephew, what had happened seemed vague, lost in the mists of time:

> The two states have become so combined, that there is but little difference excepting the loss of recollection. At this present time somethings will recur to mind, but I do not actually know whether they can be facts, or whether I have dreamed, for they are too much confused for me to communicate, and all will again vanish from my mind.[43]

Her nephew commented:

> She at a later period in her life said she did sometimes seem to have dim dreamy ideas of a shadowy past—which she could not fully grasp, & could not be certain whether they originated in a partially restored memory, or from the repetition of the events by others during her abnormal state.[44]
>
> She is at present in a third state, differing from either of the others. As she is cheerful, yet serious—possessed of a well-balanced temperament, perfectly rational and having not the slightest shew of an injured or disturbed mind.[45]

And in that condition she one day in 1854 said, "Oh! I wonder what is the matter with my head," fell on the floor and died soon after.

———•—•—•———

DR. JOHN KEARSLEY MITCHELL WAS A man of broad sympathies and wide interests, and member of a profession well respected in his home city of Philadelphia. Formal medical education had been established there in the late eighteenth century and had been much influenced by Dr. Benjamin Rush. Dr. Mitchell held Rush in the greatest respect and was proud to belong to and perpetuate his tradition; he also inherited Rush's interest in diseases of the mind that he passed on in turn to his son, Dr. Silas Weir Mitchell, who was later to have had a minor role in the strange case of Ansel Bourne and a rather more important one in the theoretical development of late-nineteenth-century neurology/psychiatry.

John Mitchell had become aware of exotic permutations of consciousness through his clinical work and research into the nature of mesmerism. In 1842 he read a paper before the College of Physicians of Philadelphia in which, undoubtedly alluding to Mary, he noted that lapses of memory associated with mesmeric (that is, hypnotic) trance can also be found in "cases of insanity and double consciousness."[46] Dr. Mitchell was himself a pioneer into the strange world of trance, apparently occult trans-personal influence, double consciousness, and the relation between split consciousness and mesmeric phenomena. Like his later followers in this exotic and suspect area of research, John Mitchell was regarded as an intrepid explorer into the mysterious world of the unconscious—a trade, as one of Mitchell's associates eulogized, requiring "moral courage, self-reliance, and power of logical analysis." He assembled notebooks on the Reynolds case, including Mary's autobiographical memoir, which in due course came into the hands of his son who published in 1888 what has been until now the definitive account of the matter.

Weir Mitchell's account spread Mary Reynolds's fame in psychological circles, but his was not the first to have done so. A Glasgow physician, Robert Macnish, used her case in his *Philosophy of Sleep* (1854), which examined the degrees of unconsciousness—in sleep, somnambulism, trance, and mental disorder—to which human beings are subject. From this source it entered into the awareness of the French psychologists—as the case of "Macnish's Lady"—who assimilated it to the cases currently coming to their personal attention. Macnish had concluded that "the particular state of the brain which induces such conditions will, I believe, ever remain a mystery."[47] The French were more ambitious and attempted to fuse their knowledge of such phenomena with rapidly changing understandings of how the nervous system works; out of their efforts, to be examined more closely in the next chapter, came the concept of multiple personality as it is now understood.

But there were other alternatives available, particularly for those who viewed Mary's possession by a transmigrated soul to be a real possibility. Ada Goodrich-Freer, a leading British psychical researcher and occultist, was one such. She herself undertook a journey to western Pennsylvania in 1901 to interview Mary's surviving nephew and to consult the records of the case. Her findings were published in the *Occult Review*, where she concluded that "the story is an instructive one, whatever the point of view, for the alienist, the occultist, the physiologist, perhaps above all, for the student of ethics."[48]

In America, Mary's case was presented in 1860 to the popular readership of *Harper's Magazine,* the author concluding that "the bearings of this case on the sanitive treatment of the insane, on questions of mental science . . . , on questions of conscience and casuistry, and on the religious aspect of the matter, are left to the thinking world. None will be more ready than the author to receive light on any of these important and intricate matters."[49]

The editors of *Harper's,* one of the most important forums of the day, appreciated that Mary's case would attract wide public interest. And so, from these various sources, a young Pennsylvania farm woman slowly began to assume a place in the history of psychology. A recent paper, looking back on research into multiple personality from the perspective of contemporary theory, is entitled "Multiple Personality 165 Years after Mary Reynolds." She is still regarded as a prototypical case.[50]

But even now there is much that is not known about what occurred. It is possible to see some of the important scenes of Mary Reynolds's life only in imagination: her reaction to separation from her parents, their reunion in the New World, the reaction of those about her when she seemed to lose herself. This last, given the history of subsequent cases, is of particular significance. Was Mary in some way *encouraged* to develop a rebellious new self? Mrs. Kennedy, Miss Dewey, and possibly John Reynolds were at least sympathetic to this sprightly being. Further, could Mary herself have been familiar with the empiricist concept of the *tabula rasa*? Given the sophistication of her family and her own penchant for reading it is not impossible. The artistic and religious culture that I have shown to have such an influence on the development of her case could well have provided the basic idea for her transformation—or transmigration—while the attitudes of certain of those around her could well have allowed a new self to grow and assume coherence.

Mary's parents are a nearly unknown factor, as are her siblings with the exception of John. One gets the impression that William Reynolds was an ideologue capable of carrying his beliefs to extreme conclusions; perhaps he was not an easy man to live with. Of Mary's mother we know virtually nothing save that she came from a family of Welsh evangelical Baptists. What were her attitudes toward the move to America? If family reminiscence is any guide she was at first far from happy with it. Did she communicate this attitude to her eldest daughter?

The form Mary's new self took was shaped by a literary culture in which her *first* self was well versed; instead of being a tabula rasa the second self was a mirror inversion of her predecessor—a relation of logical dependence. This new self was already implicitly known to those who beheld it: the wise madwoman, the visionary Sybil of antiquity, the wild man of the woods, have been recurrent themes in Western culture. One thinks of the works of Jean Jacques Rousseau and his vision of humankind in a state of nature free from the moral debasement brought by decadent civilization. Would a republican family have been altogether ignorant of these? From the vantage point of her second self Mary engaged in astute editorial commentary on those around her, even on one occasion calling well-deserved attention to a hypocritical evangelical preacher. Mary in her second state turned into the Meadville satirist and a public personality. "Madness," as I have suggested, has certain strategic advantages. For Mary, one of them was liberty.

If we were to follow current theories about the genesis of multiple personality we should look for trauma in her life, possibly abuse by her parents, leading to dissociation and the formation of an alter-self to deal with intolerable stress. Trauma there was, if the Birmingham riots count as such, but parental abuse seems to me improbable in the extreme. Unfortunately we will never know. A modern psychiatrist suggests that dissociation leading to multiple personality usually occurs in early childhood and wonders of Mary, "whether a contemporary clinician might not have uncovered a much earlier dissociation than the dramatic one that took place at age 18" (which in fact took place at age 26).[51] Quite possibly—if it were being looked for; multiple personalities and those stricken with kindred "hysterical" disorders have a way of giving back to observers what they expect to see. Clinicians of her own day, however, were not looking for this and focused on alleviating the obvious symptoms of a fevered brain.

There is much that will never be known about Mary Reynolds; the following is a summary portrait assembled from what is:

She was raised in an intelligent, dissenting English home in the politically self-conscious Birmingham of the early industrial revolution—of Joseph Priestley, of his engine-building friends, Matthew Boulton and James Watt, and of Thomas Jefferson's old teacher in America, William Small. At an early age she endured the riots and the dislocation of her family; she withdrew into herself and the books of which she was so fond. Her position as second eldest child of the family and first daughter reinforced her increasingly independent and aloof status. Her mind continued to develop encouraged by political debate and the general currents of English literature. She was directed toward eighteenth-century understandings of nature and nature's God and assimilated the democratic values of those around her. Through the pioneer hardships of Pennsylvania this process went on as she worked and dreamed.

As adolescence progressed the contradiction between her romantic spiritual life and her actual conditions and prospects became more acute. These contradictions, perhaps brought to focus by the question of matrimony, emerged in the psychosomatic fits of classic hysteria colored by the phenomena of her religious milieu. From this stress emerged a new self that resolutely turned its back upon the old. This new self was tolerated and even pandered to by some of those around her; through it Mary found an active social life that would have been denied to her for good if she had entered into marriage with a rural farmer. Up to a late date her self-perceptions were still in flux as she underwent a delayed passage into adulthood. Finally the contradiction lessened as Mary found her own way in the world. In the end she was simply herself—the so-called "third state"—and spent the remainder of her life happily and productively.

In some respects her fate corresponds to the classic multiple personality syndrome, but obscurities remain and I point out again that it also corresponds to a widely noted and sometimes ritually punctuated process of maturation. The problem of memory has been mentioned as has my opinion that the issue is spurious. Her two selves were in fact not mutually exclusive, since in some measure the second self had access to the first; this has been noted in subsequent cases and I will return to the matter later. The contradictory nature of the respective selves has also been noted before. However, given lack of a definite picture of how her liberated alter-self emerged it is difficult to know the degree to which this should be construed as a psychological rather than a social process; the same applies for many of the more recent cases. It is unquestionable that there were decisive situational elements in her case. Her transition to adulthood was so agonizing because she faced it relatively late in life and because only a certain kind of adulthood was tolerable to her. The solution that she attained was a mixed blessing; she was denied certain of what were considered the consolations of womanhood, but she kept her individuality. This was an individuality typical of *both* her states, though freely expressed in only one.

Mary's letters and other memorabilia give us a sense of the living person and the logic that governed her life's course: seen retrospectively this logic was a very simple one: a transition from childhood to adulthood through a "wild" intermediate phase drawing on then-fashionable attitudes toward the natural world—not the harsh symbolism of an American wilderness to be tamed, but of old England where the wilderness had been romantically transformed into the home of natural men and women opposed to the unnatural restrictions of culture: in this case the culture of evangelical Protestantism itself.

I WISHED TO SEE CHERRYTREE and Meadville and if any sense remains of what they were. In Meadville the school band still plays in the town square among statues commemorating the Civil War dead and the heroes of the Indian campaigns. Cherrytree still has a feeling of remoteness and claustrophobia about it, while nearby oil that helped make the Reynolds family rich is still being pumped from the margins of Oil Creek. Of Mary herself there is a single photograph in the County Historical Society—taken in death, a woman of sixty-nine years with angular features and covered in satin. The years through which she lived were eventful for her and for her society. Concepts took shape that would eventually lead to a very different picture of human nature than that current in 1785 when she was born. In the next chapter I document their emergence through consideration of the case of Ansel Bourne and his curious encounters first with God and then the psychologists.

CHAPTER TWO

⚙ The Passion of Ansel Bourne ⚙

Now it has long been noticed that there is something
in the influences, climatic or other, here prevailing,
which predisposes to morbid religious excitement.
                              —*Dr. Oliver Wendell Holmes*

WESTERLY, RHODE ISLAND, HAS SEEN its changes. Sited on the
Pawcatuck River at the Connecticut border, it has at times
engaged itself in boat-building. It is even now a pleasant little
city which, if one is so inclined, can be reached by the northeast
corridor rail line between New York and Boston. Its principal
fame was derived from the granite quarries that helped supply
New England with building stone; to this end northern Italian
granite workers were imported in some number in the late
nineteenth century—to the intense distress of old-line Yankees
who wondered what the town was coming to. Now Westerly's
population is largely Italian in descent; behind the elegant old
library is the inevitable statue of Christopher Columbus. Here
in the mid-1850s Ansel Bourne made his home and here, in the
eyes of many, God paid him a call. This was only a few years
before the Civil War, only a few before publication of *The
Origin of Species*, only a few before the world was turned
upside down. William James was fifteen years old in 1857 and
the Republic a mere eighty-one. Ansel Bourne himself was
thirty-one, and a man with much on his mind. In 1826, while
Mary Reynolds was teaching school near Oil Creek, Bourne
came into the world in New York; he would live into this
century. Like those of Mary Reynolds, Bourne's values were
shaped by evangelical Protestantism; also like her he would
enter into the literature on multiple personality. This is how it
was:

On October 28, 1857, Bourne—a carpenter—left his home and set off for the nearby town of Westerly, Rhode Island, but he did not arrive. As he walked quickly along, "he was conscious of no unusual feelings, until a thought came up vividly in his mind that he ought to go to meeting. This thought was connected with no conscientious feeling of duty to go to meeting, but seemed a mere internal and unaccountable suggestion. To the suggestion he answered, 'Where?' To this inquiry he was answered in the same manner, 'To the Christian Chapel.' His spirit rose up against this idea in decided and bitter opposition, and he said within himself, 'I would rather be struck deaf and dumb forever, than to go there.'"

Shortly, Bourne felt dizzy and sat down on a rock by the wayside; a wagon approached and as he watched, "it seemed as though some powerful hand drew something down over his head, and then over his face, and finally over his whole body; depriving him of his sight, his hearing, and his speech; and rendering him perfectly helpless." Bourne was taken home in the wagon and his doctor hastily summoned; tests were performed but no response could be evoked, and the doctor reported that "he was in fact perfectly insensible." However, Bourne himself would claim that, though his major senses were gone, he was fully conscious of having been taken to bed and of the ministrations of doctor and family. In this personal darkness his thoughts went back over the preceding events and he concluded that he had been touched by the hand of God.

While in blackness Bourne reviewed the condition of his soul and found it sadly wanting: he was estranged from his fellow men and from a God whom he had denied. "This silence was as though the soul had been cast into a deep, bottomless and shoreless sepulchre, where dismal silence was to reign eternally. And it was also night there without a single ray of light. As one justly cast off from God, he felt the horrors of that dreadful idea—cast into outer darkness." He fully acknowledged the justice of God in his condemnation, and spurned from his soul the thought of insulting God by asking mercy for such a sinner. The only offering he could think to make of himself was as a victim of sins too great for even the mercy of God, and as an offering fit only for the firey sword of justice. A day later, after many thoughts such as these, his sight was suddenly restored, but still he was isolated by lack of speech and hearing. In order to communicate, he requested writing materials and, while his wife was out of the room to fetch them, a new thought came unbidden into Bourne's mind: "Are you now willing to ask forgiveness of all whom you have injured?" He assented, and those whom he believed himself to have harmed were summoned to his bedside where, while silently weeping, he asked their forgiveness through the medium of a slate and piece of chalk.

Bourne was taken several times to the Christian Chapel, and there, through the minister who read what he wrote on the slate, made public amends before God and man. On Sunday, November 15, Bourne wrote: "I have been led to think, while sitting here, why I have been called from the ranks of sinners, and I have been led to think that God has something for me to do. Why I have come up here to the place of all others which three weeks ago I would have shunned, I know not. . . . Why I feel as I do this afternoon, I cannot tell, but I do feel as though God was about to speak to Westerly, in what way I know not— but oh, may God's will be done!" What then occurred was widely regarded as a miracle. Bourne's hearing and speech were instantaneously restored. He cried: "Glory to God and the Lamb forever!" and fell on his knees to pray aloud before the amazed congregation. As he went home from this extraordinary scene, "he could hear . . . the voice of the Lord in each rustling leaf."

His health steadily improved, and he rejoiced in glorifying God until, on Saturday, November 28, Bourne suffered another attack and was certain he would die on that night. But he awoke Sunday morning with the words in his mouth, "I yet live!" and then, in the small hours of Sunday night, he had a vision; as Bourne lay in bed, "suddenly his room seemed all lighted up with the most extraordinary brightness, brighter than the light of day. He started with surprise, and saw an image or appearance, like a man in form, standing by the side of his bed. There appeared nothing like a face, but in place of it there was an appearance like the sun shining in his brightness. A voice, which seemed to proceed from the image before him said: "Settle up your worldly business, and go to work for me." Bourne woke his wife and asked if she had seen anything, but she had not. Then as Bourne held his wife's hand, the vision returned, and once more he was unable to speak or move. It said: "Settle up your worldly business, and go to work for me. Your family shall be taken care of, and yourself looked out for. Go, open your mouth and I will fill it. Go, tell the world what your eyes have seen, and your ears have heard."

Ansel Bourne obeyed this command, and as his friends reported: "Mr. Bourne has left his worldly occupation—a carpenter—to work for Him who was once known on earth as 'The Carpenter's Son.' He goes out, trusting in God, to tell the story of what he has seen and heard. He is afraid to neglect, yet he loves to obey. He feels all the difficulties of his position, the lack of literary attainments, the incredulity of men; and yet he goes with the confidence that he will be sustained, if faithful, in the way which shall be best for him."[1]

Bourne then dropped out of history for thirty years, but his story was recorded, and in Westerly would be remembered again long afterward by those who were witness to these events.

What had happened to Bourne in 1857 was even then a matter for some debate. Word of this supposed miracle reached the sceptical pages of the *Providence Daily Journal* on November 17, where it was called "A Singular Case"; on the day following, the *Journal* speculated that this "was probably a case of strongly excited imagination, and perhaps after his senses came back, he concluded to make a good thing out of it. He has been admitted into the church, and many people look upon it as a miracle that may be placed by the side of the conversion of St. Paul." The paper added, "we hope it will be as lasting." Bourne's doctor contributed a letter in order "to show that Mr. Bourne's case is clearly attributable to a disturbed and disordered condition of the functions of the brain, and, if possible, to do away with the absurd and superstitious notion that there is anything marvellous or miraculous in the case."[2] Bourne's friends took issue with the doctor and attacked his medical reasoning by showing that nothing within medical knowledge could account for the suddenness of Bourne's release. The cause of the passion and transfiguration of Ansel Bourne was clear enough; it was "A Wonderful Work of God," a renewal of the age of miracles.

But, as with Mary Reynolds, we are entitled to inquire as to the background of the case. What indeed *had* happened to him? In 1857 there were rival explanations. The doctor suggested that Bourne had been suffering from "a severe cerebral disturbance," an argument if not in itself invalid, at least somewhat circular. The jaded copy writer for the *Journal* suspected a fraud on Bourne's part for which there was no more evidence than "cerebral disturbance." Bourne's friends interpreted the whole affair in terms of divine intervention, as did Bourne himself. Explanations ranged from medical materialism, to worldly common sense, to theology, and each contained its own distinct interpretation of human nature. But whatever the truth, the strange fate of Ansel Bourne must be referred to the vital antinomies of selfhood inherent in the evangelical Protestant tradition and the tensions imposed on the minds of those who are part of it.

FOR THE TWENTY YEARS THAT FOLLOWED his conversion Bourne was an itinerant preacher. He left Westerly and in 1887 was living in the little inland village of Greene. In January of that year he was transformed again, but this time no one attributed it to divine agency. In 1881 his first wife had died, and soon he married a widow who insisted that he remain closer to home; Bourne resumed the carpenter's trade and by 1887 had money in the bank. On January 17 he left home, went to Providence, withdrew his funds, and disappeared. On March 14 his nephew in Providence received a telegram saying that Bourne was in Norristown, near Philadelphia, and in some difficulty. The nephew went to Norristown to bring his uncle home again and found that once more something extraordinary had occurred: Ansel Bourne had for a time lost his identity and taken on that of an apparently fictitious person named Albert John Brown of Newton, New Hampshire.

About February 1, A. J. Brown rented a store in Norristown and set up a small variety business. He lived peacefully and did not trouble his landlord until one morning in March when he rapped on his door and asked: "Where am I?" Addressing him as Mr. Brown, the landlord told him he was in Norristown, but in a panic he replied, "My name isn't Brown!" His hosts thought him mad and called a doctor to whom Bourne related the circumstances of his prior life in Rhode Island. Bourne had total amnesia for the period of Albert Brown's existence.

The story was heard by a member of the recently formed Society for Psychical Research and, in 1890, was in turn relayed to Professor William James of Harvard College who then had the idea that it might be possible to recover memory of the life of A. J. Brown through hypnosis. On contact, Bourne, who had already been exposed to hypnosis in his earlier days, proved agreeable and was brought to Boston to begin a series of hypnotic sessions that were successful in eliciting some of the contents of his underlife. The subject was sensitive to hypnosis and by this means the Brown persona was again brought into the light and induced to recount his departure from Providence, stops in New York and Philadelphia, and settlement as a shopkeeper in Norristown. But Brown's memory contained facts that were also true of Bourne; he recalled his birthdate but said that he—Brown—had been born in New Hampshire, whereas on the same day Bourne had been born in New York. He also recalled the death of his first wife in 1881 and had a confused, inarticulate, but persistent recollection of "troubles" at home. James and his associates attempted to verify this story and with the help of the Philadelphia physician-novelist Silas Weir Mitchell they were able to establish that "Brown's" account of his movements was at least plausible. However, they could not establish any connection between Newton, New Hampshire, and anyone named Albert Brown. Bourne himself was baffled about why he, a carpenter, would have taken up a trade about which he knew nothing.[3]

Bourne then disappeared into the obscurity from which he came; all that is known of his subsequent career is that he left Greene and went to settle in or about Providence, and there presumably spent the rest of his days. A local Greene antiquarian remembered that Bourne had "erected a new house on the first lot east of the store and for several years made his home," but, perhaps charitably, did not mention the curious events that momentarily had attracted the attention of the outside world to Ansel Bourne. Back in Westerly, in reminiscences for the local newspaper, another old man recalled the days of his youth in the fifties and the strange conversion of Ansel Bourne; having heard of Bourne's later disappearance, he wrote that since Bourne "had another experience in after years, and as many of your readers are familiar with the incidents in the

premises, I will let them form their own opinions of the matter." For their part, James and his friends suspected a physical
abnormality in the case and that perhaps, during Bourne's
absence in Norristown, he was suffering from a "post-epileptic
partial loss of memory."

But there is no proof of it, and similar problems in interpreting these strange cases would echo into the future to our
own time in a continuing search for the elusive physical concomitants of multiple personality.

When word of the case of Ansel Bourne came to William
James, he was in the process of at last finishing the monumental and much delayed *Principles of Psychology* (1890). Bourne,
by his own consent, figured prominently in the famous chapter
on "Consciousness of Self," and thereafter has taken his place
in the ranks of other classic examples of split consciousness.
There in the pages of the *Principles* are the cases of the pioneer
French psychologists; there is Mary Reynolds; there is
Laurancy Vennum—"The Watseka Wonder"—who was seemingly possessed by the spirit of a dead neighbor girl; there also,
though not mentioned by name, is Mrs. Lenora Piper, a Boston
spirit-medium who James believed to possess clairvoyant powers. Finally there is Ansel Bourne. In one universe of discourse
his fate was part of a drama of sin and redemption, and in the
other a problem to be conceived in medical and philosophical
terms whereby the nature of self-identity would be empirically
studied through cases such as his.

Save for his sceptical doctor, the Ansel Bourne of 1857 had
been surrounded by members of the "Christian Church," a
body opposed to New England Calvinism but still very much
an extension of the Puritan tradition; his conversion and call to
the ministry, though dramatic and accompanied by unusual
psychic phenomena, were nonetheless within the comprehension of his brethren. His experiences fitted into an elaborate
and venerable cosmology in which the contradictions of the
human soul find resolution through surrender of self to God in
Christ.

But in 1890 he encountered representatives of post-Dar-
winian science, in whose eyes he was a part of natural rather
than supernatural history. There were three major participants
in the group that examined him. They were similar, though in

essential respects quite different men, whose various approaches to the understanding of the self express the ambiguities and difficulty of the problem in the framework of late-nineteenth-century thought. There was William James himself —philosopher and psychologist—opposed to all grandiose and unifying metaphysical systems and prepared to follow the facts wherever they might lead no matter how unpopular the direction; then there was Dr. Morton Prince—a prominent Boston neurologist concerned with the unusual mental conditions encountered in his clinical practice, but also with a metaphysical interest in the nature of mind; he would describe a case of multiple personality—that of "Miss Beauchamp"—which established a model for subsequent studies. Finally there was Richard Hodgson—an emigré Australian and research secretary of the Society for Psychical Research, broadly commissioned by it to investigate exotic psychic phenomena of all kinds, such as spiritistic visitation and split consciousness.

Though the paths of these three men crossed repeatedly, they increasingly diverged with regard to what they believed psychology had taught them. James would come to equivocally entertain the possibility that disintegration of personality allows the intrusion of supernormal forces into the mundane world, that the personality is somehow imprinted on the fabric of being and therefore may survive death, and that the universe contains a hierarchy of consciousness that matches the hierarchy of organized matter within it. Prince believed there to be a fundamental identity between mind and matter, and yet was also a respectable medical materialist who would to the end of his life fight what he took to be Freudian superstitions and the oversimplifying excesses of Watsonian behaviorism. Hodgson became a confirmed spiritist—"hardly able to wait to die"— believing that he had acquired scientific proof that the dead survive and can communicate through the living; he had his wish in 1905 and shortly appeared to return from beyond the grave through Mrs. Piper, the very spirit-medium he had been investigating. Each of these three selected certain of the currents of thought flowing through their time and, in accord with intellectual predisposition and personal need, each went his own way along with them.

Ansel Bourne was a focal point upon whom lines of chance and historical influence converged. He had to interpret his own life in terms of the shared understandings of his age. As I have said, all cultures pose questions of identity and value, and Bourne's set for him the problem of sin and estrangement while also providing, if one would only seize them, the keys to its solution. James, Prince, and Hodgson were changing the nature of the questions.

———•—•—•———

I RETURN TO BOURNE HIMSELF, to discover what may be learned of his life and the origins of his unusual experiences, then exploring the genesis of the concept of multiple personality that made him and A. J. Brown of such interest to the psychical researchers.

In 1857 Ansel Bourne was divided against himself, estranged from God and man and ultimately, in Christian belief, from his own better nature. Conversion for him was a surrender of his old egotistical isolation through realization that God is the only ground of being, without whom the soul is utterly lost. His conversion, though dramatic, was also stereotypic—fitting as it did into the pietistic traditions of New England Protestantism. Jonathan Edwards described what conversion—the central fact and turning point of life for the evangelical Protestant—is like, how it transforms the world of the believer. Edwards, like other evangelical Protestants, had a poor opinion of himself: "When I look into my heart, and take a view of my wickedness, it looks like an abyss infinitely deeper than hell." This attitude typifies what Dr. Holmes called "morbid religious excitement." However this may be, such despair was an essential prelude to conversion, when all is made new—as it was for Edwards: "God's excellency, his wisdom, his purity and love, seemed to appear in everything; in the sun, moon, and stars; in the clouds, and blue sky; in the grass, flowers, trees; in the water, and all nature."[4]

Because the soul is made new, "born again," so is the world it perceives; Bourne "could hear the voice of the Lord in each rustling leaf." The change, as described in countless New England spiritual autobiographies, was experienced as originating in power external to the self and in no way dependent on its own desires. The process is in the passive voice, a sign that the experience is truly of God, not the self; for this reason it is also the only subjective assurance of salvation. What happened in

Westerly, whether fraud, mental disorder, or true conversion, must be seen in terms of a Protestant culture without which it is meaningless. This was the culture of the Reformation: of Martin Luther, John Calvin, John Knox, and the founders of the New England colonies; also the culture of those English-speaking Protestants who enunciated this vision: of John Bunyan, John Milton, Cotton Mather, and Jonathan Edwards.

The Bible provided, as it still does, a measure for the estimation of the self and the world, an image of reality and a plan for dealing with it. It provides models, applicable through analogy to life's contingencies and recurrent existential dilemmas. In its grand though simple pattern it describes the falling away of humanity from God, the promise of reunion made through Christ, and an image of its fulfillment in the last days. Ansel Bourne, on the model of St. Paul, was enjoined to follow in the way it charted. He accordingly underwent the fundamental visionary experience of the primitive Christian Church as recaptured from corrupt Papist ritualism (such was their belief) by the Protestant reformers.

Anglo-American Puritanism established the cultural milieu in which Bourne was raised, and he became in turn the personal vehicle for transmission of its central myth. The intellectual heritage of Protestantism with its focus on the Bible and on personal religious experience provided Bourne with an image of his place in the world; he was told he had a self contaminated by the sin of humanity's common parents and was instructed to lead a life of relentless self-examination to hunt this sin down in each nook and cranny of his being. Even if Bourne himself had lacked all sense of such a radical division in his own nature—which, as a child, he must once have done —he was told it was there nevertheless; to have denied it would merely have been another sign of his unregenerate sinfulness. Through the demand that the self must first be lost in order to be found, this culture created and even required a schism fruitful in the symbolism of mental disorder.

The myth took on flesh in the persons of those it shaped and in the churches that they constituted on the basis of their shared understandings. What happened to Bourne in Westerly was the product of a particular religious tradition, but also it must be seen in terms of the social institutions that he encountered and the personal history that brought him to do so. Other of Bourne's fellows lived quietly, attempting to imitate Christ as best they could in their own churches and domestic worlds. For Bourne things were not to be so easy; though he was exposed to influences widely spread through his society, his destiny was a special summons to "go, tell the world what your eyes have seen and your ears have heard!"

The great revival of the 1740s was followed by abundant progeny. These revivals were stimulated by itinerant evangelists (such as Bourne himself became) who—labeled agitators, opportunists, and seducers by uneasy latter-day Pharisees— saw their calling in terms of the early church. This unsettled American world was alive with the spiritual descendants of St. Paul. One of them was Elias Smith, co-founder of the church and movement that in Westerly became the Christian Chapel.[5]

Elias Smith was a restless man. Raised during the 1780s near Woodstock, Vermont, he was exposed in youth to the freewheeling society of the post-Revolutionary frontier where those who first settled the land had to fend for themselves in religion as in other things. The Bible was the only book that really mattered or was accessible to them. Their preachers were self-educated and ordained by others of their number, were proud of their humble origins and happy to assert their understanding of the Bible to be, because motivated by faith, better than that of the orthodox clergy who had studied dry divinity at Harvard or Yale. Smith had his own conversion experience— "Looking around me, every object was changed, and a bright glory appeared on every thing. All things praised God with me" —and in turn was called to the ministry.[6]

But he found himself in theological doubt. Like Mary Reynolds he had been raised a Calvinist Baptist; however, a widespread American tendency in this period, arising in reaction to Calvinist predestinarianism, put more emphasis on man's own efforts in the work of salvation. Smith came to the conclusion that the New Testament, which anyone can read for himself, is the only authority in religion, and that the only name that a believer can scripturally accept is simply "Christian." He broke with the Baptists altogether and with the help of others of like mind the loosely knit "Christian Church" or "Christian Connexion" came into being and began to spread through New England to the upper South and Midwest aided by Smith's newspaper, the *Herald of Gospel Liberty.*[7]

Smith himself would oscillate back and forth between the Christians and the Universalists, another New England movement arising out of the middling to lower social strata from which he came (and, through the Spiritualist movement, of later importance to the story of multiple personality). Justified by a particular reading of Scripture consistent with American perfectionism, the Universalists claimed that it is God's intent to save all humanity and damn no one. But while still a Christian Smith converted John Taylor into the fold, who became the Rev. John Taylor of the Christian Chapel in Westerly; of all the churches in that town—Episcopal, Congregationalist, Methodist, Regular Baptist, Seventh-Day Baptist, Catholic, Christian —it was to the last that Ansel Bourne naturally turned. Taylor

> was a trifle over six feet high, weighed about 200 pounds with strong sloping shoulders and full breast. His gait was very dignified and when he walked down the aisle of his church, he had a kind of majesty about him which made a decided impression upon his audience. He wore plain black clothes with a white linen collar which turned down over a white linen stock which was starched very stiff, fastened with hooks and eyes at the back. His voice had a great deal of magnetism, was very loud, penetrating and sympathetic. He was an orator by nature—was considered in his denomination a very powerful preacher.[8]

Insofar as he could be comfortable among anyone, Bourne was comfortable among the Christians. In his youth he had already been exposed to the kind of faith the Chapel represented. The members of the Chapel known to have been witnesses to Bourne's conversion and subsequently identifiable were small merchants; others of the congregation, it may be suspected, were tradesmen like Bourne himself. The lower orders of New England—yeoman farmers, agricultural laborers, sailors, artisans, the working classes of the port towns— spawned new churches with an enthusiasm and regularity alarming to local elites. Among them, as said, were the Christians and the Universalists, and to this number should be added the Free-Will Baptists.[9] As their name suggests, they encouraged active human participation in the process of salvation while still emphasizing, as their statement of faith says, the necessity for a passively experienced conversion: "This change is an instantaneous renovation of the soul by the grace and spirit of God, whereby the penitent sinner receives new life. . . . It is called a being born again, born of the Spirit, being quickened, passing from death into life."[10]

When Bourne was fifteen he was apprenticed to a carpenter in Olneyville, Rhode Island, near Providence; there, around 1841, he was exposed to religion through the local Free-Will Baptist church under the Rev. Martin Cheney, then undergoing a revival that drew Bourne along with it to conversion and baptism.[11] Cheney provided Bourne with an example of a man twice born; in his youth the Olneyville pastor had passed through an attraction to Universalism downward into vice, thought by dubious anti-Universalists the natural consequence of a creed that had dispensed with the threat of Hell. But finally Cheney was brought into the light: "Through such a path of darkness, and out from such 'an horrible pit' of sin was the soul led forth into 'a large place,' where the light of life shone gloriously around it. The cords of sin were broken, and the spirit clapped its hands joyously in its new freedom. With scarcely less of wonder than was displayed when Saul of Tarsus knelt before the Saviour he had persecuted did Olneyville gaze at the miracle of grace in its midst, and exclaim;—'Behold he prayeth!'"[12]

Ansel Bourne's conversion into Cheney's church must have been swayed by its pastor's personal testimony, as was his later attraction to the Christians. In 1824 Cheney had evangelized with the other founder of that group, Abner Jones, colleague of Elias Smith before the latter's Universalist deviations.[13] But Bourne, discouraged by the hypocritical behavior of professed believers, fell away from church attendance and ultimately from belief itself. His chronicler concluded that "this unfortunate idea and presumption—that one can live a christian and keep aloof from christians—served to prepare the way for a deeper fall into the ways of unbelief," and soon Bourne had gone the whole way down: "In the secret chambers of his cloud-covered soul, he wrote, as with a pen of iron, the sentence of fearless and yet fearful unbelief, 'THERE IS NO GOD!'"

And this is the condition Ansel Bourne was in on that October Sunday in 1857 when he left his home to walk to Westerly where, in the Christian Chapel, yet another revival was under way. Before him on their personal roads to Damascus had walked Edwards, Smith, Cheney, and Taylor. Shortly Bourne was himself to be touched, the strength of the divine visitation overpowering the strength of his unbelief. The myth became incarnate again, and in pamphlet form was described as

Wonderful Works of God
A Narrative
of the
Wonderful Facts
in the

CASE OF ANSEL BOURNE
of
Westerly, Rhode Island

who, in the midst of opposition to the christian religion
was suddenly struck blind, dumb, and deaf; and after
eighteen days was suddenly and completely
restored, in the presence of hundreds of
persons in the christian chapel, at
westerly, on the 15th of
november, 1857

When Bourne was released from the bondage of his sensory incarceration it was as though Martin Cheney spoke through him: "Behold he prayeth!" However, Bourne's conversion, though conventional in form, was extraordinary in content. The call to the ministry that followed was also conventional enough, if a call in the shape of a miraculous vision can be so easily described. Yet to say that all this followed a stereotypic pattern is not to explain the distinctive features of what happened to Bourne; not everyone is converted nor called to the ministry in such a manner. It is only possible to guess what made him so distinctive, and there is little to go on.

Ansel Bourne joined the Christian Chapel but simultaneously maintained a peripheral status in it through the *exceptional* signs of divine grace he had been granted: "I have been led to think [he said] that God has something for *me* to do! I do feel as though God was about to speak to Westerly!" Bourne's subsequent choice of vocation maintained this position; he was to be at the head of the flock, not submerged in it: God spoke to Westerly through *him*.

Bourne was a marginal character and a clue as to why may be found in his childhood. He was born in 1826 and the marriage of his parents dissolved after his father "became dissipated" when Ansel was seven, casting the family into poverty. At ten Bourne was sent to live with another family for several years and later, after five years of factory work, was apprenticed to the Olneyville carpenter. He was set among strangers at an early age and perhaps had unpleasant memories of his own family; whatever happened, it made him aloof and reticent. It was recorded that Bourne could be "silent and stubborn, as he is wont to be in . . . matters which are exclusively 'his own business.'"

Richard Hodgson, in attempting to get at Bourne's medical history, learned that he had a few blackouts in the years before 1857, had headaches in his younger days, and that "he had been subject to the 'blues' since childhood. . . . When under them he did not want to see anybody or talk to anybody. These would sometimes last a few hours, sometimes a week. Occasionally, at such times, when walking, he would find himself two or three miles away from where he had last noticed himself as being."[14]

These headaches and lapses contributed to Hodgson's suspicion of an epileptic involvement. Equally, however, it can be suspected that here was a repressed, isolated, sometimes depressed individual who had been forced onto the sidelines in early life, later compensating for his loneliness by an ambivalent, aloof superiority tangentially expressed in his surprising conversion and itinerant evangelism: Bourne did not lose "himself" through conversion, but rather constructed in a public forum a more emphatic and also more social persona than he once had. Like Mary Reynolds, he managed to preserve a strongly defined public identity in doing so.

There was another factor at work. Eighteen fifty-seven was a year of major disturbance in national life. The stock market had crashed disastrously leaving behind the wreck of individual fortunes, the failure of banks, and widespread apprehension about what the future would hold; it was followed by one of the most striking revivals in the history of the country, extending through all strata of society and heavily concentrated in the cities. Sunday, November 15, had been proposed as a day of national humiliation, repentance, and prayer as though the crash were a direct visitation of a God punishing wayward Israel for its sins—an interesting day for a solitary man to be reborn and to find a new place in the commonweal. His own redemption and the hoped-for redemption of his national society proceeded conjointly, in confirmation of the old Platonic idea that the individual is a microcosm of society and subject to the same disorders.[15]

Several factors therefore coincided in shaping Bourne's conversion: the Protestant cosmology that made it possible and meaningful, Bourne's own aloof personality, a gross disorder in the body politic that led each to question the state of his soul in relation to the common good. But there remains the somewhat imponderable factor of physical or mental abnormality. Bourne perhaps had a tendency to respond to stress in the form of physical ailment and to contend with difficulty through abstraction and denial. When he became A. J. Brown he was sixty-one years old and going through a period of distress correlated to economic loss, his second marriage, and abandonment of his evangelistic career. William James asked the hypnotically resurrected Brown persona what he had undergone back home:

> Passed through great deal of trouble. . . . Losses of friends, losses of property. . . . Trouble way back yonder. All mixed up, confused. Don't like to think of it.

In a later session he (now as Bourne) was asked what was troubling him:

> Something I have been trying to get out for a long time— where I am and where I am going to.[16]

Hodgson found that a religious factor was also important in Bourne's 1887 transformation. When Bourne ceased his itinerant labors "he became somewhat troubled, thinking that he was not so active in religious work as he should be. This thought that he was not 'on the path of duty' weighed on his mind, and he seems inclined to think that if he had been in active religious service, and therefore contented with his work, the experiences which he subsequently underwent would never have occurred."[17]

Ansel Bourne had again fallen into sin, though in what way the enigmatic A. J. Brown—who in no essential respect save memory differed in personality from Bourne himself—represented a solution to these difficulties remains a mystery, and Hodgson could only conclude that "taken altogether, the case is not a little perplexing." It was just this quality in such cases—involving mystic visions, dramatic changes in self-perception and identity, the formation of alternate personalities, possible mental or physical pathology—that intrigued those who investigated him and for whom such phenomena suggested the complexity of the mind's operations. Underlying the concerns of the psychologists were philosophical problems of great and recurring significance. Were Bourne's experiences to be explained in terms of the mind or of the body, or was some totally new formulation called for?

The complexity of the problem had already struck Jonathan Edwards, to whom William James would prove a logical and worthy successor in the investigation of religious conversion and the unconscious processes underlying it. Edwards was well versed in philosophy and medicine as well as theology and searched for the criteria through which genuine religious experience may be distinguished from the morbid productions of a disordered mind. Edwards held that great excitement of the spirit can excite disturbance in the body by sending the "animal spirits" coursing through it to produce the physical concomitants of the affections—thus accounting for the emotional experiences accompanying conversion. But a difficulty arose from the belief that "though the affections have not their seat in the body, yet the constitution of the body may very much contribute to the present emotion of the mind." Persons with delicate "vapoury" constitutions can be deluded into believing that they are undergoing profound spiritual experiences, when actually they have been influenced by disease or the Devil: "Hence through ignorance, the person being surprised, begins to think, surely this is the Holy Ghost coming into him." The activity of the mind is raised to a new level and reacts back on the body through heightened activity of the animal spirits till "affection is raised to a vast height; so the person is swallowed up, and loses all possession of himself."[18]

Edwards knew that religious melancholia can well be followed by mania. At this point he found that the only adequate criterion for conversion is the public one, objective evidence of reformation; a person believing himself to be saved through subjective testimony is surely in error if he continues to wallow in sin. Edwards in his great *Treatise on the Religious Affections* (1808; originally published 1746), had been obliged to consider the question of how to distinguish true sanctification from the products of a disordered body or mind, and found the task by no means easy:

> Our wisdom and discerning, with regard to the hearts of men, is not much to be trusted. We can see but a little way into the nature of the soul, and the depths of a man's heart. The ways are many whereby persons' affections may be moved without any supernatural influence; the natural springs of the affections are various and secret. Many things have ofttimes a joint influence on the affections; the imagination, natural temper, education, the common influences of the Spirit of God: a surprising concourse of affecting circumstances, an extraordinary coincidence of things in the course of men's thoughts, together with subtle management of invisible malicious spirits. No philosophy or experience will ever be sufficient to guide us safely through the labyrinth and maze, without our closely following the clue which God has given us in his word.[19]

Edwards's phrasing of these problems well applies to Bourne's case, representing as it does an uneasy synthesis of theology and medical psychology. Bourne, as has been seen, was not only subject to religious experience, but to the pathological condition of multiple personality as well.

William James's best-known work, *The Varieties of Religious Experience* (1902), followed in the path of Edwards's *Treatise*, and drew upon it for insights. But James's opinions were informed by the interim development of psychology, which taught of the processes that take place outside of conscious awareness and lead to phenomena like sudden religious conversion. Though James was a representative of the new psychology he was also deeply sympathetic to the spiritual travail of those who were subjects of his book; this sympathy—based on his personal experience—led him to base the *Varieties* on autobiographical accounts from those who, like Ansel Bourne, had undergone this travail themselves.[20]

James's encounter with Bourne therefore has a considerable symbolic value in that it brought together a representative of an old theology grown uncertain and of a new psychology uncomfortable in its role as successor. Edwards's difficulties in determining the true outlines of the soul—what is specific to it, what due to extraneous physical or spiritual influence— much concerned James. But he put no credence in God's scriptural word, which Edwards held to be the only true guide in such matters, and fell back on the less certain evidences of science and philosophy. With the hope of determining the place of spirit in the natural world, James and others of his time had chosen to scientifically investigate what has aptly been termed the "secular soul," an entity still in possession of spiritual powers but ones now accessible to empirical investigation.[21] This venture took organizational form through the founding of the Society for Psychical Research in England in 1882, followed by the creation of an American branch to which Richard Hodgson was sent as research secretary by the English Society.[22]

Literary, philosophical, and scientific ideas combined in shaping the program of psychical research and the psychology of the unconscious in general. Empiricist philosophy had its impact as did the Romantic movement of the early nineteenth century and developments in neurobiology and evolutionary theory. This program was also affected by distinctly American popular movements arising in the wake of the Revolution and the disintegration of Calvinist orthodoxy—among them mesmeric curing, Transcendentalism, Swedenborgianism, Universalism, Spiritualism, and various perfectionist creeds such as Christian Science focusing on regeneration through the power of will. The concept of multiple personality was born of these influences and preoccupations, as were the preexistent understandings of those who became the reported cases and those who studied them.

I have already shown that the empiricist philosophy of John Locke had an impact on the way in which the case of Mary Reynolds was understood. British and continental empiricism looked for the origin of ideas in experience, being unable to imagine any other source. It was claimed that all ideas derive from impressions originating in the sensory world. But what, it may be asked, of the being who *has* these impressions? Does the self also originate in impressions derived from the sensory world, and if so—how? Some empiricists came to the conclusion that belief in a constant thing called "I," which underlies experience and in a sense owns it, is an illusion. Instead the ego was taken to be a product of the impression that experience flows past in a unitary manner, one perception succeeding another according to the laws of the association of ideas; by this account the relative continuity of the stream of ideas comes to be mistaken for the continuity of the being who has them. They believed that there is no such self-subsistent entity standing outside of experience and somehow observing it as though it were a motion picture. James, who later thought of himself as a radical empiricist, asked, "Does Consciousness Exist?" and answered himself: "No," in the sense of a constantly present entity assured of its own existence through introspection, "it does not." Consciousness, he found, is best conceived as a system of relations that sometimes binds impressions together in relation to a self that has them, but sometimes merely assigns them to the outside world without any clear reference to a self at all. Ansel Bourne, it should be remembered, had impressions "unaccountably" come into his head; we would be inclined to say that they were there already, but that is not how he in fact *experienced* them.[23]

James, in frustration at the limitations of our language and how easily it can lead us philosophically astray, had wished to dispose of the concept of consciousness altogether and substitute in its place a more neutral concept of "Sciousness"— awareness per se, without reference to who or what is aware.[24] Empiricism relativized the soul and made its very existence contingent on outside factors. The self came to be seen not as a *thing* (which our language deludes us into thinking it is) but as an *attitude*; one can either have experiences or be had by them. James reinforced these points by reference to the findings of the French psychologists that the supposed personal core of being is in fact quite unstable and liable to disintegration into fragments of greater or less coherence.

Romanticism collapsed the cosmic war between God and Evil—symbolized by the conflict within each soul between the Lord and Lucifer—into the antinomies of a soul at war with itself. The old dichotomies were still vital in personal experience, but were now comprehended subjectively. Estrangement from one's true being was still a central issue, with reunification of the self to be accomplished by an aesthetic assimilation to Nature (as with Mary Reynolds) or what amounts to the same thing, to a loved one in sexual union. The imagery is figurative, since self-unification was the real aim—fusion with Nature and the loved one symbolizing the fusion of complementary but alienated aspects of a divided soul.

The Romantics stressed the irrational, creative, and demonical components of the psyche and the manner in which these seem to intrude from a hidden world outside of or beneath normal experience; though irrational or even insane these forces represented liberation from the world of bourgeois constraint. Through art and literature the self-perceptions of generations were shaped by this broad cultural movement led by representatives such as Wordsworth, Coleridge, Byron, and the Brontës. The generation of the 1890s had made Stevenson's *Dr. Jekyll and Mr. Hyde* (1886), and Du Maurier's mesmeric romance, *Trilby* (1894)—with its free-spirited heroine and her evil hypnotic nemesis Svengali—into best sellers. The concept of the unconscious was born before the name for it and found a ready market.[25]

As a complementary development, scientific biology seemed to be establishing a physical basis for the divided self. In the first half of the nineteenth century, researchers in France and Germany began to uncover the nature of the functional integration of the nervous system. It was shown that this integration is hierarchical, lower levels controlling primitive patterns of behavior such as the spinal reflexes, while more complex patterns such as reflective thought are generated and controlled in the cerebral cortex as the apex of the system. The reflex arc became the paradigm of all nervous action at whatever level, entailing the proposition that thought inevitably tends toward active engagement with the world and its problems.

Cellular biology had demonstrated that nervous tissue is discontinuous, being made up of individual cells termed "neurones" separated from one another by synaptic barriers that a nervous current must leap; the existence of the synaptic barrier led to speculation that this is the site of the various repressions, blockages, and amnesias found in psychopathological states and trance. The brain itself was found to be far from simple, and that various mental functions, such as speech, are localized in corresponding centers within it. The new French science of phrenology contributed the notion that the various attributes of the personality are located in discrete areas of the brain and that the relative strength of these attributes can be apprised by the examination of ridges and bumps on the skull. This pregnant idea helped give rise to empirical studies of psychic localization and eventually of multiple personality itself, even though its central postulate—that the shape of the skull maps the psychological development of its contents—was rejected completely.

Evolutionism added to these discoveries the idea that this hierarchical organization was assembled in an ascending order through the action of natural selection over time, such that the lower centers are also the oldest and most primitive. Thus was established the material basis for the emergence of mind, and possible material explanations of mental disorder; the emergence of the mad or diabolic could be seen as a manifestation of atavistic forces—such as Dr. Jekyll's unsavory counterpart—when disease, trance, or drugs incapacitate their jailer.[26]

Mesmerism came into vogue in late-eighteenth-century France. It was soon exported to America by traveling lecturers using, as Mesmer himself had, the newly discovered animal magnetism in the cause of good health. By the 1840s, knowledge of mesmerism was widely spread and clairvoyant mystics claimed through its use the ability to see into a perfect world just beyond our own. The clairvoyants continued, in the idiom of a new age, the vision quest of their Puritan forefathers. Spirit-mediums then appeared who seemed, while in trance, to be able to carry messages from the dead. They were to all appearance literally possessed by the spirits, and underwent alterations of personality expressive of the traits of the beings speaking through them. It seemed apparent that the medium has the capacity to go into an altered state during which the waking personality is suppressed in favor of whatever powers are now in control, and that there are alternate streams of consciousness operative during trance of which the waking self has no knowledge. The related phenomena of mesmerism pointed in the same direction while, in combination with the sects claiming to work cures and other marvels through will power, suggesting that there are hidden energies within the personality at the disposal of those who care to look for them.[27]

The concept of multiple personality had multiple sources,

and the time was ripe for its appearance, since through it meta-physical and moral issues could be addressed in terms appro-priate to the age. The vital French cases occurred in an intellectual milieu agitated by philosophical criticism of the Christian/Cartesian notion of a unitary responsible self, research into the resurrected and newly respectable topic of mesmerism (now to be called hypnotism), and by discoveries in neuroanatomy and mental pathology. These discoveries were attentively noted elsewhere, and all the world came to France in search of answers to the riddle of the mind. Freud, who had already worked on the problem of cerebral localization of psychic function and the neurological basis of mental disorder, studied with the renowned Jean Martin Charcot at the Salpê-trière hospital in Paris and translated a key French work on hypnosis into German.[28] Morton Prince took his own mother to Charcot for treatment of a neurotic disorder.[29] William James freely circulated as scholar at large in European intellec-tual circles, assimilating the new findings concerning the divided self.[30] The French researchers were themselves occu-pied with speculations and experiments strange now but plau-sible and sensible then: telepathically induced hypnosis, transference of hysterical symptoms with the use of magnets, the clairvoyant powers of facets of an alternating personality. It was a heady revolutionary time, full of new forces.

However, orthodox science—including psychology—was predominantly materialistic; the mind/body problem was resolved by getting rid of the former. The spirit was perma-nently made flesh. That which gives rise to the illusion of mind came to be seen as the product of neural processes amalga-mated into a transitory and fluctuating whole. In accord with this proposition the positivistic psychologists sought to exam-ine the nature of the composite mind through the pathologies to which it is subject.[31] Psychopathology, through showing how consciousness disintegrates, was seen as showing in reverse how it is constituted.

The psychologists, now also armed with the evolutionary proposition that the simple historically precedes the complex in time and in the embryological development of individual organisms (ontogeny recapitulating phylogeny), concluded that the mind is effectively "colonial" in nature. Another French philosopher-psychologist, Théodule Ribot, epitomized this attitude:

> In the language of psychology the general meaning of the term "person" is an individual being that has a clear consciousness of itself and acts consequently: it is the highest form of individuality. Metaphysical psychology, to explain this character (which it reserves for man exclusively) merely assumes a Me, absolutely one, simple, and identical. Unfortunately, the explanation is illusive, the solution only apparent. Unless we assign a supernatural origin to this Me, we must needs explain how it comes to be, and from what lower form it springs.
>
> The Me is a coordination. It oscillates between two extreme points—perfect unity and absolute incoordination . . . ; and we find all the intermediate degrees exemplified without any line of demarcation between normal and abnormal, health and disease, the one trenching upon the other.
>
> Seeing how the Me is broken up, we can understand how it comes to be.[32]

Accordingly, when the French psycho/physiologists read of Mary Reynolds in Macnish's *Philosophy of Sleep* they were able to place her alongside their own cases as an example of one of the ways in which the personality may disintegrate. And, of these French cases, the most important was that of "Félida X." Her case, as the French psychologists themselves realized, was in most respects parallel to that of Reynolds: "Almost every day [her doctor wrote], without known cause or under the rule of an emotion, she is seized by that which she calls her *crisis*; in fact she enters her second state."

In her first state she had a sad, somewhat morose character, while in her second she was just the opposite; the first state had no knowledge of the second. Again explanations were not easily forthcoming; her physician was inclined to treat the case in terms of localization, believing that the alterations in her memory had something to do with a hysterically induced diminution of the blood supply to one of her cerebral hemispheres.[33]

Félida became the most famous example of split personality in the annals of French psychopathology, and was successfully used to evangelically publicize their new science and the metaphysical revisions it seemingly compelled. Looking back over the history of psychology in his time, Dr. Pierre Janet—

pioneer of dissociational theory and one of the leading lights of the French school and a great personal influence on Morton Prince and William James—spoke in 1906 to the Harvard medical school concerning Félida's intellectual significance (also discussing in detail the Reynolds case): "Her history was the great argument of which the positivist psychologists made use at the time of the heroic struggles against . . . spiritualistic dogmatism. . . . But for Félida, it is not certain that there would be a professorship at the Collège de France, and that I would be here, speaking to you of the mental state of hystericals."[34]

William James, greatly impressed by the French findings, provided a popular account of them in 1890 for the wide readership of *Scribner's Magazine;* once more the idea of multiple personality—of "the hidden self"—received a public hearing:

> It must be admitted [he concluded] that, in certain persons at least, the total possible consciousness may be split into parts which coexist, but mutually ignore each other and share the objects of knowledge between them, and—more remarkable still—are complementary.

James's sister Alice responded to William's observations on the hidden self as though she had seen herself in a mirror. She too had a form of multiple personality, though she was fully conscious of her internal contradictions, as she explained in her famous diary:

> William uses an excellent expression when he says in his paper on the "Hidden Self" that the nervous victim "abandons" certain portions of his consciousness. It may be the word commonly used by his kind. It is just the right one at any rate, altho' I have never unfortunately been able to abandon my consciousness and get five minutes rest. . . . It used to seem to me that the only difference between me and the insane was that I had not only all the horrors and suffering of insanity but the duties of doctor, nurse, and strait-jacket imposed upon me, too.[35]

These words are very like those used by cases of multiplicity in describing their plight, a problem of particular severity for late-nineteenth-century middle-class women pertaining to identity and vocation. Alice's vocation was her neurotic illness and her diary. She was, as Freud would put it, "marooned" in her affliction, and made a career of it.

For William James the problems posed by hysteria, hypnotism, and double consciousness—which, in addition to the
problems of his sister, he was familiar enough with on his own
accord—suggested a program for psychical research:

> My own impression is that the trance-condition is an
> immensely complex and fluctuating thing, into the understand-
> ing of which we have hardly begun to penetrate, and concern-
> ing which any very sweeping generalization is sure to be
> premature. *A comparative study of trances and sub-conscious
> states* is meanwhile of the most urgent importance for the
> comprehension of our nature. It often happens that scattered
> facts of a certain kind float around for a long time, but that
> nothing scientific or solid comes of them until some man [i.e.,
> Janet] writes just enough of a book to give them a possible
> body and meaning.[36]

James himself, though writing as an academic psychologist, was at heart no materialist—and his own equivocation on
the matter reflects a great unease spread throughout the intellectual culture of his time. Though materialist psychology
became and by and large has remained the orthodox vision of
inner reality, there were many far from happy with the assimilation of mind to matter. The causes and nature of multiple
personality and mental disorder in general could be variously
construed. James was a bellwether for the intellectual currents
blowing about and, like others, he was on the lookout for some
synthesis that might bring order to the chaos. In the *Principles*
—an astounding compilation of fact, philosophy, and speculation—he noted that insane delusions, mediumistic posses-
sions, and alternating personalities have the common feature
that personified external or quasi-external forces intrude into
the self's domain. Where *do* such forces originate? James's
characteristic opinion was that to rule out the possibility of
actual external intrusion is prejudice masquerading as scientific rationality. At the same time he recognized that the problems of Ansel Bourne, Mary Reynolds, and their like could well
be the partial result of a natural disease process within a nervous system liable to material decay and functional disintegration. In short, he equivocated between spiritism and
materialism, tending toward the former insofar as he thought
the evidence allowed.

This equivocation runs throughout his *Varieties of Religious Experience*, in which he attempted a tentatively prophetic reconciliation between religion and the new psychology. The *Varieties* deployed materialistic concepts and images—what James himself called "the hackneyed symbolism of a mechanical equilibrium"—while evoking the richness and human significance of religious experience. The "Sick Soul," the "Divided Self," the "New Birth," were central concepts in this effort and the most personally significant for James himself.[37]

James was interested in divided consciousness in all its forms, no matter how strange and superficially unrelated—the ecstasies of mystics, the transformations of the self experienced in religious conversion, the utterances of spirit-mediums and prophets, the testimonies of the mad. He saw himself mirrored in them, having passed through the analogue of a conversion experience in his own life that led him naturally to the metaphor of split consciousness and the subliminal self. In the *Varieties* James gives a disguised account of his own morbid state of mind prior to liberation through conversion to a philosophical doctrine of free will. His personal life also led him to the idea that conversion is in a sense a natural feature of growing up. Given the inevitability of the process, he called attention to "the admirable congruity of Protestant theology with the structure of the mind as shown in such experiences."[38] He became convinced that aberrant mental states can have a transformative and creative aspect, while the orthodox medical profession of his day saw in such things only neurological disorder and took unsuccessful steps to eliminate the unorthodox competition that thought otherwise. Ironically James's only academic degree was in medicine.

Through his psychological work James found possible grounds for rapprochement between science and faith:

> Psychology and religion . . . both admit that there are forces seemingly outside the conscious individual that bring redemption to his life. Nevertheless, psychology, defining these forces as "subconscious," . . . implies that they do not transcend the individual's personality; and herein diverges from Christian theology, which insists that they are direct supernatural operations of the Deity. I propose to you that we do not yet consider the divergence final.

... that the world of our present consciousness is only one out of many worlds of consciousness that exist, and that those other worlds must contain experiences which have a meaning for our life also; and that although in the main their experiences and those of this world keep discrete, yet the two become continuous at certain points and higher energies filter in.[39]

Elsewhere he wrote in a similar vein of multiple personality itself:

The same brain may subserve many conscious selves, either alternate or coexisting; but by what modification in its action, or whether ultra-cerebral conditions may supervene, are questions which cannot now be answered.[40]

Richard Hodgson would have regarded James's opinions as far too cautious, since by 1900 he had become convinced that not only are "energies" filtering in, but fully articulated personalities as well. Oddly, one of James's own last tasks on earth would be an inquiry as to whether, as it had promised in the flesh, Hodgson's spirit had indeed communicated from beyond the grave through Mrs. Piper, while one of Hodgson's last projects had been the editing for posthumous publication of Frederic W.H. Myers's *Human Personality and its Survival of Bodily Death* (1903).[41] Myers, a friend of James's and one of the English founders of the Society for Psychical Research, also attempted a synthesis that would subsume and make sense of what James called all the "wild" facts that had been accumulated concerning the human personality. This synthesis was constructed on the basis of the widely shared opinion that the personality is "federative" in nature and that there is a "subliminal" region in which thought processes go on out of the view of the conscious self. The facts to be accounted for ranged in extravagance and spiritual merit from "disintegrations of personality" to "trance, possession, and ecstasy," with hypnosis, sleep, phantasms, motor automatisms and the productions of genius falling in between.

Myers belonged to the Romantic wing of the psychical research movement. Himself a poet and literary critic of some standing, he looked for the sources of artistic inspiration in the recesses of the unconscious and yearned for assurance that he would be united with a lost love in the world to come. As a result he turned to other artists, such as Stevenson, for information about the creative process—learning that for many it often seems to spring from a realm outside the self. Not all could persuade themselves to go as far in a spiritistic direction as Myers had, but the important thing, so far as the history of the times is concerned, is that a large segment of the intellectual, cultural, even political elite thought this quest of great importance. As said, many were disconcerted by materialism, having, under the impact of the Darwinian revolution, lost the evangelical faith of their childhood; they accordingly yearned to find some new faith compatible with science. The conservatively minded worried that a working class that had lost the consolation of better times to come in heaven would turn to socialism in an attempt to create it here below; for them psychical research held out promise for political stability.

Though evolution was a dominant theme in late Victorian thought, it was possible to give it a mystical rather than a materialistic connotation. Myers was of the former persuasion, believing that evolution implies indefinite and goal-directed spiritual development (agreeing in this with Alfred Russel Wallace, confirmed spiritist, and co-inventor of the theory of natural selection). Hodgson, who thought the evolutionist Herbert Spencer to be the greatest philosopher the world had ever seen, also found multiple personality phenomena to be rich in implication. He and Myers believed—sharing in this with the more circumspect James—that the subliminal realm is not just the gateway to the unconscious but the very door through which influences can pass back and forth between it and the cosmic "metetherial" world outside. In his chapter on disintegrations of personality Myers gave an account of Mary Reynolds, Ansel Bourne, and the French cases, which seemed to him to corroborate his own opinion that

> each man is at once profoundly unitary and almost infinitely composite, as inheriting from earthly ancestors a multiplex and "colonial" organism . . . ; but also as ruling and unifying that organism by a soul or spirit absolutely beyond our present analysis—a soul which has originated in a spiritual or metetherial environment; and which will still subsist therein after the body's decay.

These disturbances of personality are no longer for us—as they were even for the last generation—mere empty marvels, which the old-fashioned sceptic would often plume himself on refusing to believe. On the contrary they are beginning to be recognized as psycho-pathological problems of the utmost interest:—no one of them exactly like another, and no one of them without some possible *aperçu* into the intimate structure of man.[42]

In the *Varieties* James provided a short list, with due credit to his late friend Myers as well, of those who had conducted, as he put it, "wonderful explorations" of the subliminal realm: among them the Americans Morton Prince and Osgood Mason, Pierre Janet and Alfred Binet in France, the Austrians Josef Breuer and Sigmund Freud.[43] This list reflects the theoretical flux then existing in this field. Myers and Prince in their different ways were concerned with metaphysical issues surrounding the problem of the relation between mind and matter; Mason probed the clairvoyant powers of an alternate self. Janet had experimented with telepathic hypnosis; Freud himself considered telepathy a possibility, as did Morton Prince.[44] But Breuer, Freud, and Prince avoided metaphysical speculation in their clinical reports, save to tacitly endorse a causal materialistic psychology that would make the future theirs.

If an encounter were to be devised that symbolizes a change in the world's affairs it would be difficult to do better than the psychological congress held at Clark University in Worcester, Massachusetts, in 1909; it brought together, among others, Sigmund Freud, Carl Jung, William James, and G. Stanley Hall, a fellow psychologist and Clark's president. Ernest Jones, later Freud's biographer, was also there and wrote of what he took to be James's attitude toward psychoanalysis: "William James, who knew German well, followed the lectures with great interest. He was very friendly to us, and I shall never forget his parting words, said with his arm around my shoulder: 'The future of psychology belongs to your work'—a remarkable saying when one reflects on his puritanical background."[45]

James was prone to hyperbole, and in his letters expressed a more guarded enthusiasm: "I hope that Freud and his pupils will push their ideas to the utmost limits, so that we may learn what they are. They can't fail to throw light on human nature; but I must confess that he made on me personally the impression of a man obsessed with fixed ideas."[46]

But his comment to Jones had at least a figurative truth,

and Freud felt that at Clark his movement began to come of age: "As I stepped on to the platform at Worcester . . . it seemed like the realization of some incredible day-dream: psychoanalysis was no longer a product of delusion, it had become a valuable part of reality."[47] Though having many of the same intellectual roots, psychoanalysis effectively displaced the older psychical research tradition and made the study of psychopathology and the unconscious a thing of this world only.

Freud, at one point a communicating member of the Society for Psychical Research, was having no truck with spiritism; for him the so-called spirits were endogenous psychological creations expressive of neurosis or worse on the part of their hosts. He was quite aware, of course, that earlier times had seen the matter differently, and he wrote a historically illuminating and provocative essay—"A Seventeenth Century Demonological Neurosis"—in which he used the new conceptual apparatus of psychoanalysis to explain a pact with the Devil.[48] On the American side this shift in orientation was expressed in attempts to give an account of the Salem witchcraft affair in psychological terms.[49] Freud had noted that the seventeenth-century idiom of neurotic distress naturally took a demonological form since there were few alternatives in that more religious age. Referring directly to latter-day Spiritualists he said that "the appearances and utterances of their spirits are merely the production of their own mental activity":[50] "The states of possession correspond to our neuroses, for the explanation of which we once more have recourse to psychical powers. In our eyes, the demons are bad and reprehensible wishes, derivatives of instinctual impulses that have been repudiated and repressed. We merely eliminate the projection of these mental entities into the external world which the middle ages carried out; instead, we regard them as having arisen in the patient's internal life where they have their abode.[51]

One of the consequences of this shift in intellectual concerns was a displacement of the concept of multiple personality in favor of other metaphors closer to the heart of the psychoanalytic movement. Freud altered the terms in which mind and mental disorder were to be conceived, and in the course of criticism of the French psychologists (and implicitly of Morton Prince, their follower), he demoted alternating selves to the status of "psychic complexes." Multiple personality, which had so much to do with the theoretical emergence of psychoanalysis itself, was assimilated into a psychological theory claiming more general powers of explanation.[52]

Freudianism nonetheless retains the basic metaphor of the divided self: the poor ego attempting to achieve a survivable balance between the inner and outer worlds was poised over the abyss of the id, plagued with an assortment of repressed ideas in the unconscious, and deafened by the demands of the super-ego with its yammering content of socially enjoined and parentally introjected moral precepts. This psychology was full of the old antinomies, but it brought them down to earth to be envisioned, in Freud's own terms, as an internalized war between nature and culture.[53] Psychoanalysis attributed mental disorder to the subterranean residue of disturbed social relations. The mind was now to be found as emergent from social life itself, and another element added to the foundation of a sociocentric world view.

It came to be realized that there are social factors that influence the subjective experience of psychic life. The nature of such experience is not self-evident but rather is subject to the interpretations that others make of its nature. Consciousness is as much a social as a psychological fact. William James was concerned with how the buzzing flux of experience becomes structured into a generally orderly inner and outer world, and concluded that the distinction between them is itself a product of experience—that the content of selfhood is something that is learned: "subjectivity and objectivity [he wrote] are affairs not of what an experience is aboriginally made of, but of its classification."[54] This entails the proposition that the content of the mind, even down to the most intimate aspects of personal experience, is greatly influenced by cultural factors—general wisdom concerning what is taken to be in the mind as opposed to coming into it from somewhere else, or not existing at all.

Freud had claimed that religion is "the universal obsessional neurosis of humanity," and aimed to educate the public out of all need for it in the same way that he taught his patients to overcome and leave behind their infantile fixations.[55] William James, on the other hand, recognized the *creative* power of

belief, the limits of the knowledge of his day, and the stultify-
ing effects of believing that all is at last clear. He responded to
Freud's attitude toward religion in kind: "A newspaper report
of the congress said that Freud had condemned the American
religious therapy (which has had such extensive results) as very
'dangerous' because so 'unscientific.' Bah!"[56]

The new sociocentric psychologies subverted the view that
selfhood must be viewed in terms of a unitary ego. Yet the
triumph of this attitude was never absolute; common sense
refuses to accept it, and, as I have suggested in the Introduction, this is one reason for the wonder that multiple personality
incites. Nor has it proved easy to convince everybody that they
have no soul. It is difficult to convince persons who *experience*
their lives in terms of forces irrupting from another realm that
these forces merely emanate from their own unconscious. The
world still has its mystics and seers who will not accept that
they are merely under the sway of narcissistic delusions or
incipient psychoses.

Ansel Bourne and Mary Reynolds grew up in a world in
which certain experiences in the passive mode were actively
sought, experiences which were as much the product of a certain world view as of their own psychological eccentricities. Yet
there is something irreducibly individual about those at issue;
they were not merely passive reflections of culturally specific
ideas, but rather active participants in finding their way
through the maze of time and situation through the concepts at
their disposal. They used paradigms and images drawn from
the culture around them. The experience of both was shaped by
evangelical religion, to which Reynolds added literary innova-
tions. The dilemmas both faced were in fair measure the *creation* of their common culture. Without the antinomies of the
Protestant soul their experience, however idiosyncratic in its
origin, would necessarily have found a different mode of articulation. In neither case is it easy to come to a firm conclusion
about the status of their presumptive "disorders"—whether
they should be considered pathological, and how they should
be explained if so. Certainly both had individual factors at
work in their lives which, whatever their cultural tradition, can

be construed as inherently stressful; but their culture also laid down pathogenically stringent demands. Such over-determined situations are inherently obscure.

These difficulties will become compounded as we proceed. My interim claim is that close attention to situation and cultural milieu makes such cases far more comprehensible than they would otherwise be. Furthermore we see through them human nature undergoing a progressive process of redefinition in the hands of the specialists: it is some distance from eighteenth-century evangelical Protestantism to psychoanalysis. As I have said with regard to the case of Mary Reynolds, it is interesting how many intellectual gods the phenomenon of multiple personality has been made to serve. Even the relatively prosaic Ansel Bourne figured, along with other examples of split consciousness, in a late-nineteenth-century popular treatise reviewing the findings of psychical research and ominously entitled, *Are the Dead Alive?*[57]

CHAPTER THREE

◉ The Return of George Pellew ◉

The gates are set ajar, and a motley company enters.
—M.A. (Oxon.)

WHEN THOMAS PAINE RETURNED from the dead in 1851 through the mediumship of an apostate Universalist minister, he reported how surprised he had been to find that there is an afterlife at all. He was gratified that it does not resemble in the least the traditional Christian vision of Heaven and Hell that in life this freethinking revolutionary—author of *The Age of Reason*—had regarded as a vestige of superstitious barbarism.[1]

What Paine's spirit had discovered was a variant of a cosmology already widely subscribed to in Spiritualist quarters: a universe consisting of a hierarchy of spheres and circles (usually in groups of seven) occupied by spiritual beings of various grades of perfection—depending on their degree of remove from the earth—engaged in ceaseless efforts to reach whatever level is next highest. Some of the more spiritual of these had made themselves known here below through their earthly mediums with messages of encouragement as to the unreality of death, the prospects for reunification with loved ones, and a promise of infinite advancement through the spheres in ever-increasing proximity to the Supreme Spirit. Some of these advanced spirits, among them a striking proportion of deceased Native Indians, became so-called controls serving as mediators with souls on the other side; each medium had his or her own controls—a secular version of the guardian angel—with whom there was a special and more or less permanent relationship.

The Fox sisters of Hydesville, New York, began the whole thing in 1848—a good year for revolutions—through the "raps" they received in a kind of telegraphic code from the ostensible spirit of a murdered peddler. This somewhat mundane epiphany was followed by the tipping of tables, the levitation of material objects, ghostly concerts on musical instruments, and edifying messages delivered through trance mediums. These messages represented themselves as emanating from outside personalities who, because of the conditions of trance, found it possible to appropriate the nervous system of the medium for their own ends. Frequently these beings were the spirits of prominent figures from the past; in America, Benjamin Franklin, widely known for his electrical experiments, was a great favorite among the Spiritualists who in general fancied themselves to be the harbingers of a new rational faith appropriate to the progressive nineteenth century. The movement became a mania, spreading soon to England and Europe, along with other American cultural exports such as Mormonism, and whatever their intellectual predeliction the intellectuals of the day were obliged to consider it.[2]

Among those so obliged were the psychologists and psychical researchers who asked themselves what these strange manifestations have in common with the alterations of personality found in mesmerism and clinical psychopathology. Multiple personality in particular bears a resemblance to mediumistic possession, and there were two general, though not mutually exclusive, ways of explaining this similarity: either mediumship involved the development of alternate personalities in the subliminal mind of the medium—and hence is a purely psychological phenomenon—or multiple personality, and perhaps other mental disorders, in some measure involve the presence of intrusive spiritual beings. Which would it be, and how to decide? Whatever the answer, whether spiritist or psychological, certain revisions to the concept of mind would be required. One of the first problems to consider was that of the relation between the medium and the message.

Progress was the ideological core of Spiritualism, and it was therefore appropriate that the Universalist ministry should have had a considerable say in the movement. Already they had done away with Hell as an unscriptural dogma; the only further innovation needed was the notion that salvation is a continuous process: enter the spirits with just this message.

Early-nineteenth-century America was attuned to progress; many had lost their taste for pessimistic un-American Calvinistic doctrines—as Mary Reynolds evidently had—and during the 1840s movements broke out everywhere seeking to establish a New Dispensation here on earth. The rise of Spiritualism —accompanied by mottoes such as "CHARITY, PROGRESS, ORDER, TRUTH"—coincided with various forms of communal socialism, women's rights movements, temperance, abolitionism, prison reform, and other such agitations.[3] One of the more practical contributions of the spirits was the diagnosis and cure of disease through natural remedies; here again the spirits of Native people, thought to be closer to the American earth through their aboriginal status, were especially helpful. In Mary Reynolds's old country, along Oil Creek, a medium named Abraham James appeared, who with the aid of his spirits developed a remarkable talent for siting oil wells.

In terms strangely like those of old-fashioned Calvinism, this was above all to be an *active* faith: "We must be reformers and progressives in all things appertaining to human welfare. . . . Spiritualism in the interiors is good for nothing, unless it flows out into the exteriors with sufficient vitality to conform them to divine order."[4]

A utopian Universalist minister, Adin Ballou—co-founder of the Christian socialist Hopedale Community in Massachusetts—found his political and social beliefs seconded from spirit-land, and turned this revelation against his conservative Christian opponents:

> As to the heresy of the spirits, it seems to consist chiefly in discarding the heathenish notions of a partial and vindictive God; the endless, useless torments of sinners in Hell; the existence of a Deific Devil, always opposed to the universal Father; and the unalterable moral condition of spirits in the next world. On these articles the spirits are very heterodox. . . . They condemn the world as it is, the church as it is, society as it is, and proclaim the indispensable necessity of individual and social regeneration. They are against *war, slavery, debauchery, intemperance, ignorance, selfishness, vindictive punishment, persecution, bigotry,* and whatever alienates man from God, from good spirits, and from his fellow human beings.[5]

In short, the spirits opposed or espoused everything Ballou did: "I look and all *good* spirits look with peculiar pleasure on the great work of Social Reform."[6] Unfortunately, in addition to these liberal spirits, some of the more earthbound types came through with less acceptable messages—often giving the impression that the "Spiritual Telegraph of the Nineteenth Century" resembled, rather more than a telegraph, a sewer with this world at the downhill end. Certainly this was the view of the orthodox clergy, who railed against a new demonstration of the continuing power of the Devil. For the parsons, who found spirit communications purporting to be from Jesus Christ himself exceptionally objectionable, the spirits were not those of the returning dead at all, but the minions of Satan pretending to be the departed to the undoing of souls.

The question of Evil presented difficulties for the Spiritualists themselves, since certain spiritual manifestations were certainly less than edifying. Believers were appalled at the blasphemies and obscenities sometimes transmitted from the spirit world. Even a sedate and highly influential Spiritualist such as the Rev. William Stainton Moses (M.A. Oxon.), formerly an Anglican curate, had trouble with spirits of this lower type: "Some of them would seem [he said] to be on a lower plane than our own; others are apparently destitute of moral consciousness. . . . Those, unfortunately for us, who are least progressive, least developed, least spiritual, and most material and earthly, hover around the confines, and rush in when the gates are set ajar."[7]

> These are they who allure to wrong paths, and suggest wrong desires and thoughts. They are usually shrewd and clever at such work, and they delight in presenting bewildering phenomena for the purpose of disturbing the mind. They victimize mediums in diverse ways, and find pleasure in the bewilderment of mind which they cause. Obsession and possession, and the various forms of spiritual annoyance, proceed very frequently from such.[8]

In an epistle called *The Menace of Spiritualism*, written pseudonymously by "a member of the Society for Psychical Research," a young man reported on the lengths to which this "obsession" could go; while experimenting with automatic writing he began to transmit messages foreign to his usual self:

> My whole being had manifestly undergone a change; I seemed to have received another nature—gross, vile, sensual, originat-

ing the most vile and abominable ideas, such as had never formerly entered into my mental life. My old self was still there, thank God! I have never quite lost that. But, although rebellious and disgusted, it nevertheless seemed powerless against the stronger evil influence which was dominating it. It was as if some unclean spirit had taken possession of me, and driven out my old self, and was using my mind and body for its own vile purposes.[9]

In tract after tract with titles like *A Satanic Delusion* and *Modern Diabolism,* the clergy responded to reports of this kind with the query: Well, what else would you expect? "These spirits are the emissaries of Satan"; "a real demonical influence"; "the delusion of demons seeking the ruin of souls."[10]

The Spiritualists inherited the Protestant tension between communal authority and individual inspiration; they had a terrible problem in imposing an orthodoxy on such an inherently heterogeneous and antinomian movement. The spirits delivered contradictory messages, had different accounts of the afterlife, were unable to prove that they were the beings they claimed; they blasphemed in one circle and preached in another. They apparently were capable of anything, and were greatly affected by the characters of those who sought them out. How to explain all this?

A progressivist cosmology coupled with doctrines concerning the nature of mediumship provided a way out. If there are different levels of spirituality in this world, why not also in the next? The spirit world turned out to be just as morally diverse as this one: "evil men become in their time evil spirits, and act accordingly."[11] If mediumship is based on a natural affinity between spirits, then following the idea that like attracts like, each given medium or spiritual circle will get the spirits they deserve: "a circle of fanatical spirits in the flesh would, by the laws of affinity, attract the same class out of the flesh."[12]

More subtle and challenging problems arose as well. Communication with the *dead,* after all, is not quite the same thing as a chat across the backyard fence. It cannot be expected that the departed will immediately adjust themselves to their new status: they may be confused, addled, even temporarily insane or hysterical—torn between their former home and the higher realms awaiting—"earthbound." Intervening conditions also set up interference; when radio supplanted the telegraph as a metaphor for spiritual communication, the problem of establishing clear contact was likened to trying to get a wireless message through a lightning-storm.

There could also be difficulties with the receiver. The medium was by definition a "sensitive," liable in trance to all sorts of influences. And there was the personal equation to consider—the possibility that some phenomena might be due in whole or part to seepage from the medium's own subliminal; this was a particularly seditious possibility, for it could be taken to undermine the spiritistic metaphysics at the root of the movement in favor of an essentially psychological interpretation; the gates "set ajar" might not be those to the next world at all, but to the subconscious and what for good or ill lurks down there.

To get around these problems the more sophisticated Spiritualists, such as Stainton Moses, placed emphasis on careful regulation of commerce with the beyond. It was noted that one of the things most likely to disrupt a seance is overt expression of doubt about what is transpiring; participants were advised to go along with the phenomena whatever their private opinions. Steps should be taken requiring that the sitters in a seance be congenial to one another and the medium, and to insure the repose and peace of mind of all concerned so that fractious spirits would not be attracted to a like-minded circle; if for some reason unwelcome ethereal guests made an appearance; they were to be politely but firmly shown the door.

With these high-minded conditions met, one could expect to attract spirits with congenial bourgeois virtues. Though absolute unanimity was neither sought for nor achieved, spirit messages settled into a fairly uniform pattern of conformity to the ideals of nineteenth-century liberal thought. Stainton Moses's spirit controls were a case in point; they identified themselves to him as luminaries so high that he refused to reveal their true identities. Instead they went under names like Doctor, Prudens, Rector, and the most impressive of them all: "+Imperator"—who, in seances conducted through automatic writing, invariably signed his name with a cross next to it.

Moses's central place in British Spiritualism, boosted by the interest taken in him by Frederic W.H. Myers and the Society for Psychical Research, ensured wide publicity for his spirit-guides—whose pomposity was matched only by the puerility of their messages; the Society for Psychical Research, through Myers, also found them of considerable interest. Mrs. Piper was their inheritor.

The Spiritualist movement, with periodic revivals reflecting local events, slowly assumed a denominational rather than a prophetic form—following in this respect the fate of the charismatic Christian movements to which it was logical successor. The apocalypse of spirit-heralded revolutionary social change ran behind schedule, just as the Second Coming of Christ had been delayed in the time of the early church. In the first days of the movement men had been influential in delivering spirit prophecies; they largely dropped from sight, leaving the field to female mediums who specialized in dispensing comfort to the bereaved and advice to the perplexed. Presumably the men of later generations went into radical politics.[13]

Looking back on a long life of failed causes, Adin Ballou tried in the 1890s to sum up what it all had taught him; though the new order was not yet to be, there was at least assurance of survival and a hope for things to come. Of his one-time friends and kin, now departed, he said that they are

> nearly all gone over to the spirit continent, a scattered remnant only remaining, like myself, on these mortal shores, and we are awaiting the summons hence. But how has it fared with the departed? Are they lost in oblivion or only gone before? Not lost, but translated to immortal fields—their spirits rehabilitated in bodies and garments suited to their present mode of being—each one in proper order progressing towards a celestial destiny of ineffable good and glory; some more slowly than others, but all surely. They have greeted each other on the eternal shore and congratulated each other upon their triumphant deliverance from the power of death and the grave, and upon the unfolding goodness of the Infinite Parent in all the dispensations of his ever-faithful providence. So may they greet us and we them, as we in God's own time shall emerge from the shadows of earth into the glorious sunlight of immortality.[14]

The psychologists and psychical researchers attempted to deal with Spiritualism in their own scientific terms. Noting the same problems as had the Spiritualists themselves, they began to investigate the mundane conditions that affect the nature and veracity of spirit communications. Some hoped that by filtering out palpable rubbish and obvious interfering influences they would arrive at a core of truth unequivocally demonstrating the existence of the spirit world.

The problem was daunting; there were great difficulties in the way of proof positive that the spirits of the dead are what they claim. The problem of communication was compounded by the covert influences exercised over the medium by the sitters in the circle. As Stainton Moses noted: "On the medium first of all devolves the effect of the conditions under which the sitting is held. If the minds be harmonious and the intentions pure, he is calm and passive and a fit vehicle for corresponding influences. If suspicion and evil tempers are predominant, he is influenced in corresponding ways. A mesmeric sensitive, he comes under the dominant influence, and too often re-presents the thoughts of those who surround him: or rather, becomes the unconscious vehicle for spirits who so act."[15]

Moses attempted, through the claim that disruptive sitters attract "tricksy" spirits, to defend the reality of the spirits in the face of the influences exercised over the course of the seance by the sitters themselves. For more sceptical researchers, however, the question of social influence became virtually predominant as evidence accrued.

Psychical research was an empirical discipline self-consciously devoted to the ideals and methods of nineteenth-century inductive science. Research into mediumship was conducted with great care by the lights of the day and often with obsessive concern for recording everything that went on in a seance, with the result that a great body of verbatim transcripts was left behind for subsequent analysis. Unfortunately, the more information accumulated about them, the less clear the nature of the phenomena became.

It was concluded that the only data that could actually be taken to *prove* the existence of a spirit was transmission of information that spirit alone could have known: a so-called test message. This was a stringent requirement, and there were others. The researchers were interested in "thought transference"—telepathy. Since they considered this a real possibility, they also had to consider the correlate that an entranced medium has access to the thoughts of the other participants in a seance. Therefore care had to be taken to ensure that spirit messages were not actually due to some kind of mind reading among the living rather than to real communication from the dead. In addition it had to be ensured that sitters did not inadvertently supply the medium with information by asking leading questions, or by responding with undue enthusiasm to vague and general messages that might pertain to virtually anyone's life.

For example, the spirit of a sitter's mother might make general statements about domestic scenes—"Do you remember the lilac garden behind the house"—trivial in themselves, but emotionally evocative and hence convincing to persons seeking evidence of their parent's survival. "Oh, yes," the sitter would answer, "of course I remember!" The danger was that a medium's subliminal might first throw out vague messages that continue until a "hit" is scored producing a response on the part of the sitter, then allowing further developments along whatever lines the hit suggests. Once this process is under way —"Do you also remember the birdbath in the garden?"—the phenomena assume a progressively greater illusion of real communication. William James summed up what the process is like:

> One who takes part in a good sitting has usually a far livelier sense, both of the reality and of the importance of the communication, than one who merely reads the record. Active relations with a thing are required to bring the reality of it home to us, and in a trance-talk the sitter actively co-operates. When you find your questions answered and your allusions understood; when allusions are made that you think you understand, and your thoughts are met by anticipation, denial, or corroboration; when you have approved, applauded, or exchanged banter, or thankfully listened to advice that you believe in; it is difficult not to take away an impression of having encountered something sincere in the way of a social phenomenon. The whole talk gets warmed with your own warmth, and takes on the reality of your own part in it; its confusions and defects you charge to the imperfect conditions while you credit the successes to the genuineness of the communicating spirit.[16]

Conversation with Mrs. Piper's control spirit "Rector" was a case in point:

> He has marvelous discernment of the inner states of the sitters whom he addresses, and speaks straight to their troubles as if he knew them all in advance. He addresses you as if he were

the most devoted of your friends. He appears like an aged and, when he speaks . . . like a somewhat hollow-voiced clergyman, a little weary of his experience of the world, endlessly patient and sympathetic, and desiring to put all his . . . wisdom at your service while you are there.[17]

In 1885 William James initiated the Piper investigations which, in other hands—principally Hodgson's—would span some thirty years in both America and England; with his perspective and knowledge of the parties concerned he faced the difficulties of proving the survival of Richard Hodgson himself. By the time the *Principles* was published in 1890 James had concluded that Mrs. Piper had access to supernormal sources of knowledge. But in 1909 when he attempted to decide, on the basis of voluminous records, whether Hodgson's spirit had indeed communicated through her, he was less than certain about what it all meant. Hodgson and Mrs. Piper had in life been simply too close for too long for it to be possible to screen out of her trance revelations what she knew or could surmise about him already. There was also a great deal of "noise" among the communications: "so much mannerism, so much repetition, hesitation, irrelevance, unintelligibility, so much obvious groping and fishing and plausible covering up of false tracks, so much false pretension to power, and real obedience to suggestion, that the stream of veridicality that runs throughout the whole gets lost as it were in a marsh of feebleness, and the total dramatic effect on the mind may be little more than the word 'humbug.'"[18]

James evidenced his fatigue in attempting to deal with such material: "One of the wierdest feelings I have had, in dealing with the business lately, has been to find the wish so frequently surging up in me that [Hodgson] were alive beside me to give critical counsel as to how best to treat certain of the communications of his own professed spirit."[19]

In 1915, Mrs. Henry Sidgwick, widow of one of the founders of the Society for Psychical Research, reviewed the entire history of the Piper mediumship and came to predominantly sceptical conclusions, though still maintaining the existence of a "veridical" core to the phenomena. As for Mrs. Piper's controls, James and Sidgwick concurred that in the main they were her own subliminal creations, "consolidated by repetition into personalities consistent enough to play their several roles."[20]

Sidgwick's analysis showed that much of the better part of what occurred in a seance could be accounted for by interaction of the medium with her clients. As had James, she noticed the effect that sitters have on the mediums solely because of the part they must play:

> That the sitters must influence the trance communications to some extent is, of course, obvious. For one thing, they are themselves personages in the drama, and the part they play in it and the way they play it must affect the way the trance personalities play theirs. This happens in ordinary conversation. We all of us inevitably talk to different acquaintances differently and on more or less different topics, and the complaisance of the controls, their desire to please, would tend to develop this tendency strongly. And in the trance drama the sitters not only largely determine the subjects of the conversation, but the personages who shall take part in it. They explicitly or tacitly demand that their own friends shall manifest themselves and produce evidence of identity, or give information on particular points. Then again, besides playing a part in the drama and influencing the selection of the other characters, the sitters and the audience. It is all played for them, and their presence and participation very likely help to prevent dreamlike wanderings.[21]

Mrs. Sidgwick constantly used terms borrowed from the theater in her analysis of the Piper mediumship. She regarded the seance as a form of drama in which the members of the audience are also actors, with the subliminal of the medium in the leading role. The play is written anew with each seance according to the needs and interests of the participants, the control spirits functioning as masters of ceremonies. Sidgwick pointed out that the controls give the medium a certain strategic advantage: "Advice is more impressive appearing to come from some one other than the medium, and . . . less is demanded from a spirit friend limited to communicating through another spirit, who may misunderstand what he is supposed to repeat, than one purporting to talk with the sitter directly. As a matter of fact, the difficulty of indirect communication is constantly adduced as an excuse for failure or confusion."[22]

With this interactionist perspective, James, Sidgwick, and others constructed a de facto sociology of mediumship—a practical application of James's discussion in the *Principles* of how the content of selfhood is acquired—even negotiated—in social situations.

One thing that was never doubted was Mrs. Piper's own conviction that her spirits were intelligences alien to her ordinary consciousness; this was reinforced by her assertion that she had no knowledge of what the spirits said through her while she was in trance. This again raises the important question of memory, and in this context it should be noted that Mrs. Piper's trance deliverances were defined—"classified"— by the situation itself as the product of external beings. Her devoted clientele confirmed this belief at every sitting and, with a situationally episodic memory, she herself denied any active role in such occasions. With one interesting exception the psychical researchers did their part also, treating Mrs. Piper sympathetically in the conviction that at least *something* genuine was happening.

Spiritualists and psychical researchers had alike noted that if good phenomena are to be elicited from a medium, there has to be an atmosphere of trust and acceptance. Mrs. Piper's daughter agreed: "If the investigator possesses a personality, which for some reason or other is antagonistic to the medium, he is but wasting her strength and his own time in continuing his experiments."[23]

Such a man was G. Stanley Hall, an acerbic individual who by 1909 when he met Freud was utterly sceptical about mediumship. It was just then that Mrs. Piper fell into his hands. Hall had arrived at an essentially sociological interpretation of the nature of mediumship. Some time before the Worcester conference he had undertaken a study of an adolescent girl claiming mediumistic powers. Since she was fully conscious of what the spirits were saying through her, Hall judged her to be only an incipient medium, "a medium in the bud."[24] The girl's spirits spoke of her personal aspirations and revealed various unpleasant matters about her family background. Hall tacitly encouraged the performance and saw the spirits develop more substance during the course of his sittings with their medium. He interpreted what was happening as a projection of the girl's inward feelings; of course, by this reckoning, she was exploring these very feelings by indirect means, splitting her personality so as to produce through the spirits an externalized and neutral

commentary on her hopes and social relations. Hall learned
that she fancied a certain young man and wished him to attend
a sitting so that he could be impressed with her spiritual abilities. At this point Freud and Jung arrived for the conference
and expressed a desire to see the medium; they had no trouble
in getting to the essence of the case—an essence consonant
with psychoanalytic theory—on their own: "In a short interview with her they at once diagnosed the true nature of it all,
and to my surprise she frankly confessed that her chief motive
from the first had been to win the love of her adored one. . . .
The erotic motivation was obvious and the German [*sic*]
savants saw little further to interest them in the case, and I was
a trifle mortified that now the purpose so long hidden from us
was so conscious and so openly confessed."[25]

Hall and a student, Amy Tanner, sought to determine the
extent to which Mrs. Piper was insensitive to outside impressions during her trances and subjected her to certain "austeri-
ties" in order to find out ("you have done diverse and
disgusting things to Mrs. Piper," wrote a critic in an open letter
to the Society for Psychical Research). More importantly, however, Hall and Tanner summoned forth the Hodgson spirit and
with some success attempted to deceive him. Hall wanted
Hodgson, now acting as a control, to get in touch with a spirit
—one Bessie Beals—who was pure invention on his own part.
This the erstwhile Hodgson did, and Hall confronted "him"
with the fact: "Well, what do you say to this, Hodgson? I asked
you to call Bessie Beals, and there is no such person. How do
you explain that?" The Hodgson spirit attempted to fudge its
way out of the blunder and Mrs. Sidgwick, who otherwise
disapproved of Hall's duplicitous tactics, was compelled to
find "it must . . . be admitted that some communicators are not
genuine." It was demonstrated that spirit-beings could be
talked into existence by a medium's sitters. In this instance,
Hall's obvious disbelief, coupled with his rigorous physical
experiments, led to a temporary suspension of Mrs. Piper's
abilities.[26]

Hall for his part embraced the new science of psychoanalysis (though later embracing its Adlerian heresy) and its apparent ability to account for the arcane in mundane terms, and in
1918 condemned as occultist the older tradition of psychical
research: "Psychic researchers to-day represent the last potent

stand of about all the old superstitions of the past, against which science had contended. The next generation will be hardly able to believe that prominent men in this wasted their energies in chasing such a will-of-the-wisp as [spirit] messages or the reality of a post-mortem existence, which they no more prove than dreams of levitation prove that man can hover in the air at will."[27]

Mrs. Piper slowly regained her powers, though her career as a test medium was nearly at an end. In later years she fell back on the Imperator Band, which had no pretense about being able to prove their identities, and with their aid she worked as a general spiritual advisor; as time went on she assumed this role as her normal waking self.[28]

> It is almost as if [her daughter wrote], since the trance state
> has been less and less resorted to, the cloak of Rector has
> fallen upon Mrs. Piper herself, and the good that she has been
> able to do along these lines . . . is almost unbelievable. I know
> of no record anywhere of anything even approaching the spiri-
> tual advice given by Rector as the amanuensis for the Impera-
> tor Group; and that this spiritual faculty, or power, has latterly
> been so largely transmitted to the waking Mrs. Piper the
> countless number of perplexed and troubled souls who almost
> daily seek the aid of this remarkable woman amply testifies.[29]

So far as Mrs. Sidgwick was concerned, the height of Mrs. Piper's powers had been reached in 1892 with the appearance of the spirit known as "G.P." Sidgwick's affirmation of super-normal involvement in the case was based on what happened then. She found that "none of the other public controls have any credentials at all."[30] The story of G.P. is of central impor-tance in the history of the Piper mediumship and the reaction of the psychical researchers to it. But also, when examined, it provides an illuminating instance of the way social interchange functions to conjure spirits into existence and to establish for medium and clientele alike the impression that they are indeed external beings. The case has an added interest in the intellec-tual and cultural ambience surrounding it—again reflecting the diversity of opinion about matters spiritual in late-nine-teenth-century Euro-American society.

In his essay, "The Will to Believe," William James wrote of how belief transforms the world of the believer, and of the validity of belief—moral, religious, or other—in the absence of positive evidence that might refute it. James found permanent suspension of belief to be an insipid and even cowardly option; sometimes it is necessary to make a leap of faith to save one's own soul. James knew what it is to choose because he had done so. He wondered what tips the balance between belief and unbelief, and it was clear to him that evidence is only part of the issue: "When we look at certain facts, it seems as if our passional and volitional nature lay at the root of all our convictions."[31] With regard to religious, moral, or (broadly speaking) psychological matters, "faith in the fact can help to create the fact."[32] Acting as if free will, for example, were a valid doctrine in effect *frees* the will, while subscription to a doctrine of mechanistic determinism may imprison it.

The founders of psychical research were not neutral about what they hoped it would teach them concerning the world and the place of the self—their own selves—within it. Myers, James, and Hodgson were stalking metaphysical game with scientific weapons. Of this group James had the strongest and most sceptical mind; he teetered on the brink of belief, while for Myers and Hodgson the evidence was strong enough to tilt the balance in favor of the spirit hypothesis. They made their choice on the basis of what they took to be sufficient grounds, and it changed the way in which they saw their world and reacted to the phenomena of mediumship. The case of G.P. involved the expectations and emotional orientations of those who studied his return. They found through Mrs. Piper what they expected to—a real spiritual phenomenon or utter nonsense. Those who believed that the spirit of the real G.P. was attempting to pierce the veil between worlds were largely responsible for creating the reality they already believed in; first among them was Richard Hodgson.

Hodgson was born in 1855 in Melbourne, Australia, and there took a degree in law; he then went to England to pursue philosophical studies at Cambridge University where he became acquainted with the psychical researchers and was recruited to their cause.[33] In this period his major accomplishment was a trip to India to investigate the claims to supernormal power of Madame Blavatsky, the founder of Theosophy; he judged the phenomena at issue to be fraudulent, a charge that rankles the Theosophists to this day. In 1887 he came to

America as secretary to the Society for Psychical Research in Boston, and spent the rest of his life there. Hodgson, with his Australian bonhomie, found the American atmosphere more congenial than he had the English. In the "large and charitable air of America . . . the real nature of the man blossomed forth."

His American friends responded to this kindred spirit in kind, "for surely friendship and brotherhood were almost indistinguishable in his relation with us."[34] Hodgson was good with children, ardent in sports, as fond of poetry as he was indiscriminating as to its quality. Above all, following his conversion to the truth of Mrs. Piper's messages, he *believed* in what he was learning with all the considerable warmth of his being. In a memorial address, following Hodgson's death in 1905 from a heart attack suffered while playing handball, one of his clubmates said: "More than one of his friends recall the eagerness with which he said only last summer, 'I can hardly wait to die.' . . . Then came that which he had desired; and neither the doubters nor his fellow-believers could wholly grudge him the opportunity to carry forward—as he would have said—'on the other side' the work to which he gave his life on earth."[35]

His personal style showed through from beyond the grave in a message via Mrs. Piper's speaking voice to Mrs. James and a son that "gave a very life-like impression of his presence": "Why, there's Billy! Is that Mrs. James and Billy? God bless you! Well, well, well, this is good! I am in the witness box. I have found my way, I am here, have patience with me. All is well with me. Don't miss me. Where's William? Give him my love and tell him I shall certainly live to prove all I know. Do you hear me? I am not strong, but have patience with me. I will tell you all. I think I can reach *you*."[36]

But this bluffness is not all there was to him. Beneath this facade lay an emotional nature that his male friends perhaps never clearly saw. James wrote: "He was indeed the most singular mixture of expansiveness and reticence I have ever known. . . . I was Hodgson's earliest American friend and until his death always imagined myself to enjoy an almost perfect intimacy with him. Since his death I have nevertheless found that whole departments of his life were unknown to me."[37]

His other nature emerged in his relations with women. Hodgson spoke to his female friends of God and God's love, of his own hopes and fears; they also responded to him, and he had various romantic involvements among them. Mrs. Piper's daughter wrote of him, that it was not "generally recognized, I think, what a deeply religious, poetical nature lay hidden under that bluff, jovial exterior, and what more and more during the last years of his life came to the fore, developed, he always said, 'by the fine, beautiful, precepts and counsels of Imperator.'"[38]

This sensitive but paradoxical character was able to elicit from Mrs. Piper what at first seemed to be uniquely credible phenomena. When he first assumed control of her sittings, she had already established something of a reputation as a medium. Up to this point her career had been conventional. Her husband's family was spiritistically inclined, and in sittings with them and other Spiritualists she discovered she had a gift herself.[39] Soon she began to acquire a group of spirit controls—among them a Native Indian maiden named (yes) "Chlorine," and a set of luminaries from the past including Henry Wadsworth Longfellow and Johann Sebastian Bach, whom the otherwise sober Mrs. Sidgwick called "the leader of the band."[40]

Before Hodgson entered the scene Bach gave way to the self-styled spirit of an eighteenth-century French physician named "Phinuit" who specialized in diagnosis and prescription. Phinuit was a forceful individual and, through her voice, addressed Mrs. Piper's sitters in a gruff but sympathetic broken English littered with gallicisms; unfortunately he could not make Mrs. Piper speak proper French, and Hodgson concluded that the language first learned by the medium must interfere with the ability of the spirits to communicate in their own.

Phinuit was in firm control when Hodgson began his work. He was at first disinclined to credit Phinuit with any reality, since Phinuit could give no satisfactory account of himself; nor was he able to justify his claim that he was a deceased human being, and still less could he justify the claim that he had been a French doctor. G.P. changed everything. Once he had made the small step to conscious belief Hodgson was increasingly prepared to accept the veracity of what Mrs. Piper's spirits were saying and finally became a personal disciple of the Imperator group. His will to believe was strong and further indecision emotionally intolerable.

On Friday, February 19, 1892, the *New York Times* reported severe weather in Europe, a French cabinet crisis, and a debate in the House of Representatives on the relative merits of gold and silver. It also took note of the death of George Pellew, a Harvard graduate and editorial writer for the *Sun*, who had been killed in New York early the previous morning upon falling into a construction site on his way home from a dinner party. On March 22 of that year the self-styled spirit of George Pellew returned through Mrs. Piper.

William Dean Howells, from his vantage point as author and editor, was a keen observer of late-nineteenth-century American life. He befriended young men with literary talents, as he had been befriended by such as Ralph Waldo Emerson and James Russell Lowell. One of these young men was George Pellew. Among other things Howells took note of Spiritualism and of the social ambience that generated some of its excesses. In his novels and stories he evoked the atmosphere of a Boston that was equally productive of reform movements and popular delusions: the greater Boston of the old Massachusetts oligarchy then in the process of being displaced by Catholic immigrants, of Christian Science, Harvard College, mind-cure cults, Spiritualism, Theosophists, mesmerists, Unitarians, Swedenborgians, feminists, philosophers, writers, publishers, charlatans, evangelists, psychical researchers, quacks, and medical practitioners of the new psychology—a city and region that were the inheritors of the intensely literate, morally restless and self-questioning Puritan tradition of New England's founders. It was a small, interconnected, and intellectually vital world only just being superseded by New York as the cultural center of the Republic.

In his novel *The Undiscovered Country* (1880) Howells described the sleazy underlife of Boston that produced fraudulent spiritualists for hire, but at the same time he personally attempted to keep an open mind about the significance of the phenomena they purported to control.[41] For his stories on psychical matters he invented a character named "Wanhope" who, as a dispassionate psychical researcher, attempted to strike a balance between credulity and scepticism.[42]

In the transcripts of the case George Pellew was covered by the pseudonym "George Pelham" (G.P., for short). However, his true identity was remembered within the Society for Psychical Research and is also evident on circumstantial grounds.[43] Pellew's father, Henry, was descendant and ultimately heir of a British naval hero in the wars against the French who, in 1816, was made the Viscount Exmouth. If George Pellew had avoided the excavation in 1892 and survived his father he would have become Viscount Exmouth in turn, a fate instead reserved for his half-brother. George's mother was a descendant of the great United States Supreme Court Justice and diplomat, John Jay; she died young, and Henry Pellew married her sister, which, since such a marriage was prohibited under the laws of the Church of England, led to their emigration to America.[44]

George was brought up in America after his father's second marriage, and graduated from Harvard in 1880, a classmate of Theodore Roosevelt's.[45] Roosevelt and Pellew shared the same "digs" for a time, and the former found him "*very* nice," though they do not seem to have become close friends.[46] Of course Roosevelt would cultivate an aggressive robustness, while Howells remembered George Pellew thus: "He had a kind of helplessness in the presence of material facts; his quick and eager mind faltered in the struggle of life, and all his talents did not avail to win him place or profit to the last."[47]

Yet as an undergraduate he participated fully in the life of his class, and wrote a curiously ominous class ode for their graduation festivities:

> The months proceed with gifts of smiles and tears,
> The seasons link fair hands and form the years;
> The years increase. This quiet eddy sweeps
> In broadening circles into life's dark deeps.
> In narrow banks the stream of life is hurled
> Down the bleak channels of the wrinkled world.[48]

Perhaps Pellew had a fatalistic or stoic streak in his character. In any event the phrase "life's dark deeps" evokes well enough his own odd destiny. And by the time he had written this poem he had already met one who was to be deeply involved in his fate and its aftermath—Thomas Sergeant Perry, boyhood friend of William and Henry James ("Sargy, Willy, and Harry" they called one another as they played together at Newport). Perry taught literature and composition at Harvard from 1868 to 1881 when a quixotic dispute led to his termination.[49] By 1879 Pellew was his student and they appear to have become fast friends, both having impractical personalities, a passion for literature, and a gift for friendship. It is probably through Perry that Pellew came to know Howells, Henry James, and the historian John Fiske.

After graduation Pellew took a law degree and stood up for the rights of women in controversies over extension of the suffrage in Massachusetts local elections.[50] But at heart he was unenthusiastic about the profession and tried his fortunes elsewhere. He persisted in his literary work and in 1883 received a prize for an essay on Jane Austen; by this time he had become acquainted with Henry James, to whom a copy was sent in England. In the same year Pellew was living in the Perry household where James from time to time sent him greetings.[51]

By 1886 Pellew was within the rotund orbit of another of Perry's friends, John Fiske, historian, evolutionary philosopher, progressivist mystic, and American evangelist for the gospel of Herbert Spencer; Fiske is still remembered for his observations on the evolutionary significance of the prolonged human infancy.[52] In addition to his other accomplishments he was one of the most popular lecturers of his day. The association between Pellew and Fiske most likely began while the former was still an undergraduate and the latter assistant Harvard Librarian. Their friendship was colored by mutual philosophical interests, no doubt shaped by Fiske, whose major philosophical work, a popularization of Spencer's "synthetic philosophy," had been published some time before to considerable public acclaim. Hodgson, in his report on George's return, would say that Fiske "was an intimate friend of G.P., and had talked much with him when living, on philosophical subjects."[53] These interests took shape in a manuscript that Pellew dedicated to Fiske.

It is not known when Pellew met William Dean Howells, but the relationship became warm and Howells, from his editorial position on *Harper's Magazine*, reviewed both of Pellew's books favorably.[54] In turn Pellew supported Howells's views on literary realism in a spirited article.[55] At the time of his death

Pellew was scheduled to move from his editorial work with the *Sun* to join Howells's staff on the *Cosmopolitan*, of which the latter was by then the editor. Howells wrote a eulogy for Pellew that first appeared in the editorial pages of *Cosmopolitan* and was subsequently incorporated into a posthumous volume of Pellew's poetry edited by Perry.[56] With this degree of support George might have become, save for a fall in the dark on a cold February night, a literary figure of some note and a viscount to boot. By the time of his death at age thirty-two he had already published *In Castle and Cabin*, a record of his conversations when traveling in Ireland, and a biography of his ancestor, John Jay, for the well-known "American Statesmen" series.[57] As Howells said: "The keenest pathos of his untimely death was in his dying when he seemed to have made even fortune his friend, and success invited him with the work for which he was always so willing."[58]

Both before and after his death, those who took an interest in George Pellew were bound to one another through the Tavern Club in Boston, a men's social institution characteristic of the day and one still extant (and still for men only). Founded in 1884, the club's early history was remembered by one of its more prominent members, M.A. deWolfe Howe: "The original membership of the club was made up of young men, doctors, painters, and kindred spirits, of an average age not far from thirty, who formed the habit of dining together in one or more of the cheap table d'hote (*vin compris*) restaurants which first tempered with a mild flavor of Bohemia the residential quality of Boylston Street in the neighborhood of Park Square."[59]

Not finding the restaurants entirely to their liking, these young men decided to form a club in which they could meet and control their own eating arrangements. Morton Prince was one of its principal founding members. The offices of the Society for Psychical Research were just next door, and Hodgson himself joined the club in 1887; a caricature on its walls depicts him with a stern and penetrating expression, surrounded by howling spooks. Hodgson's interests made a strong impression on his mates: "In all their number none seemed more extraordinary than Richard Hodgson, the voluble, warm-hearted Australian-English bachelor who was holding and reporting those sessions with the spiritistic medium, Mrs. Piper, with which Boston was for the moment agog. The Tavern

Club was a center for the resulting talk, pro and con."[60]

Another member of the club, and also of the Harvard faculty, was Barrett Wendell; he had joined in the same year as Hodgson and was occupied around 1890 with work on a biography of Cotton Mather in which he attempted to interpret Salem witchcraft and Mather's own proclivity for mystic visions in terms of the new psychology:

> In the light of autobiography the book bears a definite relation to the keen interest which Wendell, at about the time of writing it, was taking in the whole question of psychical phenomena. The activities of Richard Hodgson in connection with the trances of Mrs. Piper were then absorbing the attention of a considerable circle in Boston, with which Wendell had many contacts. His whole treatment of the Salem witchcraft tragedy was accordingly, and most intelligently, colored by his knowledge of psychical matters under modern investigation."[61]

Howells served as first president of the Tavern Club from 1884 to 1887 and, given the membership of the Tavern, it is no wonder that his character "Wanhope" and those with whom he argued pro and con about psychical research and the occult were portrayed as fellow clubmen. Howells set the scene for his tales in the following manner:

> We had ordered our dinners and were sitting in the Turkish room at the club, waiting to be called, each in his turn, to the dining-room. It was always a cosey place, whether you found yourself in it with cigars and coffee after dinner, or with whatever liquid or solid appetizer you preferred. It intimated an exclusive possession in the three or four who happened to find themselves together in it, and it invited the philosophic mind to contemplation more than any other spot in the club. I could be pretty sure of finding Wanhope there in these sympathetic moments."[62]

With the stage set, the reader would then learn from Wanhope and his friends about something strange and equivocal like, one imagines, the tale of G.P.

The survival of George Pellew was of special concern to Hodgson because of ideas that they shared with Fiske and Prince concerning the relation between mind and matter. This relation was then a philosophic issue of the greatest interest; the problem was that of how material nature could have produced consciousness—self-awareness. There were a number of alternatives available, ranging from dogmatic materialism to spiritism, or various compromise alternatives in between. The doctrine favored by Pellew, Hodgson, and others was termed "panpsychism"—the idea that mind and matter are the same thing differently viewed. The basic notion was that all matter partakes of the nature of consciousness in greater or lesser degree, depending on the way it is compounded into physical systems. If it happens to be compounded in the form of a human brain, human consciousness is the result; if the structure is a more simple one, so is the level of consciousness it supports. Matter seen from the outside, from an observer's point of view—say a psychologist's—is merely matter in motion: "cerebral vibrations." But from the *inside* it is awareness.[63]

How the issue was decided affected one's estimation of the probability that the human spirit can survive death. If it is assumed, following the panpsychist option, that consciousness is dependent on a physical structure of a given degree of complexity, then death would entail the extinction of awareness as the body decays back into its elements, and the mind back into psychic atoms. This apparently was George Pellew's own opinion. Not surprisingly, Richard Hodgson was more hopeful: they jointly undertook to make their own deaths a test case, and had conversations about this when George was a guest of Hodgson's at the Tavern Club:

> We had [Hodgson reported] several long talks together on philosophic subjects, and one very long discussion, probably at least two years before his death, on the possibility of a "future life." In this he maintained that in accordance with a fundamental philosophic theory which we both accepted, a "future life" was not only incredible, but inconceivable. At the conclusion of the discussion he admitted that a future life was conceivable, but he did not accept its credibility, and vowed that if he should die before I did, and found himself "still existing," he would "make things lively" in the effort to reveal the fact of his continued existence.[64]

And this he did. The first to witness Pellew's return were Hodgson and "John Hart," who we are told had been an "old and intimate friend" of G.P.'s. Hodgson stated that "Hart" was a member of the Tavern Club and that he had died in Europe in 1895. The list of members of the Tavern suggests that Hart was actually John Heard (joined 1886; died 1895), and this supposition is confirmed by the fact that Howells knew Pellew and Heard and considered them of great literary promise.[65]

At the first sitting Phinuit directed the proceedings and spoke for G.P., giving his full name and those of several of Pellew's close friends, including Heard's, which Hodgson believed that Mrs. Piper could not have known without supernormal assistance.[66] Also mentioned at this sitting were "James and Mary Howard" and one of their daughters. "James Howard" is Thomas Sergeant Perry, for among other things, Hodgson revealed that G.P. had lived with the "Howards" who had three daughters, as did the Perrys.

On April 11, 1892, Perry, having been informed of the situation by Heard, encountered G.P. personally: "The statements were intimately personal and characteristic. Common friends were referred to by name, inquiries were made about private matters, and the Howards, who were not predisposed to take any interest in psychical research, but who had been induced by the account of Mr. Hart to have a sitting with Mrs. Piper, were profoundly impressed with the feeling that they were in truth holding a conversation with the personality of the friend whom they had known so many years."[67]

Perry was intrigued, had a number of sittings with Mrs. Piper in his own home, and on December 22 received from G.P. a revelation that seemed to fulfill the conditions of a test message—one with content that only the real George Pellew could have known. At this point G.P. was coming through Mrs. Piper through automatic writing; during the sitting her hand wrote "private," and Hodgson was obliged to withdraw, leaving Perry to read the message alone: "He did not, of course, read it aloud, yet, the circumstances narrated, Mr. Howard informed me, contained precisely the kind of test for which he had asked, and he said that he was 'perfectly satisfied, perfectly.'"[68]

Perry's conviction was surely increased by references made by G.P. to their mutual friend Howells, who, though not himself participating in the sittings, is referred to as a "Mr. Rogers."[69] Howells's identity is apparent since the records state a number of things about Rogers that were true of him as well—

that he was a novelist who had seen the G.P. manuscript and that he had lost a daughter.[70] In fact Perry and Howells had just collaborated on the memorial volume of Pellew's poetry, in which the poem on Death has a special significance:

Calm Death, God of crossed hands and passionless eyes,
Thou God that never heedest gift nor prayer,
Men blindly call thee cruel, unaware
That everything is dearer since it dies.
Worn by the chain of years, without surprise
  The wise man welcomes thee, and leaves the glare
Of noisy sunshine and his share
He chose not in mad life and windy skies.
Passions and dreams of life, the fever and fret
Of toil, seem vain and petty when we gaze
  On the imperious Lords who have no breath:
Atoms or worlds,—we call them lifeless, yet
  In thy unending peaceful day of days
    They are divine, all-comprehending Death.[71]

The emotional factors that had bound Pellew, Howells, Perry, and Hodgson together in life were important in the development of what occurred; already it has been seen how significant a positive attitude was taken to be by the researchers themselves. This affective investment heightened expectations about the G.P. communications and, according to Hodgson, is a technical precondition for an effective seance: "The sitter who hopes for a communication from a 'deceased' friend can scarcely expect to get it unless his thoughts and emotions are directed toward that friend with longing sympathy."[72]

In this regard still another party figures in the scene— Winifred Howells—who, to the profound grief of her father, died in 1889. Dr. Silas Weir Mitchell had care of her during a long and wasting illness taken for a neurotic complaint (perhaps anorexia) and which, upon autopsy, evidently turned out to be cancer; the boundaries between the psychical and physical were ill defined at best: neurosis can be taken for physical illness, and the organic for the neurotic.[73] In the year of her death Howells gratefully received the consolation of William James, "one of the few scientific men who do not seem to snub one's poor humble hopes of a hereafter."[74] In a letter to James, Howells wrote: "I wish to thank you for a word that gave us a moment of distinct relief in the anguish which we have been called to suffer. Some time if you can tell us why you think that our Winny somewhere survives in 'permanent form' you will be doing a deed of great kindness and helpfulness. Do you speak from some experience in your late researches, or from some deeply-rooted instinct?''[75]

Howells never accepted spiritism but kept alive in himself the "wan hope" that surrounds his occult tales. Given his emotional stake in Pellew, I wonder if Howells was made acquainted with G.P.'s report that "Martha Rogers [Winifred Howells] is here. I have talked with her several times. She reflects too much on her last illness, on being fed with a tube. We tell her she ought to forget it, and she has done so in good measure, but she was ill a long time. She is a dear little creature when you know her, but she is hard to know. She is a beautiful little soul. She sends her love to her father."[76]

It is not known what effect these communications had on Howells, but if a feeling of assurance as to the reality of G.P. was growing in his friend Perry, it approached conviction in Hodgson. This was furthered by experiences had by George's parents in sittings with Mrs. Piper in April 1892. Henry Pellew wrote to Mrs. Perry that "such extraordinary evidences of the intelligence exercised by George in some incomprehensible manner over the action of his friends on earth have given food for constant reflection and wonder. Preconceived notions about the afterlife have received a severe shock."[77]

However, such a favorable impression was not to be universal. Scepticism or open hostility resulted in the failure of Mrs. Piper to go into trance, in garbled communication, or even sea changes in the pattern of her messages. James Mills Peirce, mathematician and collaborator in the educational reforms of Harvard president—and later Tavern Club president—Charles Eliot, was also a friend of Perry's and the living G.P.'s.[78] He too had sittings with Mrs. Piper but his presence disturbed her, since on the first occasion she could not go into trance, and on the second delivered messages that he considered to be worthless. G.P. was confused that day and at first did not recognize Peirce, who concluded that "in regard to the indefinable, unreasoned impression made by the interview, I must say that I received [nothing] that tends to strengthen the theory of a communication with the departed. No personal trait, no familiar

and private sign, no reminiscence of old affection, no characteristic phrase or mode of feeling or thought, no quality of
manner was there, to make the presence of a beloved spirit
seem real. I never for one instant felt myself to be speaking
with any one but Mrs. Piper."[79] Peirce found that Mrs. Piper
altered her use of spirit names in accord with subtle indications
he himself gave as to their personal relevance; she realized that
a blockage existed for she called on Hodgson to guide the conversation when things became difficult.

Charles Eliot Norton, again of the Harvard faculty and a
well-known defender of the arts against the philistinism of the
Gilded Age, had a similar experience in a sitting at the home of
William James; here G.P. was unable to identify what he had
won a prize for while in the flesh—the essay on Jane Austen.
Norton recalled that the sitting was "not regarded as altogether
satisfactory," though acknowledging that at least Mrs. Piper's
delusions were honest ones.[80]

But the most interesting negative experience is that of "Mr.
Marte." Marte is John Fiske, whose true identity was again
known by the Society for Psychical Research; it is also discernible through Hodgson's record, which relates that "Marte" was
a public figure involved in philosophic concerns who had made
a contribution to the doctrine of evolution. His fame was
known to Mrs. Piper as well, for when Fiske entered the room
during a sitting her writing hand trembled with excitement;
but Hodgson explained that "Mr. Marte is so well-known both
as an author and a lecturer that any mere knowledge of his
name and work cannot be regarded as having any evidential
value."[81]

Unlike Hodgson and Perry, Fiske had a violent antipathy to
Spiritualism, which in his view posited an unspiritual affinity
between mind and matter and an insipid vision of the future
life. He had already written sarcastically concerning "gross
materialistic notions of ghosts and bogies, and spirits that
upset tables and whisper to ignorant vulgar women the wonderful information that you once had an aunt Susan." "Spiritualism," he concluded, "is simply one of the weeds which
springs up in minds uncultivated by science."[82] Fiske was prepared to find nothing in the Pellew phenomena and his experiences lived up to expectation. However, his interchanges with
G.P. are revealing in their philosophical emphasis; Fiske chose

to ask only certain things and failure to obtain adequate responses was a negative test of G.P.'s reality.

In December 1892 Fiske asked G.P. about the manuscript that the latter had prepared in life, but was unable to elicit any memory of it. This manuscript was apparently entitled *The One or the Many* and was a treatise on panpsychism that embodied the idea expressed by Pellew in the line of his poem on death that begins "Atoms or worlds—we call them lifeless." Inability to remember a work on such a keenly debated issue was ground for suspicion; (G.P., on the other hand, had been remarkably precise about the location of a metal letter box in his parents' home).[83] Another topic of conversation was the thought of Chauncey Wright, an important early figure in pragmatism and a friend of James's and Norton's. Wright had been hostile to philosophical systems because he did not believe that current knowledge of the universe allows the conclusion that there is a single set of natural laws acting uniformly in all times and places; there may be temporary and local manifestations of order, which he termed "cosmical weather," but there is no reason to suppose that these apply to nature at large.[84] The same attitude led to James's belief that overemphasis on system may blind one to the "stray" or "wild" facts, such as those of psychical research, which stand outside the boundaries of the publicly accepted world order.[85] But in the seances G.P. did not comprehend the meaning of the notion of "cosmical weather," supposing instead that it referred to the *constancy* of physical law.

In sum, Fiske's attitude was contrary to that thought by Hodgson as necessary for the successful reception of spirit messages, and it was reported that "Mr. Marte formed an opinion entirely unfavorable to Mrs. Piper." Following the experience with Fiske, G.P. got "further away" and eventually was displaced by the Imperator Band, spirits with no philosophical pretensions and hence no capacity for philosophical error.

Opinions about the probability of the survival of George Pellew contrasted markedly: Perry, Heard, Pellew's parents, and Hodgson found the G.P. communications suggestive if not convincing, whereas Peirce, Norton, and Fiske were sceptical if not hostile. Norton was reserved and Peirce seems to have been uninterested in what could not be adequately known through assured scientific method; Fiske had already elaborated his own beliefs about the future life within a system uncongenial to Spiritualism. On the other hand, Perry, Heard, and Pellew's parents had an emotional stake in the question. Heard and Pellew were age-mates of similar literary-esthetic tastes; Perry, though older, shared them and had George under his own roof for a time. Perhaps he also had more of the accepting human responsiveness so necessary for a successful seance.

Perry had sittings with Mrs. Piper in the comfort of his own home and dealt with her sympathetically; Mrs. Perry and the daughters were also there, and all were receptive to G.P., who drew strength and coherence from interacting with them. As Hodgson said, "what change has been discernable is a change not of any process of disintegration, but rather of integration and evolution."[86] G.P., being treated as real, came to exhibit the behavior, knowledge, and attitudes expected of him.

A picture therefore emerges of how a semblance of life was breathed into G.P. and by extension any other "spiritual" being of like nature. However, it is not possible to obtain the full picture, and in essential respects the transcripts are unhelpful; there are a number of hidden factors that could well have affected the proceedings. Undoubtedly, as Peirce noted and Mrs. Sidgwick noted after him, the sitters provided cues to the medium. Also, the sitters were part of a small social and cultural world and some of them had been known to each other. What information did G.P. give that Perry found so satisfying? How did it happen G.P. had such a facility in recognizing Pellew's earthly friends?[87] There is much subtlety in personal interaction that cannot be recorded even in the most verbatim of transcripts; for this reason the record of the G.P. seances is entirely worthless with respect to proving George Pellew's survival. Hodgson himself evokes the difficulties here:

> Most of these communications are of a personal nature and cannot be regarded as evidential from the ordinary point of view; but the continual manifestations of this personality with its own reservoir of memories, with its swift appreciation of any reference to friends of G.P., with its "give and take" in little incidental conversations with myself, has helped largely in producing a conviction of the actual presence of the G.P. personality, which would be quite impossible to impart by any mere enumeration of verifiable statements. It will hardly, however, be regarded as surprising that the most impressive mani-

festations are at the same time the most subtle and the least communicable.[88]

There is not a complete picture of who sat with Mrs. Piper during this period, nor of their motivations and their relations, if any, with one another. That very intimate matters were discussed is revealed by those occasions when Hodgson was asked to withdraw. Mrs. Piper surely had her ear to the ground both in trance and outside it, and while in trance she was regarded as having been more oblivious to the outside world than was actually the case. Idle talk on the sidelines, such as between Perry's daughters; information inadvertently relayed to her by other sitters; the guidance which it was agreed Hodgson unconsciously provided her; all these things, coupled with a native sensibility and intuitive understanding of the social relations between her sitters and the cultural attitudes they shared, made Mrs. Piper an effective tribal soothsayer in the middle-class society of late-nineteenth-century Boston.

Finally, there was a will to believe. The middle classes of those times were troubled by new scientific developments and the questioning of old religious values to a degree not now easy to imagine. Once a willingness to entertain a belief in the possible existence of spirits is established, perhaps accompanied by the desire to again meet a loved one, the path is made ready for conviction. In Hodgson's case his experiences with Mrs. Piper had the decisive role. By 1898 he had concluded that "I cannot profess to have any doubt but that the chief 'communicators' . . . are veritably the personalities that they claim to be, that they have survived the change we call death, and that they have directly communicated with us whom we call living, through Mrs. Piper's entranced organism."[89]

Almost immediately after Hodgson's own voyage to spirit-land he returned through Mrs. Piper and henceforth featured prominently among the spirits of dead psychical researchers bringing word of the reality and nature of the future state. Yet he was dearly missed; Morton Prince, upon completion of his study of the Beauchamp case of multiple personality in 1905, wrote William James about how deeply Hodgson's loss was felt: "Dick's death has taken out a good deal of the joy that would have come from completion of the work. There is nothing more that I need say to you about our loss, as you share with all of us the shock and the sorrow."[90]

———————◆•◆•◆———————

MRS. PIPER REGARDED HER COMMUNICATORS as no less real than Hodgson did; there is no reason not to believe that she was truthful when she stated in her waking state that she was oblivious to what her spirits were saying through her in trance. Her spirits were imaginative constructions negotiated into existence in a supportive context of others ready to accept their reality. Mrs. Piper cannot be regarded as having been suffering from a mental disorder, no matter how domesticated. Yet her phenomena are diagnostic criteria for the multiple personality syndrome.

The psychical researchers of her time interpreted her abilities in terms of dissociative trance akin to that of hypnosis. Isolated parts of the mind were seen as developing internal structures capable of representing themselves as distinct personalities, an interpretation consistent with late-nineteenth-century understandings of the anatomy of the nervous system. William James, though spiritistically inclined, stated that as a *psychologist*—as a scientist—he had to accept this type of materialistic formulation himself. But he and his fellow psychical researchers, however much they may have vacillated with regard to the spirit hypothesis, were pointing toward a sociology of mind. Research on mediumship showed that important aspects of psychological structure—what is to count as self or other, for example—are socially acquired, and that the exercise of mental "faculties"—such as memory—function relative to social situation. Hall, Sidgwick, James, even Hodgson, had shown how these strange fluctuations in the content of selfhood are accomplished in a climate of belief supportive of it. Psychical research and much of late-nine-teenth-century psychology opened up an interactionist perspective on human affairs and the mind placed in context.

Spiritualism, which had begun as a loosely knit progressivist sect with radical undertones, was a very American thing. Through the suppression of her selfhood in favor of communications from another world Mrs. Piper provided a vision of hope for her anxious or bereaved clientele. She appeared to have been tailored for this role from a young age and to have been both sympathetic and suggestible. She came to believe in the reality of trance and was able to display it convincingly to others who interacted with her spirits and taught them how to behave. When Mrs. Piper's "self" was ritually defined as in abeyance through the trance-induction procedure and the general context of the seance, she—like those exposed to hypnosis —turned her attention only in certain directions: thus her lack of memory, thus also the impression that her spirits were indeed external beings.

There is philosophical instruction to be found in all this. Are our perceptions "out there" in the external world, or actually "in here" in the percipient? This fundamental problem pertains to all experience. Is a thought *my* thought, or did someone put it there? This way lies madness. Nevertheless such questions again show how what we like to think of as psychological experience is influenced by social factors. The locus of experience is a matter of definition, or what William James called "classification." The self is part of a wider cultural world. Mrs. Piper's and G.P.'s world, like that of Mary Reynolds and Ansel Bourne, legitimated and—just as had the Puritan pietist tradition—even made desirable certain experiences in the passive voice. The Spiritualists and many of the psychical researchers construed the boundaries of selfhood as embracing a trans-mundane reality of spirits and telepathic influences. With this attitude the phenomena of multiple personality appear in a very different light than for those more worldly philosophers such as Morton Prince—whom I consider next—and who have held that the world of the inner psyche is the only psychic world there is.

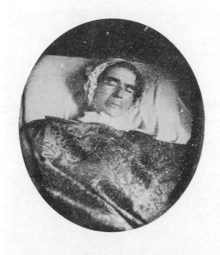

Mary Reynolds in death, 1854

Ansel Bourne, about 1900

Richard Hodgson at the Tavern Club

William James, about 1905

Mrs. Piper

George Pellew

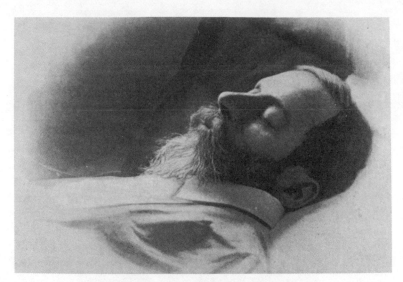

William Stainton Moses (M.A., *Oxon.*) in death

Morton Prince, about 1920

CHAPTER FOUR

✿ The Hidden Self ✿

*But I say put your trust in Princes and thy faith
shall make thee whole.*
—B.C.A.

STANDING ON THE HIGH GROUND near the Civil War Memorial one looks northward across the Boston Common to Beacon Street and westward to the Public Garden. Walking down Beacon, Charles Street is crossed and then, on the way to the Back Bay—a development of opulent row houses built in the 1870s —one passes Morton Prince's former home and office at number 458. Charles leads off toward Massachusetts General Hospital and the river; Richard Hodgson had his flat at number 15.

This was the heartland of the late-nineteenth-century Boston elite, as evoked in novels and stories. William Dean Howells's upwardly mobile but socially inept Vermont paint manufacturer, Silas Lapham, celebrated his status by building a new house on the water side of Beacon. John P. Marquand's representative old Bostonian, George Apley, lived in the Back Bay long enough to face with puzzlement the ascendancy of the Irish diaspora. Henry James located on Charles the house of the aristocratic feminist Olive Chancellor, who—in *The Bostonians*—fought a losing battle for the allegiance of the trance-speaker Verena Tarrant, daughter of a Cambridge mesmerist.

The concerns that motivated James's characters in *The Bostonians* were extracted from the actual Boston of the 1870s and 1880s, a Boston of noblesse oblige, of spiritualistic charlatans and utopian enthusiasts; a Boston of social causes and social change. James saw enthusiasts as unbalanced, hence his satirical attitude toward a city he knew well but had rejected in favor of permanent residence in England. He had a sense of what a whole personality might be like. But his characters Olive Chancellor and Verena Tarrant were only part-personalities, each supplying what the other lacked: Chancellor the intellect and purpose, Tarrant the extroverted charisma. This, though cast in the idiom of a clash of external characters, is the dynamic of multiple personality as well. The personal dynamic that James made the heart of his great novel emerged in a transmuted form in Prince's medical reports; both reflected the dilemmas of their age.

Morton Prince also believed in a whole true self, "the normal real self . . . best adapted to *any* environment."[1] Yet in times like these when the concept of selfhood was itself in flux, when there were conflicting and contradictory visions of how life should be lived, a normal real self was often more the object of an anxious quest than the expression of a naturally existing state of affairs. On the small stage of Morton Prince's consulting room the women known as Miss Beauchamp and B.C.A. conducted an internal struggle between conflicting objective possibilities. In the symbolically transformed shape of medical disorder Prince encountered one of the representative problems of his age and became the inadvertent director of a play with a peculiarly creative cast of characters; the climax, as in the novel, took the form of self-realization, a partial resolution of existential and objective contradiction; how this happened we shall see.

Neurologist and novelist were describing the same social world, though only one explicitly intended to—a world of obsessions and neuroses, of practical insecurities and philosophical disquiet, of mind-cure cults and proto-modern psychiatry. And it was a society agitated by the "woman question"— the society to which George Pellew pitched his sympathetic observations on female suffrage. Multiple personality is mainly an affair of women (or perhaps I should now say an affair of women and their doctors). The cases at issue in this chapter were the product of personal, intimate, and emotionally loaded interaction between physician and patient; their mutual attitudes, experiences, and characters are the key to the dynamic of what occurred between them.

MORTON PRINCE WAS A MAN with life on his side. Son of a three-time mayor of Boston, he "received the classical education of Boston's professional and social elite."[2] He graduated from Harvard in 1875 and from Harvard medical school in 1879. During the course of his medical studies he wrote a prize essay—*The Nature of Mind and Human Automatism*—on the subject of the unconscious and the relation between mind and matter; it was published in monographic form in 1885 and was the basis of Prince's philosophical attitudes to the end of his life.[3] In 1928, a year before he died, he was still defending a "panpsychist" metaphysics espoused fifty years before to get around the apparently insoluble problem of how matter can give rise to mind.[4]

Prince was generally remembered as Ernest Jones did: "a thorough gentleman, a man of the world, and a very pleasant colleague." A friend wrote of him that "Dr. Prince was of an extremely sociable temperament, and his interesting personality, with his friendliness and boyish enthusiasm, assured for him a warm welcome wherever he went."[5] These traits made him an admirable clubman and, as the surviving letters of his patients show, a man with a considerable influence on women.

Prince's first medical practice was in diseases of the nose and throat, but by 1890 he was devoting himself solely to the study and treatment of nervous disorders. He was in the advance wave of a new kind of psychotherapy fueled by dissatisfaction with the physicalist remedies of the older neurologists and built upon French innovation.[6] In order to understand what Prince accomplished it is also necessary to understand the implications of what he had rejected. Looking back on his psychological career, Prince wrote: "In this country the influence of the distinguished and able Weir Mitchell, of whom I was originally a disciple, and whose conception of the psychoneuroses was that of the now discarded neurasthenia, was also all-powerful; and his so-called 'rest-cure,' based upon the therapeutic physical principle of making 'fat and blood,' had spread throughout Europe as well as America."[7]

Weir Mitchell has been encountered before in regard to the cases of Reynolds and Bourne; his influence was pervasive in

American neurology at the time. The patients known as Miss Beauchamp and B.C.A. first presented neurasthenic symptoms and, at that point, Prince was still applying this diagnostic label in a way he later came to reject under the influence of the psychology of the unconscious.

Mitchell began his career as a toxicologist and neurologist; in his later practice, as he branched out to become a popular novelist and poet, Mitchell specialized in nervous complaints —an amalgam of physical disorders and what would now be considered neuroses, particularly those of women. He persisted in viewing neurotic complaints in physical terms: "I look [Mitchell wrote] upon most cases of confirmed hysteria as finally dependent on physical state or defects which may first have been directly or indirectly due to moral causes, or to these in conjunction with variously produced constitutional conditions."[8]

Mitchell's approach to such complaints was like that of his contemporary, Dr. Oliver Wendell Holmes—quite a student of female complaints himself—who regarded hysteria as a mixture of nerves, shock, and what he called "moral vampirism"— sucking the energy of one's family and friends through self-serving pseudo-illness rich in secondary gain through the loving attention it attracts. The energy necessary to sustain psychic balance was seen, in the nature of the case, to be a fluctuating quantity in women, who should regulate their lives accordingly. One consequence of failing to do so was neurasthenia.

This was a protean disorder, having symptoms as diverse as these: "insomnia, mental irritability, nocturnal emissions, tenderness of the teeth or gums, fear of society, fear of being alone, fear of being afraid (*phobophobia*), fear of everything, sensitiveness to changes in the weather, difficulty in swallowing, feelings that life is worthless, vague pains and flying neuralgias" (etc., etc.).[9]

The term "neurasthenia" had itself been popularized by another of Mitchell's contemporaries, Dr. George Miller Beard, who related this nervous affliction to the sociological conditions of the age (and went considerably beyond some of his colleagues in doing so). For him neurasthenia was nervous exhaustion—"nervelessness"—a depletion of the vital forces essential to well-being. Beard had seen so many patients complaining of the symptoms of this disorder that he was inclined to regard it as *the* problem of the age—a disorder endemic to nineteenth-century civilization and particularly to America, its most progressive representative: the home of a distinctively *American Nervousness* (as one of his books was titled): "The chief and primary cause of this development and very rapid increase of nervousness is *modern civilization*, which is distinguished from the ancient by these five characteristics: steampower, the periodical press, the telegraph, the sciences, and the mental activity of women."[10]

These views were widely shared. The doctors, impressed by the law of conservation of energy in physics, applied this law to the functioning of the nervous system. If there is only a certain amount of energy available, the channeling of a quantity of it in a given direction necessarily entails the withdrawing of it elsewhere. When a limited amount of energy is channeled into too many interests and concerns—into too much mental work—the system is overloaded, with one or another form of neurasthenic debility the inevitable result: modern women, whose mental activity had been so greatly increased in comparison to their preindustrial sisters, were in particular jeopardy. Beard believed that "in civilized lands, women are more nervous, immeasurably, than men and suffer more from general and special nervous disorders."[11]

The cure of nervous disorders therefore focused on regaining the energy whose loss had led to the disorder in the first place. If Weir Mitchell, for example, had been given care of Morton Prince's patients he—using his famous rest cure—would have kept them in seclusion and fed them on milk with an admixture of massage, baths, and electrotherapy so as to increase their nerve force and remove them from the social milieu that had led to its depletion. For Mitchell the key to nerves was nutrition—as the title of one of his well-known works suggests, a matter of *Fat and Blood.*[12]

George Beard himself recommended treatments for neurasthenia that were as eclectic as the disease: electrotherapy, hydrotherapy, bromides, rest, exercise, travel, rich diet, tonics, administration of cannabis. What neither he nor Mitchell nor others of their generation recommended was the use of techniques to get at the unconscious causation and symbolism of mental disorder.

These early neurologists were bogged down in a physicalist paradigm. Psychology was in the process of being discovered or (depending on one's point of view) invented. Yet in their own ways Mitchell, Beard, and Holmes gave nervous Americans of the post–Civil War era an explanation for what ailed them and the hope of a cure for it. Perhaps the most interesting aspect of their accomplishment was the *medicalizing* of this inchoate problem, taking it out of the realm of vague emotional distress and placing it squarely within the purview of materialistic medicine where it could be treated by rational technical means. The problem was not to be found in the condition of the soul but in that of the nervous system. The neurologists ("psychiatry" did not yet exist as a popular term) were self-consciously evangelical about their new solutions to old human problems. As Beard wrote: "Neurasthenia is indeed passing through, in this generation, the same history as insanity in the last. The time was when the symptoms of insanity were believed to indicate, not diseases, but the possessing of an evil spirit; so now, very many of the symptoms of neurasthenia have been regarded by men of science as imaginations of the patients, proofs of hypochondria—a vague term which, in this generation, covers all symptoms which the physician either doubts or misinterprets."[13]

Morton Prince was coming to see the world differently. I have shown in the chapter on Ansel Bourne how and why the new psychology took shape, and in that on G.P. the contribution made to this by the study of spiritistic phenomena. By 1898, when Prince first encountered the woman who would be called "Miss Beauchamp" he had already departed significantly from the older neurological tradition. Now, buttressed by studies of cerebral localization, unconscious psychic processes had moved to the forefront of neurological speculation. Prince was abreast of work on this subject and would write intelligently on it; he concluded in an article written at Hodgson's behest for the *Proceedings* of the Society for Psychical Research that all dissociational phenomena—hysteria, hypnosis, multiple personality, mediumship—are "probably after all a question of cerebral localization."[14]

This was all cast in terms that were no less respectably materialistic than those of the older neurologists: "The phenomena of disintegrated personality [Prince wrote] suggest that our characters are wholly a matter of brain associations, and that they may be altered for good or ill, by anything that will bring about a rearrangement of these associations."[15]

From the point of view of psychopathology Prince saw the most important factor in effecting such rearrangements to be trauma: "Particular emotional states, like fear or anxiety, or general mental distress have the tendency to disintegrate the mental organization in such a way that the normal associations become severed or loosened. Thus it happens that a mental shock like that of an accident, or an alarming piece of news, produces a dissociation of the mind.... A doubling of consciousness is thus brought about."[16]

The physician's task was seen to be bringing about more favorable concatenations of the associational network of the brain. In mundane language it would be called re-education, and hypnosis was one way in which this was accomplished. Hypnosis was seen as a dissociative phenomenon through which access could be gained to the hidden store of covertly active neural processes; in Prince's view this technique allowed the fusing of functionally disintegrated parts of the nervous system, and therefore he persistently and unreflectively used it as an adjunct to therapy—just as he, James, and Hodgson had done in the Bourne case.

When the woman who would be called "Miss Beauchamp" came Prince's way, the road was already paved for her. The drive for female emancipation, the rise of new religions, the accommodations that medicine was being forced to make to these new conditions, the internal course of its own theoretical development—all fell together in April 1898 in a classic case of multiple personality.

Prince's understanding of this case was at first shaped by the concept of neurasthenia. On initial acquaintance he characterized his patient as "a neurasthenic of the extreme type." She suffered from a typical variety of complaints—headaches, bodily pains, persistent fatigue, and poor nutrition. The case seemed conventional enough, since this patient was just the sort, a mentally active woman, whom contemporary doctors such as Mitchell expected to suffer from the disorder. Prince described her as a "religious prig," repressed, sincere, and dedicated, having "marked literary tastes and faculties.... She is essentially a bibliophile, and is never so happy as when allowed to delve amongst books, to live with them and know them." In spite of her medical problems, "nothing could dissuade her from diligent and, in fact, excessive study."[17] Prince soon came to think that her neurasthenia, and perhaps that of others, was not an expression of nervelessness but of an underlying and hidden psychic dissociation. Prince would set up the conditions for the translation of the idiom of what he would later term "so-called" neurasthenia into that of "multiple personality."

Weir Mitchell had to his own satisfaction already identified part of the problem. Speaking as a guest lecturer in 1895 he warned the women of Radcliffe College that

> women have terrible consciences and decline to waste time as so many young men do and have done, this present preacher among them. Hence women at college work harder than men; out of their eagerness arises disregard of physiological limitations. . . . I see women fall into ill-health . . . from self-devotion unintelligently guided, from emotional causes such as rarely injure the lives of men, from lack of willingness to yield to the just demands of their own physiological conditions.

Do not, he continued:

> conclude that the whole mass of you can assume the man's standard as to what you do in the way of mental labor. It will be at your peril. Some of you can. There are days for most of you when to use the mind persistently is full of dangers. You are women, not men. She who forgets it is foolish; she who persistently and intentionally ignores it is worse.[18]

Miss Beauchamp ignored it, and paid what contemporary "lady doctors" took to be the inevitable price. She had a neurasthenic breakdown, was referred to Morton Prince because of it, and by a chance coincidence of circumstances was born again via an episode of multiple personality.

Morton Prince brought to their unusual encounter his personal vitality, his theoretical preconceptions, and a desire to make the new psychology more publicly known. Miss Beauchamp brought a widely shared readiness to believe that she was already a divided soul. Prince's theoretical orientation gave this readiness substantial form.

Miss Beauchamp was actually named Clara Norton Fowler, a fact only recently clarified after a period of some confusion

on the matter.[19] Save for Prince's own account there is little
known of her, though it has been possible to find out something about her family background, earlier life, and subsequent
career. Prince stated that she was a college student when she
first came to him, and in Boston medical circles it came to be
understood that she was at Radcliffe.[20] If so, this appealed to
me, since she well could have heard Weir Mitchell's discourse
on feminine limitations in 1895 (what would Fowler's liberated alter-self have made of *that*, I wondered). Unfortunately it
is not the case. She was, however, briefly a student at Radcliffe
in 1906 after leaving Prince's care. Tracing her records back
from this point reveals that in 1898 she was at Bradford Academy (now Bradford College) north of Boston, where she is
described as a "sophomore special student" (probably being
special because of entering the academy at an age above the
norm and by some unusual route—not, in other words,
straight from her regular schooling).[21]

The records at Radcliffe show that Fowler was the daughter
of Mary Norton Fowler and John Conway Fowler of Beverly,
Massachusetts, near Salem. These further show that she was
born in 1873 and therefore was twenty-five when she began
treatment with Prince, who states that her parents did not get
on, that her father had a violent temper, and that she had been
rejected by her mother "for no other reason, apparently,
excepting that the child resembled her father in looks." Prince
records that Mary Fowler died when her daughter was thirteen,
and that Clara received a violent shock when an infant brother
died in her arms. Mary Fowler did indeed die when her daughter was this age—the Massachusetts vital records showing that
she died at age thirty-nine of "puerperal fever," hence as a
result of infection following childbirth. There also had been a
son born in 1880 who died only four days later of "congenital
debility" and who is probably the child to whom Prince
refers.[22]

John Fowler's parents were both born in Ireland and he in
Massachusetts. It appears he had an identity problem of his
own, since in 1872, when twenty-two years old, he changed his
name for unknown reasons from Richard Conway to John
Charles Fowler. In 1871 Conway/Fowler was a mason practic-
ing his trade in Beverly, and there he stayed for the remainder
of his life—dying in 1921 without remarrying. An advertise-

ment from the Beverly town directory describes him as "John
C. Fowler, jobbing mason, practical working bricklayer and
plasterer."

Prince states that Clara ran away from home when sixteen,
after living with her father for several years following the death
of her mother; these years when she was alone with her father
"were characterized by nervous stress and strain, a succession
of nervous shocks, frights, and unhappiness. At sixteen she ran
away from home and never saw her father again."[23]

This again appears to be correct, because she is next to be
found engaged in 1893 at some form of nursing training in a
place that (hiding its real identity) Prince calls "Providence."
This was actually Fall River, an industrial town in southern
Massachusetts near the Rhode Island border. This period in her
life, when she was twenty, proved of considerable importance
in her case since in Fall River she had an encounter with a man
named "Jones" to which Prince, in accord with his theory of
traumatic neuroses, attributed the onset of her psychic dissociation. The latter discreetly obscured the facts of the matter,
only later, in the 1920s, alluding to sexual factors in response
to Freudian theory.[24] Certainly Jones's influence was considerable during Fowler's time with Prince; there was apparently
some degree of conflict between the two men, whom she
tended to identify with one another.[25]

Whatever the facts in the Jones affair, it is certain that at
the time of Clara's encounter with him in Fall River she had
severed ties with her father completely and never renewed
them, for in a will dated May 1921 (when he was terminally ill
with cancer) John C. Fowler leaves "First. To my daughter
Clara N. Fowler who last lived in Fall River, Massachusetts,
when last heard from the sum of Five Dollars." Scarcely an
impressive amount. The remainder of the estate is left to
another daughter who is made executor of the will.[26]

What is known of Clara Fowler from sources external to
Prince's writings (and for that matter from within them) is
tantalizing and inconclusive. At a fairly young age she developed an idealistic affinity for medical work. After leaving her
father's home she had a bad time of it in life and, if her report to
Prince is accepted, had a traumatic and apparently sexual
encounter with an older man while engaged in nursing work,
one that recurred during her time under medical care. Five

years after Fall River she is to be found at Bradford involved in studies of which we are assured she was fond, but which placed her under considerable stress, apparently from just the factor against which Mitchell warned the Radcliffe women: overconscientious dedication. Her bibliophilic tendencies seem to have emerged as a refuge from an unhappy family life. She was also for a time the only child: "a neurotic, sensitive, visionary child, brought up in an unsympathetic atmosphere. . . . The effect of all this upon the child was to suppress all disclosures of her own mental life, and to make her morbidly reticent. She never gave expression to the ordinary feelings of everyday child life; never spoke to say she was tired, hungry, or sleepy. She lived within herself and dreamed."[27]

Clara Fowler was a young woman very much on her own, both practically and emotionally. She was without independent resources and dependent on her own abilities in making a success of life or even getting by at it. Therefore how extraordinary what befell her. By 1921, when her father died, she had left Fall River, entered Bradford Academy, passed through Prince's care in Boston, become one of the most famous cases of multiple personality on record, studied briefly at Radcliffe, been the subject of a hit stage play produced by the renowned David Belasco of Broadway, married a man named R.E. Forrest, was in 1915 remarried to one of Prince's own close associates —another practitioner of the new psychology—and eventually became a high-society hostess. One of the most distinguishing features of Fowler's career is its upward mobility, an interesting fate for the daughter of a mason, himself the son of Irish immigrants. The contradictions in her life began to work themselves out through her encounter with Morton Prince: her first neurasthenic personality—corresponding to James's Olive Chancellor character—shortly encountered her second, the being named "Sally"—Miss Beauchamp's equivalent of the free-spirited Verena Tarrant.

Prince would describe the case for the general public with deliberately propagandistic intent:

I remember that in 1906, when *The Dissociation of a Personality* was published, the work done outside of the psychoanalytic school was so little read that I determined I would, if possible, at least make "them" read. So in writing the *Dissociation* I purposely, with "malice aforethought," constructed it in the form of a dramatic story of great length, 563 pages. As a scientific account it might well have been condensed within the compass of fifty pages. I think my little ruse was successful.[28]

It was indeed, and his ruse elevated multiple personality to the level of a public sensation. With the Beauchamp experience behind him, Prince came to treat other cases of multiple personality. The second of concern here was known as "B.C.A." Together she and Miss Beauchamp show how the phenomenon was produced in the context of their individual lives and how it answered to their self-perceptions and objective situations.

The two cases are complementary. Miss Beauchamp is mainly known through Prince's case report and her family history; on the other hand B.C.A. left highly revealing letters that graphically show how she reconstructed her experience in terms of the concept of multiple personality—a metaphor well suited to her situation—and how she grappled with this situation with the aid of her doctor and his concepts. Yet B.C.A. and Miss Beauchamp were quite different people. There is no sign in B.C.A.'s life of the early traumas that seem to have been so typical of Miss Beauchamp's, no evidence of an unpleasant family milieu nor of having been exposed all alone to a hostile world. As with the idiom of possession, the same psychiatric concept can map different existential predicaments.

Her letters show that B.C.A. was actually Mrs. Nellie Parsons Bean. The Massachusetts vital records indicate that she was born in 1864 to Edward Parsons, originally of Troy, New York (latterly of Illinois), and Lucy Barney Parsons, of Swanton, Vermont; her heritage, unlike that of Clara Fowler, is classically Yankee. When she came under Prince's care she was forty years old, a recent widow with an adolescent son at Phillips Andover Academy. Her husband had been William G. Bean, also of Yankee stock (New Hampshire), a division supervisor for the Boston and Maine Railroad. William Bean was three years older than his wife, but apparently had a stroke at an early age. The records show that he died in 1905 of heart disease at age forty-four; his early death would prove an essential element in the fate of his wife. The Beans lived in Winchester, Massachusetts, a middle-class suburb of Boston. Mrs. Bean was still there when she was referred to Morton Prince by her fam-

ily physician—a relatively young and attractive woman showing, as Prince wrote, the "ordinary picture of so-called neurasthenia, characterized by persistent fatigue and the usual
somatic symptoms, and by moral doubts and scruples." She too
was a woman on her own.[29]

In Prince's hands the cases of Miss Beauchamp and B.C.A.
underwent a parallel creative development. William James, I
think, sensed how it occurred. Morton Prince sent a presentation copy of *The Dissociation of a Personality* to James, who
responded with characteristic hyperbole: "*J'en suis ravi*—literally. Not only is the case probably destined to be historic, but
your exposition is a perfect master piece of lucidity and narrative art. Imagine the case in anyone else's hands!" But James
then went on to make a cautionary remark that brings clearly
to focus one of the problems in interpreting multiple personality phenomena: "Of course critics will say that your subdivi-
sions [of Miss B's personality] are too distinct, that where you
see occasion for singling out definite phases, there is nothing in
Nature but a flux of incoherent memories, emotions, impulses,
and delusions. But don't mind that. One must anyhow drive
stakes in, to define any continuum."[30]

To label something is to subdivide that continuum, and it
has been suggested that Morton Prince may have fallen into a
fatal error when he allowed Miss Beauchamp's new self to be
given a name, thus allowing it to further crystallize.[31] This also
occurred with respect to B.C.A., but this was not such a bad
thing because through the assumption of a personified alter-
state (the "B" personality) Mrs. Bean at last was able to define
vague yearnings that had troubled her for years. This was true
of Miss Beauchamp as well.

William James was concerned with the flux of experience
and how the stakes get driven in that isolate it into publicly
communicable bits. Outside information is needed about the
inner life. Prince described another patient of his who was
unable to determine whether ideas developed through automatic writing were her own. If this woman had been dealing
with a Spiritualist rather than a psychologist she could well
have been educated into mediumship herself (recall Stanley
Hall's "medium in the bud"). This possibility was nearly realized through Miss Beauchamp.

Miss Beauchamp's first new self emerged in the course of hypnotherapy to be christened BIII or "Sally" (BII was merely the neurasthenic BI hypnotized). Sally would be followed by BIV whom Prince, acknowledging the degree of maturity and determination shown by this personality, would call "The Woman"; BI and BIII were respectively "The Saint" and "The Devil." Prince wrote that "these three personalities had very sharply defined traits which gave a very distinctive individuality to each. One might say that each represented certain characteristic elements of human nature, and that the three might serve as an allegorical picture of the tendencies of man. If this were not a serious psychological study, I might feel tempted to entitle this volume, 'The Saint, The Woman, and The Devil.'"[32]

Prince found that Miss Beauchamp had failed to respond to conventional methods of treatment and he resorted to hypnotic suggestion; by this means "it was found possible to convert a condition of constant physical distress into one of at least temporary comfort." Improvement continued until

> one day while in hypnosis, Miss Beauchamp surprised me by denying having made certain statements which she made during the previous state of hypnosis.... On one of the following occasions I was startled to hear her, when hypnotized, speak of herself in her waking state as "She." Previously ... she had always used the first person "I," indifferently for herself, whether awake or asleep in hypnosis.
>
> "You are 'she,'" I said.
> "No, I am not."
> "I say you are."
> Again a denial.
>
> Feeling at the time that this distinction was artificial, and that the hypnotic self was making it for a purpose, I made up my mind that such an artifact should not be allowed to develop. I pursued her relentlessly in my numerous examinations, treated the idea as nonsense, and refused to accept it.

Finally:

> "Why are you not 'She'?"
> "Because 'She' does not know the same things I do."
> "But you both have the same arms and legs, haven't you?"
> "Yes, but arms and legs do not make us the same."
> "Well, if you are different persons, what are your names?"

Here she was puzzled, for she evidently saw that, according
to her notion, if the hypnotic self that was talking with me
was Miss Beauchamp, the waking self was not Miss
Beauchamp, and *vice versa*. . . . Repeated experiences . . . made
it plain that Miss Beauchamp when hypnotized fell into one or
the other of two distinct mental states, or *selves* [my empha-
sis], whose relations to the primary waking consciousness, as
well as their memories, were strikingly different.[33]

"Sally" was vivacious, adventurous, and by her own
account amoral; she enjoyed playing practical jokes on her
strait-laced sister who found herself baffled as to who or what
might be responsible for them. Sally, as in Mary Reynolds's
second state, thought of herself as a spiritual being having no
integral connection to the body in which BI was placed. She
also claimed to be co-conscious with BI who, however, was not
co-conscious with her; of BIV, "The Woman," she had less
knowledge. At first Sally was solely present as a hypnotic state;
only later did she, as she herself put it, get "her eyes open" on
her own. By June 1898 Sally was assuming clear dominance
over Miss Beauchamp's life:

All her life she had been in the habit of falling into . . . states
of abstraction (for such they were), when she lived in the
clouds. Here was [Sally's] opportunity. The physical and mental
conditions were ripe. [Sally] was not one to let such a golden
chance slip by. So while Miss Beauchamp was dreaming in her
chair, [Sally] took both her hands—Miss Beauchamp's hands—
rubbed her eyes and "willed"; then, for the moment, Miss
Beauchamp disappeared and "Sally" came mistress of herself,
and, for the first time, able to see.[34]

The stage on which all this was played out was a very small
one: Morton Prince's consulting room. Very few other people
knew of Miss Beauchamp's condition, and those she did not
want to know about it she kept in the dark. As Prince said, her
personalities "have endeavored by every artifice to conceal the
knowledge of their trouble from friends, and have done so with
a success that is astonishing."[35] The fact is that when Miss
Beauchamp was around her doctor she got markedly sicker.
"With me and with those who know her trouble, she has a
depressed, rather weary, expression and manner. Her voice,
too, is strongly indicative of this frame of mind; but I am told

that with strangers who know nothing of her infirmity she is more buoyant and light-hearted."[36]

That summer Miss Beauchamp went to Europe on holiday, Prince reporting that "aside from a few exceptional hours remained herself during the rest of the summer." But when she returned to Boston, and was again near Prince, "her comparative health soon came to an untimely end."[37]

Morton Prince made no attempt to hide the fact that he was quite charmed by Sally, who exhibited "a lively vivacity, boldness, and saucy deviltry, difficult to describe"; when Sally had departed the scene for good he would say, "and to think that Sally has 'gone back to where she came from' when she might have told so much that I wished I knew!"[38] Sally found her doctor equally charming, but also was demanding of him; in a biographical memoir Prince's daughter recorded what it was like:

> Miss Christine L. Beauchamp . . . came at all hours to the house. In fact, all the patients came so frequently to the house, that we were never surprised to find them anywhere. Miss Beauchamp appeared frequently at my father's house. She was tall, willowy, with a die-away, plaintive, high-pitched voice—(not especially pretty but pleasant-looking, as she was quite young). At odd moments of the day or night she would appear, according to the crisis that her multiple and diversified personalities chose to present. . . . "Sally" was the most obstreperous and the strongest of all her diversified personalities. Sometimes if "Sally" was too obstreperous, odors of ether would emerge from the office. At such times she was resisting hypnotic suggestion, and Doctor Prince was using ether as a quietant to subjugate this mischievous nature who could and did resist hypnotism in order not to be as she herself said "gotten out of the way." . . . "Sally" was more entertaining than Miss Beauchamp. Her whole manner changed from a die-away out-of-luck sort of person to a very active, mischievous and self-assured being who might do anything.[39]

Prince comprehended his unusual case in terms of hypnotic dissociation and traumatic neurosis. He believed in a common-sensical manner that everyone has a normal "true" self and that cases such as multiple personality represent a disintegration of that self. "Common experience shows that, philosophize as you will, there is an empirical self which may be designated the normal real self. . . . I . . . assume that there is a normal self, a particular Miss Beauchamp, who is physiologically as well as psychologically best adapted to *any* environment."[40]

Therapy therefore was to be a quest for this true self, and Prince could not be satisfied until it was found; nor of course could his subjects. His theory of psychic trauma provided a therapeutic entry into the problem; he would have to hypnotically probe into the past of his patients until the precipitating trauma was brought to light. In the case of Miss Beauchamp, Prince thought the crucial episode to have been the encounter with the enigmatic "Jones" in Fall River. BI was not the normal true self, nor were Sally and BIV; the original self was the one that had fallen apart in 1893 under the impact of emotional shock. This is the one he believed himself to have restored, a restoration that constituted her cure.

This can be seen differently. Sally, it should be noted, came into the world *during* her time with Prince and became progressively articulated into a personality with distinct qualities. So did BIV, and hypnosis was the means through which this was brought about. Hypnosis—being an "altered" state—granted Miss Beauchamp the poetic license to experiment with the content of her selfhood. Here it is necessary to follow in detail the way in which the inner experience of Prince's patients, and others like them, comes to be registered in terms of the concept of multiple personality. This can easily be done through Mrs. Bean. Spiritistic imagery had a role in both cases, and this suggests that both, in other hands, could have gone in rather a different direction.

The Boston of this time was alive with concern for spiritistic phenomena; Richard Hodgson was given a hand in the Beauchamp case when the Piper investigations were at their height and he was increasingly giving control of his own life over to the direction of the Imperator Band. Morton Prince was a member of the Tavern Club along with Hodgson, Howells, and others interested in occult phenomena. It is known that Miss Beauchamp visited Hodgson at the Society for Psychical

Research, whose offices immediately adjoined the club; she was well aware of the spiritist hypothesis and, in her guise as Sally, played at mediumship while in treatment with Prince.

Miss Beauchamp wrote to Prince in her primary state that "I do really think that, like those poor people of old, I must be possessed of devils—possessed of forty devils."

> Her feelings of being "possessed" she connected in an indefinite way with her trances and realized that from time to time her mind and body were controlled much as one might be controlled by convulsive phenomena. Although her idea was somewhat vague, she inferred that this control was due to one part of her mind acting upon the other part and on her body. This really was the actual feeling that she had when "possessed," and against this possession [by Sally], when it came upon her, she struggled with all her will. I think this conception, too, was vaguely connected with the ethical ideas of punishment for sins, and hence the diabolical nature of the possession.[41]

Prince accordingly set himself up as an exorcist: "Putting my finger to her forehead, I made her believe [while hypnotized] I had the power of exorcism. The effect was remarkable. She shrank from me as the conventional Mephistopheles on the stage shrinks from the cross on the handle of the sword, at the same time complaining that it made a 'terrible' painful sensation run through her body."[42]

An old metaphor was used in a novel context. Such theatrics—obviously based on the popular media—show again the degree to which the culture of the time penetrated into the physician's consulting room. Morton Prince was scarcely a detached scientific observer; he and Miss Beauchamp mutually, though unconsciously, colluded in the composition of a medical drama based on stereotypic nineteenth-century roles.

Hodgson was a bit-player in all this. Throughout 1898 and 1899 he was intimately involved in the case and served, as Prince put it, *in loco parentis*, when Prince could not be around himself. In her (that is Sally's) letters to Prince, Hodgson is present as "Dicky." Hodgson's other female friends looked back on him with affectionate remembrance of his sympathy and warm nature. Prince gave Hodgson great thanks for his help in the matter. Ironically Hodgson by this time, on the basis of the G.P. affair, was a confirmed spiritist while Prince maintained a materialist stance based on the psychology of the unconscious. However, though apparently quite different, these two theoretical options are not all that dissimilar in effect; each allows for the exploration of hidden possibilities beyond the normal self.

This was not passive observation. Both Prince and Hodgson interacted with Sally and the other personalities as though they were real. There is an intimation, however, that the Prince-Hodgson collaboration was not without stress. It would later be reported that Hodgson was shut off from further "experiments" at Prince's request. I have suggested elsewhere that, if this were the case, its probable cause was that Hodgson had come to consider Sally an intrusive spiritual being.[43] There are signs that Sally found this the most plausible explanation for her own existence also.

Prince had primary control of the case and its spiritistic potential was aborted. Nevertheless Sally remained an enigma with regard to what Prince took to be the dissociational character of multiple personality phenomena. Sally, with her co-conscious abilities, functioned as Prince's assistant in managing the other personalities and even in their analysis. She did not quite seem to fit in as a piece of fragmented self; when BIV and then Miss Beauchamp's "true" self emerged, Sally seemed to have no place at all in the final synthesis. When BIV came into being, Prince at first thought her to be the true self he was looking for. But it was only Sally who knew when the true Miss Beauchamp had been restored, a synthesis of BI and BIV. The real Miss Beauchamp who emerged in 1902 knew everything about Miss Beauchamp's past lives; her neurasthenia was gone and her memory restored to its pre–Fall River integrity. To Prince it was apparent "that what Sally asserted was true," that a cure had been accomplished:

> "Who are you?" I asked.
> "I am myself."
> "Where is BI?"
> "I am BI."
> "Where is BIV?"
> "I am BIV. We're all the same person, only *now I am myself*."[44]

There were still difficulties ahead and Prince had to wait

until 1905 before he could say with confidence that Miss Beauchamp was whole once more. Sally then faded from view:

> And Sally, what has become of her? With the resurrection of the real self, she "goes back to where she came from," "imprisoned," "squeezed," unable to "come" at will or be brought by command. . . . It has not been possible as yet to communicate with her, and determine what part if any she plays in Miss Beauchamp's subconsciousness, or whether as a subpersonality she exists at all. . . . The resurrection of the Real Miss Beauchamp is through the death of Sally.[45]

William James was puzzled as well: "*who* & *what* is the lovely Sally," he wrote to Prince, "that is a very dark point." James was alluding to the possibility, taken further by others, that Sally was indeed an external spirit. What can also be said, however, is that Sally bore a marked similarity to her doctor in her vivacity and *joie de vivre*, and became Prince's paraprofessional assistant, colleague, and friend.

In later years another colleague had occasion to ask Prince whether he had ever "found it necessary to inhibit the resistance or to facilitate the recall and cure by drawing the patient's *libido* yourwards?" Prince replied:

> No, never. Like every physician I have had patients develop an idealism, or, frankly stated, an affection for the physician but this I have always considered a handicap and to be avoided. Of all the obstacles to effective treatment I consider this one of the greatest. . . . My rule, therefore, is keep yourself as detached as possible.[46]

No mean feat when faced with Sally Beauchamp:

> I love you always, you know *always*, but best when you you [sic] are strong and splendid, when you are tired and people are not nice to you. I can't bear to think of going off under Papa Leo's wing again [?] never seeing you again, never hearing your voice. I can't do it Dr. Prince, I can't and I won't. I want *you* not any nasty old priestly man. I hate them all. Aren't you the least bit sorry for me? Because I have behaved badly to you? I'm going to take FI [BI] to the architecture thing now to divert her mind—you like that don't you. Do poodles have to have morals too? Isn't there any place free from them? I don't want them nor anything not *you* and I can't see why it should be wrong for me to love you. But right or wrong, I don't care.

Please forgive me again . . . and let me stay with you. <u>Please</u>
<u>please please</u>.[47]

Sally did in fact get to stay with a doctor, but it was not
Morton Prince.

———◆———

MRS. BEAN'S CASE DEVELOPED as Miss Beauchamp's had: neurasthenia transformed into multiple personality during therapy.
As a neurasthenic Mrs. Bean had no amnesia for the other
facets of her existence even though, following her widowhood
in 1905, she had undergone marked shifts of mood—alternating between euphoria and neurotic debility. Before meeting
Prince she had no labels for her experience—had, by her own
account, never heard of "a change of personality"—yet she did
things she had never done before, "enjoying life to the utmost
in a way entirely foreign to my natural inclina-
tions . . . walking, boating, etc., living solely out of doors. . . . I
lost the formality and reserve which was one of my traits. My
tastes, ideals, and points of view were completely changed."[48]
The second Mrs. Bean rejected the black of widow's weeds and
wore nothing but white in its place.

While in her euphoric condition she took under her wing
someone (presumably male) whom she determined to save
from himself; however, he deceived her in some undisclosed
manner and she went into a depressive reaction later to be
called the "A" state. "When you first saw me," she wrote, "I
was A at my worst."[49] This, however, was her hindsight view
since only in therapy did she learn from Prince himself how to
clearly differentiate these several states: to drive the stakes in
around her respective selves.

> Shortly after I came to you I began to alternate frequently and
> it is well to emphasize that one marked change in the state of
> A developed. In this state I now had *complete amnesia* for my
> whole life as B; for everything I thought and did.[50]

B, on the other hand, was fully co-conscious of A; A's
amnesia was the prerequisite for B's liberty:

> After amnesia and unawareness I became a distinct personality
> in my own thought because I had a life completely my own, of
> which A was unaware. My thoughts, my experiences, she knew

nothing of. The unawareness removed all inhibition of my thoughts. . . . The fact that A did not know them gave them greater freedom.[51]

Again this was brought about by hypnosis, during the course of which the full-blown "B" state first emerged, "characterized by changes of facial expression, manner, speech, etc."[52] B.C.A. in retrospect found it difficult to put into words what had occurred, though she was sure that hypnosis had been the key to her cure: "Every improvement in my condition has been made by the use of hypnotism."[53] One thing she was also sure of is that B's behavior was utterly incomprehensible to A and even to C, her restored "normal" state: "I do not *understand* myself as B. . . . A seems exactly like myself in an absurdly morbid, emotional, and unreasonable condition, but B seems foreign."[54] Given this foreignness, this outside quality to her forbidden or repressed desires and activities, she turned, as others had before her, to the imagery of possession: "I *am* possessed by *something*." B more realistically commented that "I am not a demon at all. I only like fun and a gay time."[55] And whatever this "something" was, no one save Morton Prince knew about it:

> During all this time I lived my life to all appearances like any ordinary person. I directed the daily routine of my household, took entire charge of extensive repairs to my house, and managed my business affairs to a large extent . . . but not one of my family or friends suspected the true state of the case. I have done my best, indeed I have Dr. Prince, and have managed to keep things straight enough so that no one suspects—not even Dr. Cummings [her general practitioner], I think. It's marvelous that they don't, isn't it?[56]

Her passion, her doubts, fears, and pain were reserved for her doctor. She poured out to him the ambiguity of her situation, all the things she had been and might be.

> As B, I felt very grateful to you for treating me as if I were a "real" person and allowing me to express my own personality. With every one else I had to pretend to be A, and my feeling of gratitude and the fact that you asked for my co-operation— put me on my honor as it were—was the underlying motive in telling you so much of A's inner life.[57]

Prince allowed Mrs. Bean to attain distance from herself through his encouragement of the B persona. He also encouraged a theoretical attitude through which she grappled with her situation. She, as B, came to a theory of "repressed ideas" parallel to the understanding she achieved through Prince of Freudian psychoanalysis ("It is very queer, is it not?" she asked).[58] The concept of the unconscious gave her the means to shape an as yet inchoate hidden self, one that had lain dormant in the objections she had to her fate in life. The self she was striving to attain was not the true self she already was or had been at some earlier time, but the one she might be or was becoming. "How can any one say that there is not in his own mind a second stream of thought of which he is not conscious?"[59] Precisely; one cannot in fact say this, since by definition it cannot be known. But to *affirm* it is also to create it; the idea of the unconscious allows a redefinition of one's position in the world and a restructuring of a personal life history in terms of supposedly repressed ideas.

As a young woman around twenty, Nellie Bean received a "shock" that both she and Prince came to view as the genesis of her subsequent split. This otherwise unspecified shock was described by Prince as arousing "certain emotions which, besides a mild degree of fright, were intense repugnance or disgust, and another affect which we will term X."[60] Prince was being cagey and the suspicion arises that these affects pertained to sexual relations with her husband. However this may be, this shock was held to have aroused a sentiment of rebellion against her fate, which only came to be fully expressed through B. During the time when her husband was ill, Mrs. Bean's feelings of resentment grew, and she commented that "all these things were like floating thoughts. I never thought 'I' do not like this or that then; it was like an impulse in the other direction. I think A was conscious of these impulses and thought she was wicked to have them. . . . She felt double all those years when Mr. [Bean] was ill. It seems to me as I think of it now that I was always there—sometimes more, sometimes less—in the form of conflicting impulses."[61]

The public emergence of the B personality took place under hypnosis. But Prince and B.C.A. believed that B had already taken shape because of another shock pertaining to betrayal of a trust that Mrs. Bean revealingly described as "of an intensely emotional nature. It brought to me, suddenly, the realization that my position in life was entirely changed, that I was quite alone, and with this there came a feeling of helplessness and desolation beyond my powers of description."[62]

Mrs. Bean was indeed helpless and alone—at war with contradictory tendencies. Prince's theory of dissociative traumatic neurosis brought these tendencies to focus. With B's help he set to work to reintegrate Mrs. Bean's personality. C finally emerged and had full memory of her past life and of all the doings of A and B. She then wrote an essay—"My Life as a Dissociated Personality"—autobiographically describing her experiences as a multiple personality.

Compared to Miss Beauchamp's this case was straightforward and, because of Mrs. Bean's letters, the factors that conditioned its development can be clearly perceived. The basic point to be made is also the most obvious. Nellie Bean was a woman. Furthermore she was a young widow. These two factors in combination were quite sufficient to generate a nasty case of neurasthenia; however, Prince's theories allowed her to freely explore the contradictions of her situation in a way that the older theory of neurasthenia could not have done. What was her own view of what it meant to be a woman? As usual B had the answers:

> Something is happening to me, Dr. Prince. I don't know what it is, but—I am frightened—I am afraid I am going to be a woman just like A & C. I don't want to, Dr. Prince, I can't. I want to be just what I have always been—just "B," free as the wind, no body, no soul, no heart. I don't want to love people for if one loves one must suffer—that is what it means to be a woman—to love and suffer. . . . *Please* help me not to feel anything.
>
> I do maintain that I am as real as A and better fitted to live —really. I am *much* more as A used to be than she is. . . . You will find that everyone of us, A, B, and C, feel the same about living but we all want a different kind of life. For my part I would quite as soon be a good lambchop as an angel—it is the only chance I'll ever have to be anything but a woman and I have had enough of that now. I hate to sign myself "B"—it makes me feel like a beetle on a pin—can't you give me some other name?[63]

She groped for a name appropriate to her circumstances and found one through literature. Mrs. Bean turned to a novel that well expressed the contradictory situation of middle-class women in the late nineteenth and early twentieth centuries. Through this novel she found a paradigm for her experience and, at least temporarily, a name for herself. In a letter to Prince, Nellie Bean signed herself "Bertha Amory," commenting that perhaps this name could be used as a pseudonym in published accounts of her case and concluding in a postscript that "it's lovely to have a name."[64]

The novel was *Through One Administration,* published in 1881, and its author Frances Hodgson Burnett (also the author of *Little Lord Fauntleroy*). The plot was set in Washington D.C., whose politics and intrigue are a backdrop to the action. It is the story of a talented and beautiful young woman married to a superficial, fatuous, and indifferent husband. She has a platonic relationship with an Army officer (a bit of an anthropologist as it happens) who has all the qualities her husband lacks. Of course the story cannot come to a good end; the conventionalities must be observed. The soldier is killed in battle against the Indians and Bertha Amory must reconcile herself to her fate as best she can. In the novel Bertha's father remarks of her:

> The trouble is, that the experience of a woman of forty is what a girl needs when she chooses her husband at twenty, and, as the two things are incompatible, the chances are always against her. Bertha had the faults and follies that I told you go to make a martyr. When she had made her mistake, she was strong and weak enough to abide by it. It is mostly imagination in matters of this kind; it was imagination in hers. She was young enough to believe in anything. . . . She had no conception of a feeling stronger than herself, and held curiously obstinate and lofty views of the conduct of women who did not hold their emotions in check.[65]

Bertha is made to speak of the "other Bertha" and to begin showing neurasthenic symptoms that she does not understand: "I think I am not well at all. I—I am restless and nervous—and —and morbid. I am actually morbid. Things trouble me which never troubled me before. Sometimes I lose all respect for myself. . . . Women are not happy, as a rule . . . they are not happy. I have learned that."[66]

Nellie Bean was a Bertha Amory, and she seized on the parallels between them. Mrs. Bean married when she was about twenty, as Bertha Amory had; there are signs that her marriage was imperfect as well. She was sincere and dedicated, having literary, philosophical, and religious interests—"lofty views." B characterized the A state thus:

> She thinks like this: "my life is being wasted, all my hopes, ambitions, aspirations have come to nothing. Is this all there is to life? sorrow, disappointment, suffering? My whole life is spoiled, and why? because I set myself a standard too high. It is cruel. My heart aches so. It is so heavy. How are the mighty fallen," etc.[67]

But Mrs. Bean had a feature that Bertha lacked; she was a widow, and this presented radical problems of its own. What to do now? Find a new mate, seek a career, sell the house and move to the city? The B state mirrored Mrs. Bean as she was on the eve of her marriage—a girl of twenty; with Mr. Bean gone she was in this condition again, facing life on her own and uncertain of how to go about it. B commented on A's plight:

> I say she ought to sell if she gets a good chance, and have some money to spend for pleasure. She thinks that when the house is gone all the old life will be gone; she can't bear to become a member of what she calls "the vast floating population of widows and old maids who have no root anywhere and belong nowhere"—but who cares about the "old life" anyway? I am sick and tired of it and want a new one.[68]

B experimented in relationships with other men, even at one point allowing a Mr. Hopkins to kiss her; A was naturally aghast.[69] B was aghast in turn when she co-consciously found A actively thinking about marriage:

> Oh, Dr. Prince, for heavens sake, send for A and bring her to her senses—what do you suppose she is thinking of doing now? Getting married! Yes, she is. Did you ever hear of anything so ridiculous? Why, if she got married I would be married too I suppose, and I won't. I *can't*. . . . She doesn't really care anything about him, and she thinks she can't be happy anyway so might as well take what she can get. Isn't it horrid of her? She is deterred by the fact that she has a "B"—thank

heavens; and that she would feel she ought to tell him about Mr. Hopkins—Silly thing! As if that made any difference. Is she the only woman who ever kissed any man except her husband? And is kissing a crime? And she didn't do it anyway—I did it myself, and it never hurt even a bit—I am glad of it—and she didn't have a husband anyway.[70]

There was another, less conventional possibility, and as she assimilated the new psychology she saw a new kind of career ahead of her:

I am feeling very well and full of enthusiasm and interest in the work which seems opening before me. It is rather late, at forty, to begin one's "life work" but that is what I mean to make this if I am at all capable of doing what you say I can. At times like this, when I seem so completely myself, I realize to the full how much you have done for me—how much time and how much patience it has required. I can never, *never* make you understand the depth of my gratitude, and say what you will Dr. Prince, I *know* that no one else in the world could have done for me what you have done. . . . I am building much, perhaps too much, on the hope of being able to assist you in some way. Am I too presumptuous in thinking myself capable of doing so? . . . It is because you have opened a new world and a new life to me and given me the hope that I can be something worth being. I am shedding the old life like a husk. . . . The intellectual life for mine.[71]

Nellie Parsons Bean became Morton Prince's research assistant and typist, and through him a published author in her own right, an example of the curative power of the psychology of the subconscious. She never remarried and died in 1950 at age eighty-five.[72]

In 1912 Mrs. Clara Norton Forrest was married to Dr. George Waterman (Harvard 1895), and so by a different means was linked to the new psychology as well.[73] In the years that followed, Dr. Waterman (himself a witness to the case of B.C.A.) became an influential psychiatrist, having patients such as Robert Frost and the general-to-be, George Patton.[74] In the fiftieth report of the Harvard Class of 1895 George Waterman wrote in 1944 of what his life had been like:

My practice has kept me in my chosen field of neurology, and the last twenty-five years most of my time has been spent in

helping my patients learn to adapt themselves to life as they
find it—some under prosperity and some under adversity. In
so doing, I find myself fairly well steeped in the philosophy of
living as presented by my patients and in my reading. Many of
my patients have been men of letters and learning, some of
them men of science, some in business to accumulate wealth
or power—and also a large group primarily interested in the
pursuit of happiness, as justified by our Declaration of
Independence.[75]

Dr. Waterman and his wife played host and hostess to his
influential patients and to other society figures, moving with
the seasons between Blue Hill, Maine, and Palm Beach, Florida.
Of the former Miss Beauchamp—now so risen in life—little
further is known. Dr. Waterman's niece writes that "even my
Uncle did not know all the background of her troubles. Every
time she tried to tell him the tragic reasons she became so upset
that he would not let her continue." Waterman's nephew gave
much the same picture: "His wife, Claire Waterman, was
always something of an enigma to us and even some terror
when we were very young. She had an acid tongue and considerable malevolence."[76]

Morton Prince served as way station for two lives in transition, each achieving with his help something of a reconciliation
of their dreams, prospects, and actual situations. What he
meant to them is obvious from their letters; but they also
meant something to him (not merely, I think, as clinical test-
cases), and he was prepared to take the time and considerable
trouble to see it out. Through his labors Miss Beauchamp
became a classic case to which, though doubts have been
expressed about his analysis, contemporary writers frequently
refer.

AROUND THE FIRST WORLD WAR interest in the multiple personality syndrome began to flag, and until the 1950s reported
cases occur only seldom in the literature. But in his day Prince
was a very influential practitioner and made successful efforts
to get the new psychology more widely known, which he did
through his teaching, the founding of the still extant *Journal of
Abnormal Psychology*, and above all through his report on the
Beauchamp case. *The Dissociation of a Personality* was

reviewed widely both in medical circles and in popular magazines and newspapers, evidently tapping with its informal and dramatic narrative style a lode of public concern for selfhood.[77] However, he was finally buried under the rising Freudian tide and a new way of conceiving the mind's operations in their social context.[78] Unlike Freud, Prince was not prone to making systematic theoretical statements and for the most part had an abominable prose style; nor did he found a school. Freud was not only a gifted prose stylist, but also a gifted organizer and propagandist.

Freud, in the *Studies in Hysteria* (1895), in all but name an examination of multiple personality, remarked how striking it is that his case reports should read like novels. He disavowed any responsibility in the matter, claiming that this was merely the way in which they developed, and that it was his responsibility as a scientist to simply report it.[79] However, when cases of this sort are carefully studied they are shown to be the co-productions of physician and patient, no less in Freud's case than in Prince's.

At the beginning of this chapter I said that studies of multiple personality draw upon the same dramatic elements as does literature. In turn literature and drama have drawn upon multiple personality. So far as I am aware Prince's study of Miss Beauchamp was the first case of multiple personality to have such an effect, though hardly the last. A British playwright named Edward Locke came upon the Beauchamp case and saw a play in it. In 1910 he approached David Belasco with a script entitled "The Case of Becky," and Belasco instantly detected the potential of the theme. In an essay for *McClure's*, Locke recorded his conversation with the producer concerning the scientific status of his work: "As the play had been suggested by actual scientific experiment, I gave him my authorities. I told him about Dr. Morton Prince of Boston, and how the physician had successfully disassociated one of two personalities, in a single identity, in the 'Miss Beauchamps' case. . . . 'Remarkable,' he said."[80]

"The Case of Becky" was first put on stage in Washington D.C., and then in 1913 brought to the Belasco Theater in New York where it received widespread attention though somewhat mixed reviews. An approving one commented that "the uncanny fascination of the unseen forces that rule *Becky* in the new play of dual personalities by Mr. Edward Locke . . . will be a signal for much speculation and discussion. The question of mental suggestion is quite sure to be disputed as vigorously and also to as little purpose as the topic of the survival of personal energy after death."[81]

Another review was less enthusiastic: "'The Case of Becky' demands medical attention, and very little other. . . . 'The Case of Becky' is unimportant if true."[82] This reviewer thought the whole thing superficial, contrived gimmickry. It must be confessed that Locke wrote a potboiler, but one that is highly revealing about what the public at that time thought possible and dramatically acceptable. The three central characters are Becky, a girl with two selves, one of them decidedly "obstreperous"; Emerson, a neurologist skilled in hypnosis; and "Professor" Balzamo, an evil stage-mesmerist and peripatetic charlatan. Becky, needless to say, has a secret. Her normal self, Dorothy, is sweet, while Becky finds her decorous companion markedly uninteresting:

> "Oh, I got her number! She thinks she's foxy, but I know. She can't hide anything from me. . . . The damned little fraud: That's what I detest about that woman: That's what gets me going. Oh, she gives me the ginks. She's so sweet, so sedate and good, so damned nice!"[83]

Dr. Emerson is asked: "Subconscious mind—just what is that?" and answers:

> "The vast warehouse of the brain, where everything is stored— the things we need—the things we don't need—all the bad we know and force ourselves to forget—with lots of things we know that we really don't know we know—the conscious mind having forgotten them. To apply the story to the present case: Dorothy is Dr. Jekyll; Becky, her other self, is Mr. Hyde."[84]

The problem for Emerson, as for Prince, was to determine where the alter-personality had come from. Here Locke drew not on Prince but on George du Maurier's *Trilby*, and on a theme already widely known in popular culture—the innocent young girl in the thrall of a mesmeric seducer. The denouement comes when Emerson confronts Balzamo directly, determines that Becky has been created through hypnosis, and defeats Balzamo by the same means. Through an electric hypnotic-induction machine he implants a posthypnotic suggestion that ends Balzamo's power forever.

However, it did not end the power that multiple personality has periodically exercised over the public imagination. "Becky" and "Dorothy" have been reincarnated in our time as "Eve Black" and "Eve White," as "Victoria Scarleau" and "Sybil." In the interim between 1913 and 1957, when *The Three Faces of Eve* was published, multiple personality nearly disappeared both in the public eye and as a medical concept. Now it has come back more strongly than before, and it behooves us to ask why.

CONCLUSION

❧ When Doctors Disagree ❧

"Hi there, Doc!"
—"Eve Black"

ON THE EDGE OF THE PUBLIC GARDEN derelicts sleep under the majestic stone gaze of the Unitarian preacher William Ellery Channing; inside the Garden the swanboats ferry tourists about the pond much as they did when Richard Hodgson was alive. The old city has changed both in the direction of growth and decay but it still retains its vitality and intellectual dynamism. The subjects of my book have all gone to their respective fates while the living must face the problems and obsessions of their own time. Boston is no longer the center it was; the country has grown but, though more diffuse, it still retains the heritage of those who came in the seventeenth century to establish their City on a Hill—in doing so exporting a distinctive vision of human nature to the New World. In the interim since B.C.A. wrote up her unusual story there have been the Freudian revolution, a depression, and four wars—and now the return of multiple personality.

Since 1811 the vicissitudes of this concept have been about as tortuous as the fates of those to whom the idea has been applied. In France, where it achieved its first theoretical articulation, "multiple personality" has disappeared entirely from the intellectual framework of psychotherapy and apparently from perceived clinical manifestation as well.[1] But, in the United States, the early French theories of dissociational phenomena are being rehabilitated, while multiple personality is clinically undergoing an efflorescence unparalleled since the late nineteenth century. As mentioned in the Introduction, a modern author writes of a "multiple personality epidemic," one measured by an increasing frequency of reported cases and theoretical pronouncements based on them.[2] What can at least be said is that there is a current epidemic of *interest* in this arcane topic, one taking organizational form in 1984 with the creation of an International Society for the Study of Multiple Personality, lately extended to include—"and Dissociation." (Pierre Janet would have been pleased).[3]

Yet for quite some time the syndrome was in eclipse, only sporadically represented in case reports. Now it is the object of a growing psychiatric industry, the subject of an intriguing literary genre, and an element in contemporary symbolic discourse concerning the changing family, the relations between the sexes, and the treatment of children. In addition, a process of adjusting the conceptual boundaries between mental disorders has begun, which promises through this process alone to give the multiple personality syndrome a greater prominence than it formerly had. Once a thing is clearly defined it becomes easier to see.

I have shown how the concept of multiple personality arose, how it matched the experience of individuals and the circumstances of the societies in which they lived. Ideally, to complete the job, a similar procedure should be applied to the cases of current issue. But the literature is burgeoning and, since this literature is really much of a piece, it would be unprofitable and tedious to do so; in any event I do not seek to write the history of the present, merely to show how the past illuminates it. Therefore, instead of examining particular modern cases in detail, I will be content to characterize the current state of affairs in terms of the case studies I have presented and the propositions set forth in the Introduction, then discussing the conclusions and theoretical implications of this study as a whole.

The very existence of the multiple personality syndrome remains a debatable issue—in relation to other alternatives such as fraud, self-deception, misdiagnosis, and transient cultural fashion. In the wake of the tendentious not-guilty-by-virtue-of-insanity verdict that acquitted John Hinckley of the attempted murder of President Reagan, the American Psychiatric Association recently generated a declaration stating that "psychiatry is a deterministic discipline that views all human behavior as, to a good extent, 'caused.' "[4] There are of course different theoretical and practical approaches to the problem of multiple personality—some biomedical, some more humanistic—but in any event the medical model imposes a deterministic world view on those who subscribe to it. Therefore the search for the causes of multiple personality goes on, but as yet theory remains incoherent, its predictive value nil, and its therapeutic application a matter of some debate. The keynote speaker at the 1985 meetings of the International Society pointed out that, as yet, theorists in the area of multiple personality are unable to explain why one abused child becomes a multiple personality while another does not. I do not doubt that the traumatic factors held to be productive of multiple personality are likely to be productive of *something*. My case studies have shown that there is a fit between a certain life experience and the aptness of certain metaphors in describing it. There is a statistical overrepresentation of lonely and imaginative children, of evangelical Protestants and women; contemporary therapists associate multiple personality with high intelligence, suggesting—among other things—a class bias in their sample.[5] I have maintained that the form mental disorder takes is influenced by the acquisition of a culturally specific idiom of distress in collusion with local circumstances. This is hardly a mechanical process of causation, nor is any lip service to the value of deterministic causation likely to make it be.

Mary Reynolds was imaginative and isolated; so were Miss Beauchamp and the modern case of "Sybil"; such circumstances have been found conducive to the formation of the "imaginary companions" that many children have, and which have been associated with the etiology of some cases of multiple personality.[6] Reynolds, Bourne, Eve, Sybil, and others came from an evangelical background disavowing emotional spontaneity as a fleshly evil. As Jeremy Hawthorn observes: "The reason why religion is omnipresent as an apparent causal factor in these cases is that, paradoxically, it encloses individuals in 'totalizing' beliefs in which contradiction and variation are impossible."[7]

But in all the publicly well-known cases of multiple personality the causal sequence of events leading to it remains quite obscure. Current theory has it that a dissociation and splitting of consciousness begins as a defensive reaction in childhood or as an indirect way of expressing otherwise inadmissible impulses and desires. Alter-personalities often claim that they have been around from an early age, hiding their strange secret from an inquisitive world. Some therapists hold that without proper treatment this disorder may never be publicly manifest unless a given personality turns out to be noticeably sociopathic. Multiples are often remarkably well-adjusted neurotics, skillful at concealment; modern commentators refer to this as a "disorder of secrecy." It is suspected that only those experienced in the detection and treatment of the problem are likely to see it for what it is, that it is much more common than has been thought, and has been concealed or mistaken for something else—usually schizophrenia; it has been pointed out that many of the standard diagnostic signs of schizophrenia apply to multiple personality as well, as do those of what is termed "borderline personality disorder"—a twilight zone between neurosis and psychosis.[8] Yet the majority psychiatric opinion still seems to be that it is so rare that a given practitioner is unlikely to ever encounter multiple personality at all.

Here is the rub. Reported cases of multiple personality tend to cluster around a growing number of specialists who believe this is due to their special expertise in detecting it. In addition a sensitized public is increasingly ready to view its problems in terms of this evocative idiom. As Morton Prince's daughter noted long ago, many well-placed Boston ladies wrote appreciative letters to Prince thanking him for at last putting words to their otherwise inarticulate affliction through his account of Miss Beauchamp.[9] This effect seems to obtain now as well. Case reports tell us that some multiples were directly influenced by the media—by having encountered this phenomenon through literature or film; this probably occurs with a frequency far greater than the reports indicate. One psychiatric authority who has seen a considerable cohort of multiples remarks that "naive" patients are now hard to find. Popular psychology has begun a feedback process between theory and clinical reality that produces through resonance a heightened incidence of multiple personality. One can sense the market to which this popular literature appeals through a look at the best-selling nonfiction of 1973, the year in which *Sybil* was published:

1. *The Living Bible*
2. *Dr. Atkins Diet Revolution*
3. *I'm O.K. You're O.K.*
4. *The Joy of Sex*
5. *Weight Watchers Program Cookbook*
6. *How to be Your Own Best Friend*
7. *The Art of Walt Disney*
8. *Better Homes and Gardens Home Canning Book*
9. *Alistair Cooke's America*
10. *Sybil*[10]

The American obsession with selfhood is evidently alive and well; of these works all but three pertain to interpersonal relations and the problem of self-image, a bias that has remained prevalent in the popular media since the nineteenth century. Even the popularity of the redoubtable Alistair Cooke may owe something to this narcissistic cultural insecurity; Americans have always taken a keen interest in what others think of them—perhaps because they are not altogether sure what they think of themselves (I trust that we can at least absolve the home canners from this obsession; I am not so sure about the Walt Disney enthusiasts).

There is also the problem of conceptual redefinition to consider. The standard North American classification of mental disorders is established by medical committee, and this process has resulted in three editions of the *Diagnostic and Statistical Manual* of the American Psychiatric Association (DSM), with the fourth in preparation. This manual classifies disorders into major categories and subcategories along with diagnostic criteria and, in its current form, a handbook of brief case studies illustrating symptomatology. These classifications ("nosologies") have two major functions: expediting diagnosis, and the gathering of epidemiological statistics. Though the Introduction to the most recent edition of the manual (DSMIII —something of a best seller in its own right) warns against imagining that the diagnostic categories are clearly separable from one another, the headings are arranged in a numerical order lending itself to a checklist approach; if the symptoms are such-and-such, the disorder is such-and-such and enters the statistics accordingly.[11]

There were two previous editions of the manual, one published in 1952 in response to a pressing need to standardize terminology, the other in 1968. In the former the major category "Dissociative Reaction" (000–x02) is placed under the "Psychoneuroses" (as distinguished from the psychoses and various organic conditions): "This reaction represents a type of gross personality disorganization, the basis of which is a neurotic disturbance. . . . The repressed impulse giving rise to the anxiety may be discharged by, or deflected into, various symptomatic expressions, such as depersonalization, dissociated personality, stupor, fugue, dream state, somnambulism, etc."[12]

Multiple personality is not mentioned by name at all, a fact reflecting the extreme improbability of such a diagnosis in the period at issue (perhaps in the age of Ozzie and Harriet children were less abused). By 1968 things had changed somewhat. Now (ten years after *The Three Faces of Eve*) multiple personality is directly mentioned under the general heading of "Neuroses," subheading "Hysterical Neuroses" (300.1), sub-subheading "Dissociative Type" (300.14): "In the dissociative type, alterations may occur in the patient's state of consciousness or in his identity, to produce such symptoms as amnesia, somnambulism, fugue, and multiple personality."[13]

In DSMIII the classification of multiple personality under "Dissociative Disorders" is retained, though now "dissociation" has moved up in taxonomic status and "neuroses" altogether dropped as a major category. Of "dissociative disorders" in general, the manual states: "The essential feature is a sudden, temporary alteration in the normally integrative functions of consciousness, identity, or motor behavior. If the alteration occurs in consciousness, important personal events cannot be recalled. If it occurs in identity, either the individual's customary identity is forgotten and a new identity is assumed, or the customary feeling of one's own reality is lost and replaced by a feeling of unreality."[14]

The "Diagnostic Criteria for Multiple Personality" are then grouped as follows:

A. The existence within the individual of two or more distinct personalities, each of which is dominant at a particular time.

B. The personality that is dominant at any particular time determines the individual's behavior.

C. Each individual personality is complex and integrated with its own unique behavior patterns and social relationships.[15]

Multiple personality has shifted from (in 1952) what I take to be a subcategory of "Dissociated Personality" to (in 1968) a named subcategory of "Hysterical Neuroses, Dissociative Type," to (in 1980) a subcategory of "Dissociative Disorders."[16] Writers on multiple personality have themselves taken note of this shift, and with a new prominence enhanced by magazine articles, dramatizations, and radio and television interviews, multiple personality has again become much discussed.

I should now examine this process a bit more closely. All authors agree, whatever their opinion otherwise, that the number of reported cases has soared since 1970.[17] As I have said, this is generally seen to be the result of a combination of factors—the myopia of inexperienced therapists, the ability of multiples to screen their problem, inappropriate diagnosis, and so on. It is also widely agreed that there is a hidden population of sufferers badly in need of help—to which there is urgent need that the medical profession and the public at large be alerted. As one influential survey article states: "If this rash of new cases arises out of improved diagnostic techniques and improved clinical awareness—and I think this is where the case is to be made—one may surmise that there are scores, possibly hundreds of persons suffering at any given time from this painful, puzzling, and often disabling personality condition, and who, as either undiagnosed or misdiagnosed, are failing to reap the benefits of appropriate treatment."[18]

The same author points to a lack of therapists—"all of whom can be counted on one hand"—experienced enough in this area to have a clear understanding of the obstacles in the way of correct diagnosis.[19] This was written in 1980 and, as the author predicted, with refined diagnostic criteria and a greater number of specialists trained in their use, the presently reported cases of multiple personality number in the hundreds, with a concomitant rise in the average number of personalities per case; it is said that, unlike the nineteenth-century norm, dual personalities are simply not seen any more.[20]

The reasons for this are less than clear. One author will state that multiple personality is hard to detect and may be missed for years, even after a given case has encountered the mental health care system; another finds that (if hypnosis is used), "to enter the domain of the personalities is childishly simple."[21] As noted in the Introduction, it has long been thought that hypnosis should be employed with caution in such cases lest it contribute to the elaboration of the phenomena or even bring new personalities into existence through its action alone.[22] Others claim that it is the *only* adequate therapy, the only way to effectively crack the amnesic barrier between personalities and promote their reintegration or "fusion."[23] Whatever their doubts and their theoretical attitudes toward it, most practitioners apply hypnosis in practice and the general view seems to be that it indeed produces an altered state of consciousness in which different rules apply.[24]

As might now be suspected, my own opinion is simple and parsimonious: hypnosis as a special or altered state does not exist. What happens in so-called hypnosis is that the hypnotic subject is convinced—either through preexisting assumptions or through the messages sent by the practitioner (or both together)—that he or she is in a special state in which different rules do indeed apply, in which certain unusual subjective experiences are expectable. The subject receives information about the state he is in and experiences it accordingly: wandering off into poetic reveries, not because some hidden part of the mind has been unsealed, but because poetic license has been granted to dream; to undergo amnesias, not because some part of the mind has been closed off, but because access to it is defined as impossible. I regard hypnosis as an interesting cultural delusion—a part of what Berger and Luckmann termed a "psychology." Recent practitioners are aware in varying measure of these difficulties, but nonetheless their therapeutic procedures seem capable of influencing the phenomena in unintended ways.

One of the most insidious ways is implied by the very terms of reference in which therapy is conducted. It is the therapist's responsibility to elicit information allowing for appropriate diagnosis and treatment. The way in which this is done is shaped by currently fashionable theories. Not just any question is asked of a patient; not just any procedure is used. There is the risk that "leading questions" may steer the patient's perception toward what the investigator has already come to expect—that, as in the case of B.C.A., experience may be restructured around a peculiarly evocative idiom. Freud, for instance, found certain "resistances" in his patients which, given his theory of repression, only convinced him all the more that he was on the right track when they were encountered; the more the patients fought his interpretation the more (so he reasoned) they had to hide. It has been noted that multiple personalities sometimes react to the doctor's interpretation of their situation with angry denial.[25] However, once the interpretation is accepted a new life history may be constructed on its basis; hypnotic regression is exceptionally productive in this regard. Many patients state that their first alternate appeared as a defense against adult aggression. It is possible, however, that retrospection in the therapeutic context has—as with B.C.A.—produced a pseudo-memory consonant with current theories about the etiology of multiple personality; therapists attempt to overcome this possibility by seeking independent confirmation of typical multiple personality behavior evinced prior to entering therapy, but I do not know how often or with what rigor.

An unintended influence stems from the problem that—as in the Spiritualist seance—treating the facets of a multiple on their own terms may have the effect of further solidifying their reality. One therapist, for example, states that as a rule of method one should "call the patient whoever he or she wants to be called. Treat all alters with equal respect."[26] Of course this is aimed at their eventual fusion, it being necessary to evoke the contradictions of the patient so that they may later be resolved. Yet there are dangers in this: "It is essential [a sceptical observer writes] for the therapist not to succumb to the temptation to take the patient's symptomatology at face value."[27]

Another practitioner believes that he has found in each of his patients an "Inner Self Helper" (ISH), a personality akin to a guardian angel or spirit-guide that always has the best wishes of its host in mind, no matter how many other co-residents there may be. This meta-personality is transcendent to all the other neurotic souls fighting out their contrary tendencies within their shared body. The author in question tends toward spiritistic imagery and states that he cannot rule out the spirit hypothesis in giving an account of at least some multiples.[28] To the degree that the appearance of such a helper becomes an expectable part of the therapeutic process, the more so it is likely to be found when actively sought.

Because of the ability of a meta-personality to make aloof transcendent commentaries on the desires and social relations of its host, therapeutic encouragement of this stance is not necessarily bad medicine. In fact it reflects a common feature of the multiple personality syndrome more generally—the presence of at least one personality claiming co-conscious knowledge of its mates. Once it is suspected that a given patient is indeed multiple, active efforts may be taken to evoke the hidden self and to find a meta-personality who can function, like Sally Beauchamp or "B" did, as co-therapist.[29] In this role such a personality functions as an introjection of the therapist himself, and in at least one case was deliberately cultivated as such: "I induced [the therapist writes] another personality, 'Dr. Bliss,' through hypnosis to assist me in therapy. This was done rapidly through a hypnotic trance and my colleague, 'Dr. Bliss,' has been living with 30 other personalities since that date."[30]

A popular account of multiple personality—"Inside the Divided Mind"—appearing in the widely read forum of the Sunday *New York Times Magazine* states (I do not know with what truth) that the source from which the above quotation is drawn is regarded as "the classic scientific article on multiple personality." Dr. Bliss is quoted as commenting on as yet undiscovered cases of multiplicity that "there is a galaxy of them out there."[31] With therapeutic procedures such as these, if such a galaxy of untapped talent is not already present it soon will be.

This raises a further problem: the degree to which the incidence of multiple personality is influenced by a climate of public expectation fostered by the media itself. The *Times* article is only one example of a growing number of publicly available accounts of multiple personality; we also have our equivalents to Edward Locke's popularization of the fortunes of Miss Beauchamp. Together these productions have a considerable impact on the general culture at large, and the therapeutic community in particular (in which I include both therapists and clients). Doctors Hervey Cleckley and Corbett Thigpen, the physicians who described the case of Eve and in so doing contributed a great deal to these developments themselves, look upon the current multiple personality epidemic in dismay. In 1984 they say that, in the thirty years since Eve, they have seen only *one* other case of multiple personality they regard as genuine, and wonder why others see so many more. Their answer is direct—it is a fad: patients wish to be diagnosed as multiples; doctors attuned to the times wish to diagnose them as such:

> It seems that in very recent years there has been a further increase in the number of persons seeking to be diagnosed as multiple personalities—some patients move from therapist to therapist until "achieving" the diagnosis—and similarly, among some patients who ostensibly have the disorder there is a competition to see who can have the greatest number of alter personalities. (Unfortunately, there also appears to be a competition among some therapists to see who can have the greatest number of multiple personality cases).[32]

Thigpen and Cleckley's reference to patients shopping among therapists until the correct diagnosis is achieved suggests another factor that seems to be at work in the current epidemic—the fact that many of those who eventually *do* get diagnosed as multiples have been in psychotherapy for years. An investigator who has attempted to obtain a sample of multiples large enough for statistical analysis finds that out of a research group of seventy-three patients "more than half of them had come from a cohort of neurotic patients refractory after ten or more years of verbal therapy! Fifty-nine percent of the research series admitted they had withheld data which might have suggested the diagnosis."[33]

According to findings presented at the second annual meeting of the International Society (Chicago, 1985), an average of 6.8 years intervenes from the time of the first diagnosis to the final and correct diagnosis of multiple personality. It would be naive to assume that in a large group of patients already steeped in psychological lore there were not a great deal of sharing of information outside the therapeutic context, of anxious self-motivated searching for the roots of their difficulties, and in the matter of course a good deal of contact with the idea of multiple personality. Unfortunately case reports do not allow insights into the subculture of mental patients.

Eve's doctors were modest about their abilities to explain what had happened to her; when the case was presented to the general public in 1957, it was as a psychological marvel of nature—a human drama at once mysterious and profound—and so it was received. Thigpen and Cleckley were at pains to disavow that they had inadvertently influenced the direction of the case. True: hypnosis had been employed before the case was revealed to be one of multiple personality, but when the "Eve Black" personality emerged her sweet sister "Eve White" ("the damned little fraud," as Becky would have said) was not at the time under hypnotic influence. True: multiple personality is a rare and striking phenomenon, but the doctors did not think that their amazement at encountering such a case—the reaction it aroused in them of "wonder, sometimes of awe"—had encouraged Eve to become more florid in order to please them.[34] True: as the case developed, the doctors found it possible to elicit Eve's various personalities with the ease of flicking a light-switch; yet they continued to insist on the true separateness of Eve's personalities. The case of Eve became a media event and, given the quasi-novelistic form in which it was presented, evidently it was meant to.

Perhaps it is a coincidence that the woman who would become known as "Sybil" first revealed her multiplicity to Dr. Cornelia Wilbur in December 1954, shortly after the first account of Eve was offered to the psychological community in the uniquely appropriate forum of Morton Prince's *Journal of Abnormal Psychology*.[35] Like Thigpen and Cleckley, Sybil's analyst was "overtaken by an uncanny, eerie feeling" when exposed to an unexpectedly multiple self.[36] Perhaps it is also a coincidence that before this key event Sybil "indulged in the ritual of making frequent pilgrimages to . . . the university psychological library, where she steeped herself in psychiatric literature, especially case histories."[37]

Some cases are clearly based on precedent. For further example, Henry Hawksworth (whose story—*The Five of Me*—was presented in novelistic form and made into a television film) had been frequently "misdiagnosed" as something other than a multiple; he had read *The Three Faces of Eve* and, given his long experience with the mental health establishment, was well acquainted with psychology and, I assume, the theoretical orientations of his therapists.[38] Hawksworth, whose violence ran him afoul of the law, was induced by his doctor, Ralph Allison, to demonstrate while hypnotized his multiplicity from the witness stand for an amazed jury and a sceptical prosecution. Kenneth Bianchi—the "Hillside Strangler"—was aware of Eve. Martin Orne, who was instrumental in providing evidence that Bianchi had been dissimulating, states that "he's seen 'Three Faces of Eve,' the film which is like an education on how to fake a multiple personality."[39] A psychiatrist asked himself rhetorically whether it might be possible to fake multiple personality; so far as a California jury was concerned the answer turned out to be a resounding "yes!"[40] Billy Milligan— "The Man with Ten Personalities"—was, with the aid of the testimony of Sybil's therapist, Cornelia Wilbur, acquitted of rape on grounds of insanity.[41] Alarmed by this increasing tendency for multiple personality to be employed as an insanity defense, Thigpen and Cleckley would suggest that Billy Milligan was also a fraud.[42]

I do not mean to imply that all or even many multiples are frauds; I imagine few are. It should be remembered that my concern is with how self-experience is culturally and socially shaped. However, the current state of debate (1985) remains clouded by conflicting claims about the status of the multiple personality syndrome. When doctors disagree, outsiders are entitled to their scepticism.

It is clear that multiple personality can become a role, a valued part of one's self-definition. "Eve" (Chris Costner Sizemore) is a case in point. Corbett Thigpen gave a talk on her case before the American Psychiatric Association accompanied by a film in which Eve's personalities were put through their paces, an episode that apparently first drew media attention to her. Thigpen and Cleckley reported that "Eve Black took great interest in the news items that appeared in the press about the case of which she was a part. Indeed, she seemed to be fascinated by the anonymous fame she found for herself in these accounts."[43] Later, as the Eve sensation gathered momentum toward its culmination in an Academy Award winning film, she began to feel hard done by, nonetheless remaining in the shadows—hiding as before her multiplicity from all but a few.[44] Evidently the publication of *Sybil* in 1973 was too much for her. (Here I might parenthetically note that the therapists in question saw fit to assign their patients pseudonyms drawn from the world of myth: "Eve," the archetypal woman in all her moods; "Sybil," a Greco-Roman trance oracle, a seer of truth. These women in turn have become mythic paradigms for the rest of us.)

At the end of *The Three Faces of Eve*, Doctors Thigpen and Cleckley speculate about Eve's future, stating that whether she "will continue to enjoy a happy life we are unable to predict."[45] Eve's own point of view was that she had not been cured at all, even though her doctors received the glory for supposedly having done so. In the interim from 1957 until her true identity became public in 1975, Eve's personalities multiplied like rabbits until she acquired twenty-two, thus upstaging Sybil's mere sixteen. Her behavior became increasingly histrionic and finally caught the attention of the press. Once out of the closet she made the *Washington Post* and the popular CBS news magazine *Sixty Minutes*. Currently Eve is on the executive board of the International Society for the Study of Multiple Personality for a second year.

The publicity accorded to Eve and her subsequent political emergence within the Society may have helped precipitate a new organization. A group of multiple personality patients at the Chicago meetings of the International Society announced the creation of a newsletter for people such as they: *S4OS— Speaking for Our Selves* ("A Newsletter by, for and about people with multiple personalities"):

> AT LAST!!! There is a written forum for people with multiple personalities to learn from each other about their experiences and to educate helping professionals about the diversity and range of experiences of people who have multiple personalities. We have entitled the Newsletter *Speaking for Our Selves* since our goal is both to speak for the many selves inside us and to speak for the many individuals who have Multiple Personality Disorder.

If this group lives up to its program, patients will henceforth have a say, as educators no less—as an advocacy group—in the future elaboration and development of the multiple personality syndrome; I wonder how many of them will also become therapists who, like the African with whom I began, gain their credibility from being able to treat as injured healers what they once suffered from themselves.

An associated current feature of the multiple personality phenomenon is the resurgence of occultist theorizing. One of the best-known therapists in this area came to entertain the spirit hypothesis because he found it difficult to explain certain features of his cases otherwise.[46] Thigpen and Cleckley found themselves besieged with correspondence from occultists full of good advice about what their famous case *really* was.[47] Multiple personality patients seem to have a tendency to dabble in the occult themselves, especially if from California.[48] Reincarnation is also much in the air. Dr. Ian Stevenson, who has himself investigated a case of multiplicity, has been working over the years in a cross-cultural study of reincarnational phenomena such as cases in which children claim to embody the returned spirits of dead ancestors. Stevenson notes the occasional similarity to clinical multiplicity: "In most cases, the subject experiences the previous self as *continuous* with his present personality, not as substituting for it. The substitutive kind of identification does, however, occur occasionally in spontaneous cases suggestive of rebirth; and it occurs usually in hypnotically induced regressions and nearly always in mediumistic trances. It also occurs more or less in 'ordinary' cases of multiple personality without claim to a previous life."[49]

This type of finding provides yet another possible avenue for the extension of an essentially occultist theory of multiple personality. Possession, of course, is another possibility. A recent book—*Multiple Man* by Adam Crabtree, a Canadian psychotherapist—reflects the recurrent equivocation between spiritistic and psychological modes of interpreting multiplicity. He deals in his practice directly with those who experience themselves as possessed, and cites Dr. Ralph Allison's kindred work with approval. Crabtree, who was once a Benedictine monk conversant with Catholic opinion on exorcism, describes a therapy that is quite explicitly for "cases of possession by human spirits, living and discarnate." Elsewhere his book runs through the standard litany of possession-type phenomena, including a good deal of material on multiplicity, but he fails in the end to positively opt for one mode of explanation or the other (though I think I detect his preference).

Chris Costner Sizemore provided an imprimatur for this work, stating that "his [Crabtree's] concepts of possession are not only intriguing and thought-provoking, but highly illuminating revelations of the innermost recesses of the mind." Crabtree's conclusions are not in themselves particularly remarkable nor, since she has lately been making something of a profession out of lecturing on multiple personality, is it any great surprise that "Eve" has gotten into the act. What is perhaps of greater significance is that he, and others interested in such things, were in 1985 invited to discuss their findings on the popular mainstream Canadian Broadcasting Corporation radio show *Ideas*, again suggesting the degree of public interest that these phenomena arouse.[50]

Finally, there is the issue of childhood sexual abuse. Dissociation in response to such abuse is becoming the dominant paradigm in explaining the origin of multiple personality. Here *Sybil*, with its powerful images of a little girl tortured by her own mother, seems to have set the tone. The first new personality that many multiples can remember often makes the claim that it came into existence in response to some specific trauma. Since they pertain to a period of life of which adult memory is by no means certain, such claims are difficult to judge; it is possible, as I have said, that in some instances they are based on pseudo-memories evoked by the therapeutic context itself.

One symptom of the popularity of the child-abuse issue is the impressive public effect—strongest I think in feminist circles—of the 1985 publication of Jeffrey Masson's *The Assault on Truth*, in which it is claimed that Freud suppressed the evidence that his patients often *had been* sexually molested in childhood in favor of the more palatable idea that such memories are actually wish-fulfilling incestuous fantasies—(silly women!).[51] However, the problem goes considerably deeper than the acrimonious controversy that this book aroused (the covert questions being: "How have we come to such a pass that children are tortured, abused, and molested in such numbers?" "Why are contemporary *men* such brutes?" "How can women and children be protected from them?" etc.). Concern for abuse, whatever its actual significance as a problem, reflects a sociological climate of confusion over self-identity and of restless search for clarification, whether in the medical or the political arena. The keynote speaker at the Chicago meetings spoke of attempts to get the problem of child abuse more widely known; speaking of her own personal encounter with the woman known as Sybil, she didactically instructed her audience that it is their role to tell the public about the relation between abuse and multiple personality. My impression is that they are ready to do their best.

And in doing so they legitimate themselves. Multiple personality has already been legitimated as a defined syndrome in DSMIII, but until now the segment of the psychiatric profession interested in this problem has existed in a psychological state of siege in the face of colleagues who refuse to believe that the object of their inquiry is real. One speaker in Chicago spoke of what he called the "Israel Effect," solidarity created through encounters with a hostile world. The impression gained from such images is that of a small intrepid band of explorers slowly gaining ground on the philistine opposition through the very fact that they were able to create an international organization, hold two successful and well-attended meetings, and achieve a high degree of media attention; "we really are in a frontier area," said another speaker. The apotheosis of Dr. Cornelia Wilbur is an interesting sign of this new confidence. In one of her own talks at the meetings she spoke of how, since 1963, she has "fought for multiple personality." Dr. Frank Putnam, pioneer of the use of the EEG in multiple personality research, gave an interesting insight into what she meant by this. The case of Sybil was never presented in a professional journal, and it saw the light of day only through Flora Schreiber's popular account. Putnam stated that the reason for this is that the organizers of a symposium for which Wilbur originally presented the case actually *refused* to have it published. The tables have surely been turned, and Dr. Wilbur revealed as a prophet.

However, popularity has its costs, and professional respectability is a difficult attainment in an area that has always had a touch of the occult about it—and now satanism as well. The organizers of the 1985 meetings were taken aback by how many questions they were receiving, from the press among others, about cases of multiple personality that are held to have originated in abuse by satanic cults. I got the impression that— like demon-possession and exorcism in the modern Roman

Catholic Church—this is a question that many would rather just have go away. The following press report indicates the difficulty:

> A 14 year-old novice devil worshipper who carved the satanic symbol 666 on his chest with a knife, shot a gambling expert, his wife and their daughter last spring after the angry half of his personality told him the killings would set him free, a family court judge was told Thursday. He pleaded not guilty Thursday to three counts of first-degree murder. He told police after his arrest that he killed [them] to vent anger stemming from an argument with his parents over smoking and girls. Family court judge C.R. Ball heard how the violent side of the youth's personality was given a name by a psychiatrist several months before the shooting. The youth referred to this angry second person as Eddie, a name borrowed from the mascot of the heavy-metal rock group Iron Maiden.[52]

Satanism, hard rock, and psychiatry are certainly a heady brew, and I would imagine that the doctor who gave Eddie his name is—like some of those involved in the Bianchi case—in for some hard sledding with regard to possible accusations of iatrogenesis.

However, even with such difficulties the activities of those working in the field of multiple personality bid fair to create a subprofession within the disciplines of psychiatry and clinical psychology. What occurred in Chicago indicates an important waystation in the process: the creation of a professional association with annual ritual meetings. They will soon have a journal (*Dissociation*) and now need the most important criterion for a profession as sociologists define it—an independent process of training and certification governed by a legitimating body that controls just who has a license to practice the trade and to drum out those, such as the occultists, who fail to toe the professional line. Through meetings and journals an orthodox paradigm is forming, as is a group of recognized specialists. There is fair consistency, though not absolute unanimity, about what this disorder is and what causes it. The danger is that the experts will run out of things to say; with a theory of traumatic neurosis in place as the fundamental explanatory principle, theory development could degenerate into mere case lore. There must be *new* ideas to sustain professional momentum, and it will be interesting to see what these are.

One possibility is an enhancement of neurophysiological research; already there is work being done with the EEG suggesting to the researchers' own satisfaction that multiple personality has a neural basis with unique features. This is encouraging, because it allows work to go forward on normative positivist lines that produce experimental *results* rather than mere qualitative observations. Mainstream psychiatry is already oriented this way, and adoption of its methods by the multiple personality researchers may in itself encourage the legitimation process. Another possible avenue for advance is appropriation of other paradigms. "Schizophrenia" is one obvious target, since there is much overlapping in diagnostic criteria between it and multiple personality.[53] For example, multiples often report inner voices, whereas one DSM criterion for schizophrenia is "auditory hallucinations in which either a voice keeps up a running commentary on the individual's behavior or thoughts, or two or more voices converse with each other."[54]

Even the classic cases of multiple personality such as Miss Beauchamp and B.C.A. report a sense of having their thoughts interfered with, yet again a diagnostic sign—even a primary one—of schizophrenia: "bizarre delusions ... such as delusions of being controlled, thought broadcasting, thought insertion, or thought withdrawal."[55]

When it is noted that the DSM requires only the presence of *one* such criterion for a proper diagnosis of schizophrenia, the boundary between it and multiple personality seems very fine indeed.

Another possible and probably softer target is "borderline personality disorder"—in itself an equivocal concept—which the DSMIII characterizes as follows:

> The essential feature ... is instability in a variety of areas, including interpersonal behavior, mood, and self-image. No single feature is invariably present. Interpersonal relations are often intense and unstable, with marked shifts of attitude over time. Frequently there is impulsive and unpredictable behavior that is potentially self-damaging. Mood is often unstable, with

marked shifts from a normal mood to a dysphoric mood or
with inappropriate, intense anger or lack of control of anger.
A profound identity disturbance may be manifested by uncer-
tainty about several issues relating to identity, such as self-
image, gender identity, or long-term goals or values.[56]

With the solitary exception of amnesia this could just as
well be a description of multiple personality. Multiples show
shifts of mood; one personality often persecutes another to the
point of physical mutilation; one personality is often an angry
one; the personalities may be of different sexes, suggesting a
profound disturbance of gender identity. If the therapist
becomes convinced that there is a dissociated personality
behind such borderline behavior, it is but a small step to a
diagnosis of multiple personality.

The so-called affective disorders also contain features of
multiplicity such as radical mood shifts. But it is pointless to go
on; I have only wished to demonstrate that the diagnostic criteria for quite a number of disorders overlap considerably. Many
investigators have shown (I am scarcely the first to do so) that
psychiatric nosologies are sensitive to cultural fashion and
even to political pressure. Homosexuality, for example, which
was once regarded as a disorder in itself, is now only to be
considered such if the homosexual is worried about being one,
if—as the DSMIII puts it—this realization is "ego-dystonic."
This change was a direct response to gay activism within the
American Psychiatric Association.[57]

With all these factors working in conjunction, the concept
of multiple personality and the group treating it have indefinite growth potential. This concept and the sociological milieu
in which it functions have all the features of a classical Kuhnian
paradigm, one well on the way to becoming "normal science."
There is a concept, an increasingly normative ideology, and a
socially interlinked troup—made up of patients, therapists,
and theorists—which together function to both generate and
propagate this particular idiom of distress for a public well
ready to subscribe to it and demonstrate its truth.

The current popularity of multiple personality is the product of the disorder of our times. But in the present debates on
the subject I find myself engaged with a microcosm of the
entire history of the subject: medical materialists debating

with psychologists and spiritists. Dr. Daniel Bemus, who treated Mary Reynolds by bleeding, has his modern analogues. It has been reported that many multiples regard hospital psychiatry as abusive in itself:

> Calomel, Tartar and Gamboge
> He deals me out good measure
> Could I the dose to *him* infuse
> Would be to me a pleasure.

Interaction among patients, specialists, and popular culture, as well as general social unease have set a process in motion that I mean to follow into the future—and I anticipate that this book will itself have some interesting effects on the process. The modern counterparts of the nineteenth-century psychical researchers and psychologists hope to achieve a more adequate model of mind; as the lead caption of the 1983 Hale article in the *New York Times Magazine* says, "once the stuff of pop literature, multiple personalities are the subject of new research that may help explain consciousness." I am less than certain that this will be the outcome. As I have said, metaphors have the capacity to mystify and compel—to convert an image into the illusion of a fact.

Multiple personality is a play on social roles and it can be properly understood only in reference to the set currently available—the cultural "ideal types," the "root paradigms," which allow us to structure our experience and render it comprehensible and predictable to others. The perennial conflict between Jekyll and Hyde is currently acted out in the consulting rooms of the therapists and increasingly in courts of law. We still have a sense of the inner demons which, like Dr. Jekyll, we would release if we could. The oppositional logic of multiple personality is a derivative from Christian Euro-North American culture. Other places, other cultures and times—other demons, other psyches.

I must admit to a sense of fatigue with the current issue of multiple personality—as though this has all happened before to little avail. I am much inclined to react as William James once did —*Bah!* However, my own culture should be accorded the same tolerant benefit of the doubt which, as anthropologist, I am obliged to accord to others. It is easy enough to indict one's own fellows for superstition and happily condone the same aberrations in foreigners. A reviewer of the first draft of this Conclusion commented that "the author doesn't strike the right balance between literally 'bah-humbugging' the issue of multiple personality and achieving an anthropological perspective on it as a functional social illusion."

I appreciate the difficulty, but insist that there is no "right balance" here. The study of multiple personality purports to be science; so in another way does anthropology. I have attempted to achieve a sympathetic cultural understanding of a phenomenon that I cannot accord the same ontological status as those who believe in it. However, there is also the question of truth, of explanatory adequacy. I wish to replace a deterministic ethnocentric explanation of multiple personality with a contextual interpretation I take to be more appropriate. On the one side I address members of my own culture as though they were members of an alien society. I see the Western psychotherapists dealing with multiple personality as healers, a role found in many if not all societies; I see those they treat as genuinely disturbed; I see the methods of the therapists as effective and sometimes life saving. However, when I see them as my colleagues—engaged with the same cultural tradition, having many of the same values, including the values of scientific inquiry—then I am inclined to criticize in a way that I probably would not if they actually *were* members of an alien society. I see them as engaging culturally specific problems with culturally specific tools while construing themselves as practitioners of a universalistic value-free science. This dual quality to the argument is therefore not equivocation, but as far as I am concerned absolutely unavoidable.

My criticisms are straightforward. The inductive causality-oriented study of multiple personality has so far proven unsuccessful. The data are not up to the conclusions drawn from them. The sample, insofar as there is one, is class biased in much the same way that Freud's was—toward interesting patients with the same culture and values as those who treat them; this I suspect to entail a covert process of selection that directs certain kinds of patients to therapists inclined to diagnose their problems in terms of multiple personality. Statistically the sample is worthless. Cultural factors compound the problem: a climate of media attention, the moral dualisms of our culture, the odd and increasingly well-publicized role of the forensic psychiatrist, a sociological milieu rendering self-identity acutely problematical, an activist patient subculture. The interactional framework of psychotherapy also remains an issue: the use of hypnosis, the increasing acceptability and coherence of the multiple personality paradigm, the increasing use of the paradigm by therapists—all these contribute to breathe life into a phenomenon which, if it were differently regarded, would manifest itself in some other way. Categorical boundaries between mental disorders are currently in flux in such a way as to make multiple personality a more popular diagnosis and to steer both therapists and clients toward its use as an interpretive device.

These criticisms are judgments drawn from the same inductivist intellectual tradition as the theories of those whom I criticize. But to make such points is not my main purpose, though certainly ancillary to it. I have no wish to be understood as engaging in a Szaszian antipsychiatric polemic; I am not. Nor do I want to be understood as saying that multiple personality is only an iatrogenic artifact; the culture at large is more than capable of generating experiential schism on its own without the help of doctors. Following William James, George Herbert Mead, and others, I perceive the more important and subtle issue to be that of the relations between "mind" and society, between concept and self-experience—those processes that result in the parceling up of an apparently unitary flow of consciousness (James's "stream of thought") into sensibly discontinuous experience in accord with culture, role, and the individual vicissitudes of fate. I therefore also perceive that multiple personality is in one sense genuine, but in another spurious. It is genuine insofar as it lives in experience, and this it does. It is spurious insofar as it is taken to be the result of a causal psychological process, and this it is not.

The "self," to be sure, is an unusual kind of concept in that it muddles the distinctions we like to make between the subjective and objective worlds. As a cultural construct the "self" is as "objective" as a "tree" or "dog." It reflects a certain categorization of experience which, as Berger and Luckmann said, contains an implicit cosmology. Yet the "self" seemingly contains elements that no other perception can possess, if only bodily sensibility (I cannot, at least not usually, feel what a tree feels). Further, the concept has complex ramifications based upon its profoundly social quality: the position of the individual in a total and not always coherent world of interpersonal experience. "Self," of course, is an English word—a reified abstraction that we take to summarize all that a social person is. Not all cultures have a similar term, nor even anything resembling it. The very existence of the word suggests a culturally specific problem area.

We speak of "self-knowledge," of "knowing oneself." However, the concept of the unconscious has, with whatever justice, led us to suspect that the phenomena of consciousness cannot be taken at face value. How much more difficult the problem when we look beyond our culture to others with quite different metaphysics and social organizations. Rodney Needham calls attention to the seemingly perennial problem—with which ethno-psychiatrists are more than amply familiar—of separating physiological or psychological universals from culturally specific constructs: "To the extent that inner states may be discriminable as universal natural resemblances, they are in the province of physiology. If inner states are inferred from social expressions, they are social facts like other social facts. There are presumably correspondences between physiological states and certain aspects of the ideologies by which psychological states are attributed to individuals. But in many cases there will be no correspondence, namely when the psychological concepts are purely social artifacts."[58]

Multiple personality illustrates the problem. As said, Western psychological theory makes universalistic claims, and indeed there are phenomena in other cultures—such as possession—that resemble kindred phenomena in our own. To what are these resemblances due? The theory of multiple personality is based upon the idea of dissociation and psychic fragmentation. Yet I have suggested that such fragmentation can be seen as a cultural process in two senses: (1) that the lines along which such fragmentation occurs are themselves culturally conditioned—that, as with Western African soul beliefs, the self can be locally construed as a decomposable composite entity reflective of the complex quality of a culturally embedded social persona, and (2) that certain interactional situations, such as hypnosis or the drama of possession, can in themselves lead to the phenomenological reality of inner fragmentation—to a de facto experiential division of the mind.

Of course in some ultimate sense we are talking about a basic and universal human reality that underlies culture and makes it possible. I, for one, have been accused of extreme cultural relativism, as though I believe that such an underlying reality does not exist.[59] An absurd proposition, but one that brings to focus the highly ambiguous status of the relation between "culture" and "psychology." Following the deterministic world view of Western psychiatry, one would be inclined to look for universalistically applicable causal processes underlying disorder—however exotic the local manifestations of disorder happen to be. In the preceding pages I have concentrated on a given idiom of distress that has been seen to answer to the needs of individuals in marginal, ambiguous, contradictory, or transitional personal situations. The assumption has been that these situations *are* inherently stressful because in some way they disallow a coherent social life, or at least make one difficult. This is a deterministic claim, although, as I said in the Introduction, it must be remembered that what counts as stressful is influenced by what the local culture considers *of* value. Further, it is clear that there are a number of avenues open for those who find themselves in such situations, and in most cases it is less than clear why one route is chosen over another; if this is determinism, it would seem to be of rather a weak kind. I have concentrated on the concept of "meaning," particularly on those conditions that bring the meaning of the self's relation to the world into question. In addition, much of what is called "disorder" is logically bound to canons of orderliness; disorder is symbolically opposed to order, each bound to the other; thus Mary Reynolds's second self was a mirror of her first. An idiom of distress is a semiotic concept that must be seen as part of the greater order that we associate with culture itself.

Whatever the theoretical orientation that given researchers may hold, I—as anthropologist—would insist we can scarcely proceed without knowledge of the symbolism that structures ideas concerning disorder and the events in which these ideas are manifest. Psychobiological and semiotic modes of explanation are not inherently mutually exclusive; given cases must be taken as they come. Though it is all very well to pay lip service to multicausal determinism jointly embodying the "psychological," the "biological," and the "meaningful," in the end it is a question of evidence. I personally find it difficult to construe cases such as those of Reynolds, Bourne, Piper, Fowler, and Bean as being strictly determined by anything.[60] What I do find are persons presented by their culture and its changing circumstances with existential dilemmas and with something as simple as loneliness (is there a drug for *that*?). As something of a Durkheimian, I find it possible to consider the major function of therapy to be the construction of a basis for meaningful sociality. So far as "therapy" (whatever its cultural form) creates a therapeutic community, it creates sociality itself, giving morally validated order to what for some is a chaotically meaningless world.

It is perhaps a rather trivial point, but—to repeat—the "mind" must be located in its true home, which is society. Yes, the mind is rooted in the body, as is whatever gives us the capacity and probably the need to construct culture as a system of meanings. This, though undoubtedly true, is not very helpful. When presented with a problem like multiple personality I am inclined to suggest that what is needed is something like what William James pointed toward: a sociological phenomenology, a falling back on the social roots of experience. Various philosophically inclined sociologists have also thought so, and have looked back to James for their inspiration. The sociocentric world view emerged out of nineteenth-century philosophical criticism of the concept of the "ego" or "self"; this new "psychology" they produced is in my view as decisive as any intellectual development of our time: we see a convergence of American pragmatism, European Marxism, psychoanalysis, British analytical philosophy, and anthropology toward the common realization that society must be the beginning point of analysis, not the brain per se, not the psychology of individuals.

The "mind" we find to be an empty category, merely a potentiality. As embodied culture-bearing beings we fill this possibility through interaction with one another. But this does *not* mean that somehow we end up in the same place; as James said (and which can stand as an aphoristic synopsis of my argument): "subjectivity and objectivity are affairs not of what an experience is aboriginally made of, but of its classification." One thinks of the Balinese with their complex cosmology and ritual system, and a propensity to become personally anonymous figures of cosmic reality through their extraordinary ability to lose themselves in trance. The Balinese shift with ease between social personae. So do multiples, but the nature of the so-called switching process between personality phases is profoundly unclear; as with the Balinese entering into the ritual mode—it just happens. The reason this strikes us as odd is that we have a concept of the self that makes it appear so. For the Balinese the switch is due to the entry of a divine being; for us the emergence of a subterranean personality: and who is right? I think neither.

Our Western psychologies betray their heritage. The idea of the unitary ego with its faculties—will, understanding, memory—seems to me still very much with us; otherwise multiple personality would not be the issue it is. However, my focus here has not been primarily philosophical nor, of course, psychological: rather I have been concerned with nineteenth- and early-twentieth-century American society and the changes rung on the theme of multiple personality in a rapidly changing culture. I have used this theme as a heuristic device to trace these cultural developments. Of course, beyond this rather limited intent one can see a prospect for the future; I suspect, for example, that much philosophical and anthropological insight can be drawn from a critical analysis of the concept of dissociation. This concept is the core of what makes multiple personality so interesting, but I think it (and this is as far as I am willing to go at the moment) to be a culturally specific construct implicitly casting much light on our own culture. An analysis of this idea is at least likely to produce insights into fundamental Western ideas concerning the nature of the person. I do not know if I will undertake an analysis of this idea myself; the next project on line (and a logical complement to this one just ended) is a social-historical biography of the above-mentioned Rev. Elias Smith who so much influenced the destiny of Ansel Bourne; this is likely to take time, and will throw me back still further into the murky convulsive world of late-eighteenth-century evangelical religion and radical politics.

NEARLY SEVEN YEARS AGO I BEGAN WORK on this book through an examination of the fate of Ansel Bourne. It led down some odd byways of the history of my own culture and of a personal past, and now I am glad to be free of it. It is difficult, however, to know how to conclude; a part of my own life is dropping away. So, I will return to Boston and evoke an image that appeals to me. Freud once likened the unconscious to the city of Rome; he created the powerful image of a present in which all of the city's history is in mind's eye at once, the bygone buildings and the society that created them standing as shadows among the constructions and activities of the living. In his vision of the unconscious the entire history of the person is co-present, but not all of it is consciously recognized. Standing on the walkway under the bridge that leads from Cambridge to the south bank of the Charles, one looks on a clear winter's day down the river toward Boston and the sea. From this vantage point are seen the gold dome of the State House, the steeples of the old city, and the towers of the new. I see this evocative city in the same way as Freud saw the unconscious, as encapsulating an entire past from the founding of the Massachusetts Bay Colony to the raucous present. I prefer to see the continuities in this, and through this book have recovered them for myself.

But I also think of Mary Reynolds putting down one of her much-loved books—the poetry of Cowper perhaps—to look (as I imagine my mother to have done in kindred circumstances) at the snow falling over the Pennsylvania wilderness. As for Ansel Bourne, what he made of his stay on earth we do not know. His intense preoccupied eyes look out from the old photographs as though he were trying—and failing—to remember something important.

Notes

INTRODUCTION

1. I think here of the debates sparked by I.M. Lewis's work (1971) on ecstatic religion in which he advances the proposition that some possessed states are indirect strategies for the redress of adverse distributions of power—used for example in patriarchal societies by women against men. However, is this type of possession to be properly viewed as due in some measure to an automatic psychological response to deprivation or to a conscious manipulation of a cultural idiom? This issue has been interestingly discussed by Newman (1964) and Langness (1965) with respect to "wild man" behavior in New Guinea. The former argues for an essentially sociological interpretation of this type of apparently psychotic episode whereas the latter sees such an outbreak as a transiently psychotic release of intolerable stress through a culturally stereotyped idiom.

2. Hawthorn 1983: 33.

3. Bayley 1985: 14.

4. Freud 1961a.

5. Turner 1974: 25.

6. McKellar 1979.

7. Turner 1974: 64.

8. Perry Miller 1954: 3–34.

9. Augustine 1927: 40.

10. Bercovitch 1975.

11. Rush 1835.

12. Fellman and Fellman 1981.

13. See Kleinman 1980.

14. Perry Miller 1954: 7.

15. Horton 1961; 1983.

16. William James [hereafter "James"] 1981.

17. Berger and Luckmann 1967: 174–75.

18. Heelas 1981:3.

19. Horton 1983: 79.

20. Berger and Luckmann 1967: 178.

21. Ellenberger 1970: 126–41.

22. Hilgard 1977: 18.

23. Prince 1975:55.

24. Hilgard 1977: 1, 77.

25. Halbwachs (1980) and Neisser (1982). These works show how social factors influence not just what gets remembered but also what gets forgotten in real-world contexts; together they represent a critique of the artificiality of much laboratory method.

CHAPTER ONE

1. S.L. Mitchell 1816: 185–86.

2. Locke said: "For, it being the same consciousness that makes a man be himself to himself, personal identity depends on that only" (Locke 1959: 450–51). Mary Reynolds was later to attract the philosophical attention of Frances Wayland, president of Brown University; he had been informed of her case by a student and put it to use in underscoring through a practical example the importance of memory to personal identity: "Consciousness, united with memory, gives rise to the conviction of personal identity. We know by means of this faculty that certain thoughts and feelings exist, and that they are the thoughts and feelings of the being whom I denominate I, myself. Memory connects these various testimonies of consciousness into a connected series, and thus we know that our intellectual acts, from our earliest recollection, proceed from the same being, and not another" (Wayland 1854: 114).

3. *Dictionary of National Biography*, 1921–22, vol. 19: 667–68; *The Dictionary of Welsh Biography* 1959: 956–57.

4. John Reynolds 1870: 8.

5. Coats n.d.: 15; see Langley 1939: 45–48; Rose 1964: 416–17.

6. The general intellectual atmosphere of Birmingham at this time is evoked in Schofield (1963). He describes the membership, the activities, and the intentions of the so-called "Lunar Society of Birmingham," made up, among others, of Joseph Priestley, Matthew Boulton, James Watt (together making up the steam-engine building firm of Boulton and Watt), and Josiah Wedgwood, the potter, who provided Priestley with chemical apparatus. There is no direct sign that William Reynolds knew these gentlemen, with the exception of Priestley himself, but it is at least likely that he knew of their innovative activities. It is known also that early in their career on Cherrytree Creek the Reynolds family was visited by one Thomas Wedgwood who stayed some time and then, dismayed by the conditions, left for New York—there to die of yellow fever. I presume that Priestley had something to do with their contact.

7. Priestley 1806: 118; see Rose 1960.

8. John Reynolds 1870: 44. A relative wrote from England commenting on the conditions of those who remained: "The distress already in this country can better be conceived of, than described. The poor must perish when my mind is engaged in contemplating the most probable events to take place. Judging from causes, nothing but horror and devastation presents itself to my gloomy imagination. The wicked rule, but that the Lord still reigns is my consolation. If I had not sisters who are so dear to me, I would not hesitate about leaving this most wicked land. We are such an

insulted, oppressed people" (Esther Adams to Mrs. William Reynolds, February 24, 179?).

9. John Reynolds 1870: 20.

10. John Earle Reynolds 1938: 79.

11. The following describes Meadville in 1816: "Meadville, forty miles from Erie, is situated on the east bank of French Creek. It is a county town composed of several streets, and consists of one hundred and fifty houses. The land is too flat to be pleasing. The streets are also narrow, and the proper formation has been neglected. An eastern population which is pouring into this place, may however soon remedy the latter evil. . . . At present, we think the appointment of scavengers would be useful. Though there are many decent frame houses, and some of them evidently occupied by persons of taste, yet neatness appears less prevalent than at Waterford and Erie. The practice of erecting houses of hewn logs, and plastering the chinks with clay, which is so common in the newly settled parts of Pennsylvania, obtains even here, and gives a solitary aspect to the builings" (Thomas 1970: 38).

12. The poem in question is entitled, "Verses supposed to be written by Alexander Selkirk, during his solitary abode in the island of Juan Fernandez." Cowper/Selkirk found solace in religion, but still the poem expresses the emotional isolation that Cowper felt even in the midst of society.

> When I think of my own native land,
> In a moment I seem to be there;
> But alas, recollection at hand
> Soon hurries me back to despair.

13. Mitchell Manuscripts, Historical Collections of the Library, College of Physicians of Philadelphia #8: 2 (henceforth MM); for a listing of the Mitchell collection on Mary Reynolds see the references).

14. Plumer 1860: 807.

15. Alden 1843: 254.

16. John V. Reynolds n.d.: 4–5.

17. James 1914: 167.

18. MM8: 12.

19. G.D. Smith 1977: 53–54.

20. John Reynolds 1870: 29. In England William Reynolds had also known the great Baptist minister Robert Hall, pastor of a Baptist congregation in Cambridge. Hall was a bellwether for the theological and philosophical currents of his time. He flirted with heterodox theological opinions, swaying toward the Unitarian Priestley and back again. He was at the same time devoted to Jonathan Edwards and himself had a series of "breakdowns" that expressed his own contradictions. Hall's predecessor in Cambridge, Robert Robertson—author of an influential history of baptism—went farther toward heterodoxy. He died in Priestley's home in Birmingham, and Hall wrote his epitaph (Langley 1939; Gregory 1833).

21. Cleveland 1959: 91, 95.

22. MM8: 9.

23. Ibid.: 11.

24. MM1: 13.

25. Mary's poetry is in the collection of the Crawford County Historical Society; for the most part it is undated unless part of a letter. The relationship between women and clergymen in the nineteenth century is discussed exhaustively by Ann Douglas (1977), who identifies a psychological syndrome she calls "pulpit envy."

26. I thank Francis Dallett, Archivist of the University of Pennsylvania, for this information. He also informs me that in 1806–1807 Rush taught two courses, which Bemus presumably attended: "Institute of Medicine and Clinical Practise," and "Theory and Practise of Medicine." Unlike the *History of Crawford County* (1885, vol. 2: 713–14), which shows that Bemus took a degree from the University of Pennsylvania, the archives show that in fact he did not receive a formal degree, and was there for only one session. In those days this was not unusual, since licensing of doctors was still in the future and medical education was largely conducted on an apprenticeship basis (see Starr 1982: 30–59, on this formative period of American medicine). It is possible that Bemus heard of something resembling multiple personality phenomena from Rush himself; Carlson (1981) points out that Rush had become aware of such cases and lectured on them to his students at the University of Pennsylvania. In one case Rush knew of, the Reverend William Tennant went into a comatose state such that his relatives took him for dead; fortunately the funeral was delayed and three days later Tennant revived, "but large gaps in his knowledge and capability became apparent. He had complete amnesia for all aspects of his life before the deathlike state" (Carlson 1981: 667). Like Mary Reynolds he had to be partially re-educated and, again like her, he experienced a sudden restoration of memory. Rush encountered other instances of periodic amnesia. "In discussing this kind of phenomenon, Rush commented on the continuity between spells of somnambulism and the awakened somnambulist's inability to recall what had transpired. He admitted that it appeared as if there were 'two minds' but believed the phenomena occurred because of excessive motions in different parts of the brain, which Rush in his typically monistic fashion believed contained only one mind" (Carlson 1981: 668). For the place of Rush in the intellectual world of the day, see Boorstin (1960), and for the general background to this world, Wills (1979).

27. Rush 1835: 281, 172–201.

28. *Calomel*: mercurous chloride, a purgative.

    Tartar: potassio-antimonious tartrate, "a poisonous substance used in medicine to induce vomiting."

    Gamboge: a gum-resin used as "a drastic purgative" (*Oxford English Dictionary*).

    In another episode one Dr. Blossom, apparently Bemus's assistant, called Mary "an insignificant thing." She took her revenge by summoning him out to treat a nonexistent patient:

So now friend Blossom, that have I
An *insignificant* thing you know,
Have made you both scold and cry,
And into passion go (MM1: 18)

She enjoyed practical jokes on her doctors. On one occasion she decided
to get back at them for all the bleeding to which she was being subjected:

I thought to make the Doctor an April fool, accordingly I sent for him,
knowing he was in the habit of bleeding me when I would pass from my
second to my first state, and he knew I had a great aversion to being bled
when in the second state, so I proposed to Miss Dewey to send for the
Doctor to bleed me. I put on a very sober face, and told him I wished to
be bled. He expressed great pleasure to find I had once more been
restored to my natural state (MM1: 15).

Mary then revealed her deception when the doctor—who believed she
could hide nothing from him—was on the point of bleeding her: "'April
Fool!' You may be sure the two Doctors felt pretty cheap."

29. Rush 1835: 152.

30. MM1: 4. As Karl Miller says (1985: 333), "The new woman was cheerful,
a 'perfect stranger,' Mitchell says, a born-again romantic who looked on
nature with the eye of the child in Wordsworth's 'Immortality' Ode, on a
world 'apparelled in celestial light.'"

31. Stock 1982: 177-88.

32. MM8: 5.

33. MM1:3.

34. *Spectator* no. 343 concerns a trick played by a young man on the resistant
object of his affection. He slipped into her apartment and wrote a letter in
the name of her pet monkey, claiming to be a brahman who had been
reborn in that form. *Spectator* no. 578 relates the story of a king who was
tricked out of his body by an evil dervish and won his way back through
similar means.

35. The importance of light is discussed in Nicolson (1946), who notes the
influence of Newtonian optics upon authors such as Addison and Thomson. Mary's effusions about Meadville read very much like Addison
himself:

Our imagination loves to be filled with an object, or to grasp at anything that is too big for its capacity. We are flung into a pleasing
astonishment at such unbounded views, and feel a delightful stillness
and amazement in the soul at the apprehension of them. The mind of
man naturally hates everything that looks like a restraint upon it, and is
apt to fancy itself under a sort of confinement, when the sight is pent
up in a narrow compass, and shortened on every side by the neighborhood of walls or mountains. On the contrary a spacious horizon is an
image of liberty, where the eye has room to range abroad, to expatiate at
large on the immensity of its views, and to lose itself amidst the variety
of objects that offer themselves to its observation (Addison 1970: 178;
Spectator no. 412).

36. "Light is sweet, and it is pleasant for the eyes to behold the sun. For if a man lives many years, let him rejoice in them all; but let him remember that the days of his darkness will be many" (Eccles. 111: 7–8).

37. The rest of the poem speaks allusively of those she is leaving behind, particularly a "musical swain," who her autobiographical memoir informs us was actually a brother-in-law. Elsewhere in accounts of the case it emerges that this person had a great influence over Mary in the early days of her second state. My impression is that Mary had rather a crush on him.

38. Rush 1835: 172.

39. John Reynolds 1870: 53.

40. Rush 1835: 60.

41. Rush knew that the mind has considerable influence on the body. In a lecture to medical students he commented that "the influence of the will has not yet been fully explored." He rejected the "futile pretension of Mesmer to the cure of diseases by what he had absurdly called animal magnetism. But he is ready to conclude that the facts which Mesmer established prove the influence of the imagination and the will upon diseases" (Binger 1966: 180). As for the rise of mesmerism and eighteenth-century scientific attitudes toward it, see Darnton (1970: 62).

42. Silas Weir Mitchell 1889: 18–19.

43. MM1: 15.

44. MM9.

45. MM8: 11.

46. John Kearsley Mitchell 1859: 186.

47. Macnish 1854: 31. Macnish perceived a relation between mesmeric phenomena and multiple personality: "According to the report made by a Committee of the Royal Academy of Sciences in Paris, animal magnetism appears to have the power of inducing a peculiar species of somnambulism. The circumstances seem so curious, that, even authenticated as they are by men of undoubted integrity and talent, it is extremely difficult to place reliance upon them. The person who is thrown into the magnetic sleep is said to acquire a new consciousness, and entirely to forget all the events of his ordinary life. When this sleep is dissolved, he gets into his usual state of feeling and recollection, but forgets every thing that happened during the sleep; being again magnetized, however, the remembrance of all that occurred in the previous sleep is brought back to his mind" (p. 30).

   As Karl Miller shows (1985: 50 and passim) Macnish had literary interests himself, and was deeply concerned with the subject of duality. As Miller comments, "In the earlier part of the nineteenth century, literature and science could still be seen as aspects of a single knowledge: the writer and the doctor could be friends, and the sharer of a self."

48. Goodrich-Freer 1907: 101.

49. Plumer 1860: 812.

50. Greaves 1980.

51. Ibid.: 587. Carlson (1984) reviews the place of Mary Reynolds in the psychological literature, pointing out again Benjamin Rush's knowledge of such cases. However, I must disagree with Carlson on one point. He says that "the role that the nervous system played in Mary Reynolds's case was evident from the earliest accounts. Her periods of blindness, deafness, loss of consciousness, fits . . . , periods of rigidity, or trembling, all point to some kind of involvement of the central nervous system as did her mental state" (p. 77). The nature of my disagreement should be obvious; Carlson did not know of Mary's letters and what they reveal about her generally marginal situation, nor of the cultural factors that contributed to these events.

CHAPTER TWO

1. The account of Ansel Bourne's conversion and of his multiple personality episode are drawn from Cummings (1858) and Hodgson (1891–92) respectively. Other accounts of the latter episode may be found in James (1981 vol. 1: 369–71), Myers (1903 vol. 1: 309–17), and Rider (1909: 136–39).

2. Hodgson 1891–92: 227n.

3. Ibid.: 232.

4. Edwards 1817: 31.

5. A general account of the Christian movement may be found in the autobiographies of Elias Smith (1840) and Abner Jones (1842); a more general historical account that situates the Christians in the context of like-minded New England dissenting movements is found in McLoughlin (1971 vol. 2: 745–52).

6. Elias Smith 1840: 54.

7. The role of this paper and that of the Christians at large in the democratization of American religion is discussed in Hatch (1980).

8. Besse Taylor 1927: 69; and 62 for Taylor's conversion; see also Denison 1878: 198–99. "He [Taylor] belonged to the Christian Denomination, believed in regeneration, baptism, atonement, etc., but rejected the trinity, foreordination, close communion, and infant baptism" (Taylor 1927: 69; see 65–66 for the conversion of Ansel Bourne).

9. The Free-Will Baptists were fellow-travelers with the Christians, having most of the same theological and political opinions. The former, along with the Universalists and the Shakers, are discussed in Marini (1982). See also Baxter (1954).

10. Free-Will Baptist General Conference 1848: 65–66. Here I find my own family history joined to the story, since the *Treatise* from which this quotation is taken was the property of my paternal great-grandfather, Moses Kenny, a Free-Will Baptist preacher in Michigan. His own grandfather had been a Congregationalist deacon in Vermont; the progression from Puritan orthodoxy to a more democratic heterodoxy (or "purity" I suppose these heretics would have said) is fairly typical of the social stratum—small hard-scrabble farmers—from which they came during

this period of American history. One way or another Elias Smith had many peers.

11. Cummings 1858: 6.

12. Day 1853: 43–44.

13. Ibid.: 53.

14. Hodgson 1891–92: 236–37.

15. Timothy L. Smith 1957: 49 and following.

16. Hodgson 1891–92: 234, 246.

17. Ibid.: 228. "His ministrations [while he had been an itinerant evangelist] were in great request in many country towns, and for thirty years more or less he has worked hard, conducting Sunday services, speaking at revivals, officiating at funerals, and performing strenuously all the offices which the position of an unattached minister demands, not forgetting, of course, to cite his own personal experience, when necessary, to illustrate the power of the Lord. During this time he often spoke as much as six or seven times in the week; and this, with the incessant travelling, he thinks was not nearly as good a life for his health as the trade of a carpenter. . . ." How like Elias Smith!

18. Edwards 1808: 31, 165, 65.

19. Ibid.: 349.

20. James 1914. The central biographical source on William James and his philosophy is Ralph Perry (1936); a more personal account may be found in Allen (1967), while the psychological roots of James's own experience are explored in Feinstein (1984).

21. I draw this term from Cerullo (1982).

22. Cerullo (1982) discusses the origins of the psychical research movement, its relations with Spiritualism, and the social context of those who subscribed to it. The most general history of psychical research is Gauld (1968), while the best social historical account of Spiritualism and psychical research (parapsychology) in the United States is Moore (1977).

23. These philosophical problems, including that of "Does Consciousness Exist?" are discussed in James (1977; first published posthumously in 1912), and in a more empirical form in James (1981).

24. See James's chapter in the *Principles* (1981), "The Methods and Snares of Psychology," especially his section on "the misleading influence of speech." "If we could say in English 'it thinks,' as we say 'it rains' or 'it blows,' we should be stating the fact most simply and with the minimum of assumption. As we cannot, we must simply say that *thought goes on*" (1981: 220).

25. See Abrams (1971), who—because of a passionate advocacy of diversity and antipathy to all-embracing logical systems—counts William James a Romantic as well.

26. See Young (1970) who systematically discusses the impact of the concept of localization on the way the mind is understood. See also Riese and Hoff (1950–51).

27. The rise of mesmerism is charted in Darnton (1970) and its early impact in America in Fuller (1982). For more on such questions see chapter 3.

28. See Freud (1966) for his writings pertaining to this period.

29. Merrill Moore 1938: 702; Prince 1971: 2.

30. A major influence here was the thought of Gustav Fechner, a founder of what came to be called "psychophysics." A major focus of this type of study was on perceptual thresholds—how much stimulus it takes to be subjectively registered in consciousness and the intensity of this registration as a function of the original intensity of the stimulus. When James traveled and studied in Germany in the 1860s he was greatly influenced by Fechner, whose *Elemente der Psychophysik* he heavily annotated (it can now be found in the Houghton Library at Harvard). Fechner also had an influence on Freud (Ellenberger 1956; also 1970: passim). Later on Fechner devoted himself to a philosophical pantheism, which greatly appealed to James, positing as it did that the world itself is a conscious entity compounded out of the lesser consciousnesses it contains; among other things Fechner could be construed as a prophet of the concept of a global ecosystem. James devoted a lecture in his series published as *A Pluralistic Universe*, originally delivered in 1908, only two years before his death. There he said: "It is the intense concreteness of Fechner, his fertility of detail, which fills me with an admiration which I should like to make this audience share" (1977: 64).

31. As Young (1970) documents, phrenology had a considerable influence on the concept of localization, since it embryonically contains this doctrine through the idea that functions are localized. Auguste Comte, whose scientific program had a great influence on the development of French psychology and the philosophy of science in general, also subscribed to phrenological doctrines as advanced by Franz Joseph Gall. Comte claimed that phrenology provided virtually all the equipment that psychology needs to become a science rather than a body of specious metaphysical speculation.

32. Ribot 1887: 1, 52, 20. Through such cases as that of Mary Reynolds, Ribot was well aware of the phenomenon of multiple personality. In his *Diseases of Personality* he wrote, as did George Herbert Mead, concerning the *normality* of split personality: "'two souls' said Goethe 'dwell in my breast.' Not two only! If the moralists, poets, dramatists have shown us to satiety these two contending in one *me*, common experience shows yet more: it shows us many *mes*, each as it comes to the forefront, excluding the others" (p. 24). Mary Reynolds ("Macnish's Lady") is cited in another work, *Diseases of Memory* (1882: 99–101). Ribot, in his influential position as editor of the *Revue de Philosophie*, was well situated to spread the new findings and opened up the pages of his journal to others interested in such matters.

33. Azam 1887: 66.

34. Janet 1929: 78; lectures originally published in 1907. He pointed out in the same lectures the disproportional number of cases of multiple personality of American provenience: "The question presents for you, as it were,

a national interest. For some reason—why, I don't know—it is in America that the greatest number of remarkable cases have appeared, and it is American doctors, among them Macish [sic; Macnish was not American] . . . Weir Mitchell . . . and quite recently one of the greatest physicians of this town, Dr. Morton Prince, who have devoted to it the most remarkable studies" (p. 67). For more on Janet see Ellenberger (1970: 331–417) and Hilgard (1977).

35. Alice James 1964: 148–49.

36. James 1890: 369, 373. As with Mary Reynolds, the propositions of John Locke concerning continuity of personal identity also surfaced in the context of James's discussion. When speaking of amnesic multiple personalities, James wrote: "It is, after all, only the fulfillment of what Locke's speculative genius suggested long ago, when, in that famous chapter of 'Identity and Diversity' which occasioned such scandal in its day, after saying that personality extended no further than consciousness, he went on to affirm that there would be two different selves or persons in one man, if the experiences undergone by that man should fall into two groups, each gathered into a distinct focus of recollection" (p. 367).

37. James 1914: 1997.

38. Ibid.

39. Ibid.: 519.

40. James 1981 vol. 1: 379.

41. Myers's biography and his contributions to the foundation of psychical research are treated in Gauld (1968), also Cerullo (1982).

42. Myers 1903 vol. 1: 68. This is an extraordinary work, seen by Cerullo as the epitome of nineteenth-century psychical research. I am inclined to agree, though would give James's *Principles* honorable mention. Myers, basing his argument on the concept of the subliminal, wished to show the continuity of what might be called paranormal experience, from minor disintegrations of consciousness to more extreme conditions. Of course he ultimately put a spiritistic interpretation on these things; in doing so, however, he assembled a compendium of late-nineteenth-century psychological knowledge concerning the unconscious, one valuable to this day. He also elicited the unease that motivated the enterprise in the first place: "I need not here describe at length the deep disquiet of our time. Never, perhaps, did man's spiritual satisfaction bear a smaller proportion to his needs" (Myers 1903 vol. 2: 279).

43. James 1914: 234.

44. Ernest Jones 1955 vol. 2: 375–407.

45. Ibid.: 57.

46. Letter to Theodore Flournoy, September 28, 1909 (James 1920 vol. 2: 327–28.

47. Freud 1959.

48. Freud 1961a.

49. See Beard (1882). This work is concerned with the psychology of public hysterias and draws an explicit parallel between the Salem affair and the

hysteria following the assassination of President Garfield. Just as in the attempted assassination of President Reagan, the successful attempt on Garfield led many to question the insanity laws and the entire concept of psychiatrically defined diminished responsibility; in the Garfield case, the assassin was hanged. Also see Wendell (1891) who examined Cotton Mather's propensity to mystic visions in the light of the new psychology (for more on the intellectual climate that shaped such inquiries see the next chapter).

50. Freud 1955: 48.
51. Freud 1961b: 72.
52. See Cerullo (1982: 159–66). The history of Freud's increasing acceptance in the United States is given in Nathan G. Hale (1971). This matter is returned to in chapter 4.
53. Freud 1955.
54. James 1976: 71.
55. Freud 1955.
56. James 1920 vol. 2: 327.
57. Rider 1909.

CHAPTER THREE

1. Hammond 1850. Capron (1855: 99–100) in his sober insider's review of the Spiritualist movement was less than enthusiastic about the Rev. Hammond's performances: "Mr. Hammond has produced three books. . . . He also claims to be empowered or assisted by spirits to heal diseases, talk in unknown tongues, dance and perform various gymnastic exercises, such as shaking the arms and hands, perform Indian dances, whooping, & c."
2. Hardinge 1870; Capron 1855: 99–100.
3. There are a number of histories of Spiritualism. From a believer's standpoint the most important is Hardinge (1870), which gives a review of the entire movement from its beginnings until the time of writing. A later one, bringing matters up to date, is Arthur Conan Doyle's *The History of Spiritualism* (1926). Frank Podmore, one of the key members of the Society for Psychical Research, wrote a number of works on the history of Spiritualism, mesmerism, mesmeric healing, and the activities of the psychical research movement (Podmore 1902; 1908; 1910). The best overall social historical account of American Spiritualism, psychical research, and parapsychology is Moore (1977); for the relations between Spiritualism and science see Moore (1972). Howard Kerr (1972) has provided an account of Spiritualism in American literature, while Nelson (1969) attempts a sociological explanation of the Spiritualist movement in Britain. Anthropologists have also had their say; the best single work on Spiritualism and Spiritualists is Macklin (1977); Biscop (1981; 1985) has studied a church in Vancouver, British Columbia, and shows how the reality of the spirit world gets to be constructed and reaffirmed in the context of this and other churches.
4. Ballou 1853: 254.

5. Ibid.: 88.

6. Ibid.: 225.

7. Moses 1879: 16. Ballou noted kindred difficulties: "It seems reasonable to believe that the lower secondary spheres or circles of the spirit-world are filled with gross and crudely developed human spirits—with almost countless multitudes of souls, whose ignorance, or moral deficiency, or positive perverseness, still remain such, in spite of the general tendencies favorable to progress, as predispose them to sympathize with congenial spirits in the flesh, and to repeat, when opportunity will allow, their old follies, deceits, and mischievous exploits" (Ballou 1853: 62). Emma Hardinge faced the problem also: "The world had to learn that the spirit country is peopled from earth, and that spirit-life commences from the point where mortal existence ends. Unconscious of this solemn truth, the early communicants with the unseen world were unprepared for the visitation of *dark spirits* whom the sad experiences of earth had manufactured into criminals. Unaware that life, whether here or hereafter, is *progress*, not violent and unnatural change, investigators were appalled at the representations, produced through media, of the same vicious tendencies in spirits which they had beheld with indifference from the same spirits whilst inhabitants of earth" (Hardinge 1870: 58).

8. Moses 1894: 243. For more on Stainton Moses see Gauld (1968 passim), Cerullo (1982 passim), and Myers (1903 vol. 2: 585–87).

9. Raupert 1914: 53. Raupert made something of a business out of writing propaganda against psychical research and Spiritualism; though he was not a Catholic, his work on the dangers of Spiritualism received an imprimatur. Another of his tracts was entitled *The New Black Magic* (1919).

10. A.B. Morrison 1873: 125; Berg 1856: 5. The former was a Methodist, the latter Dutch Reformed.

11. Moses 1880: 71.

12. Capron 1855: 234. "It may be proper here to state that whatever may be the facts in regard to the wicked intent of any spirits, there is danger of great annoyance, and even injury, resulting from free communications with spirits of a coarse and undeveloped character. Either ignorantly or wilfully—I am hardly able to decide which—they seek to get and keep control of the medium, making angular, discordant, and even vulgar and obscene communications" (p. 117n).

13. The spirits continued to show flashes of political concern, as in one case in the 1890s during the height of the Free Silver agitation when the *soi-dissant* spirit of Abraham Lincoln advocated nationalization of the railroads. In the 1920s American spirits showed a strong antipathy to Bolshevism.

14. Ballou 1896: 156.

15. Moses 1880: 120.

16. James 1909: 32.

17. Ibid.: 3.

18. Ibid.: 115.

19. Ibid.: 19–20.
20. Ibid.: 3.
21. Sidgwick 1915: 294.
22. Ibid.: 77.
23. Piper 1929: 200–201.
24. Hall 1918.
25. Ibid.: 156.
26. This exhaustion and temporary cessation of powers happened more than once, as Mrs. Sidgwick reported: "One reason given in January, 1897, for the taking over by the Imperator Band of the management of medium and sittings was that the medium had been worn out by sittings for tests of identity or of supernormal power" (1915: 110).
27. Hall 1918: 154.
28. This problem seems to persistently bedevil Spiritualists. Though claiming to be scientific in their attitudes toward mediumistic phenomena they can be less than enthusiastic about attempts on the part of the more sceptical to get positive and replicable results. In fact such results are not obtainable. However, with respect to conversion to Spiritualism at least some "evidential" material is usually required as a demonstration of the movement's truth. Following this demonstration less emphasis may be placed on evidence per se and more on the personal content of the communications.
29. Piper 1929: 88.
30. Sidgwick 1915: 78. "The extraordinary vividness and truth to life—to judge from his friend's accounts of the 'G.P.' control make me think that in 1892 occurred probably the culmination of Mrs. Piper's automatic powers" (p. 10).
31. James 1897: 4.
32. Ibid.: 25.
33. For biographical details of Hodgson's life, see Baird (1949), Gauld (1968: passim), Hyslop (1907), and Sidgwick (1905–7).
34. Howe 1906.
35. Ibid.
36. James 1909: 11.
37. Ibid.: 22.
38. Piper 1929.
39. Tanner 1910: 160.
40. Sidgwick 1915: 9.
41. Howells 1880.
42. I would like to thank Professor Edwin Cady for his useful observations on the fate of Winifred Howells. He points out that her father, given his devotion to his daughter, would not likely have been informed of Mrs. Piper's contact with her ostensible spirit. Nevertheless, it is interesting that Howells and his daughter were brought into the matter at all. This at

least suggests his influence on those who were a party to these curious events.

43. Gauld 1968: 259.

44. Malone 1934: 409–10; Townend 1967: 913–15.

45. Morison 1951: 21.

46. I do not know if Pellew had taken courses from William James, but Roosevelt took at least one; Roosevelt was also for a brief time a member of the Society for Psychical Research.

47. Howells 1892a.

48. Pellew 1892: 8.

49. Harlow 1950: 33–60.

50. Pellew 1888a.

51. Edel 1975; Harlow 1950: 313–14.

52. Perry later wrote a biography of his friend (1906). Spencer was also the intellectual idol of Richard Hodgson, who wrote, "of course I hold that Spencer is the greatest thinker the world has seen" (letter to "Jimmy" in Australia, November 14, 1887; letter in files of the Society for Psychical Research, New York). For the influence of evolutionary theory on this group see Wiener (1965).

53. Hodgson 1898: 422.

54. Howells 1888; 1890.

55. Pellew 1888b; see Cady 1956: 146 and passim.

56. Howells 1892b: 527–30.

57. Pellew 1888c; 1890.

58. Howells 1892a.

59. Howe 1934: 3. This work was printed privately for members of the club.

60. Howe 1941: 219; 1934: 95–96.

61. Howe 1924: 80; see Wendell 1891.

62. Howells 1907; "Braybridge's offer." Other Wanhope stories appear in the same collection and in another anthology of Howells's stories, *Questionable Shapes* (1903). Wanhope is presented as a dispassionate investigator and is played off against the enthusiasm or scepticism of his clubmen.

63. "Panpsychism" much appealed to those distressed by the supposed consequences of the doctrine of evolution with regard to mind and free will. The major intellectual source of this doctrine seems to have been William Kingdon Clifford, a Cambridge mathematician, philosopher, and evolutionary theorist (Clifford 1886; Fiske 1874: passim; 1896).

64. Hodgson 1898: 295.

65. Mildred Howells 1928: 388. I think it probable that Heard cross-connects to a number of other literary figures, especially to the Scots writer William Sharp who wrote much of his work under the female *nom de plume* Fiona Macleod. Heard and a couple named Janvier had lived in Mexico and the latter were very close to Sharp who in turn had visited the United States and met Howells a number of times. After the real identity of Fiona

Macleod became known, psychical researchers regarded his case as on the borderline of multiple personality phenomena; Sharp believed that a female soul lived within him and wrote Fiona's mystical Celtic stories. Morton Prince, when exasperated with the Freudians, wrote their convert and his former colleague J.J. Putnam, using the pseudonym "Fiona Mac-Prince." Evidently he found it easier to say harsh things in an alternate persona.

66. Hodgson 1898: 297.

67. Ibid.: 300.

68. Ibid.: 322.

69. Howells and Perry were also close (Harlow 1949: 135–50).

70. Ibid.: 312–13.

71. Pellew 1892: 54.

72. Hodgson 1898: 371.

73. Mildred Howells 1928: 92; Cady 1958: 96–99.

74. William Dean Howells to William James, March 18, 1889 (letter in William James Collection, Houghton Library, Harvard). These sentiments are duplicated in a letter from Howells to James's sister Alice, who had also written consolingly upon Winifred's death: "Your brother William [Howells wrote] said something that more than anything else enabled our hearts to lay hold on faith again, and supplemented with a hint of hope those perfect terms in which Harry [Henry James] expressed our loss. And now your message, with its memory of another world, completely past, is an intimation that we may somewhere else survive that of today too, and of all earthly morrows" (Strouse 1980: 224). Alice, however, was quite sceptical about William's interest in the spirits (Strouse 1980: 256).

75. Howells to James, March 18, 1889.

76. Hodgson 1898: 301.

77. Ibid.: 362; see Gauld 1968: 362.

78. Byerly 1906; Whittemore 1906.

79. Hodgson 1898: 461–62.

80. Ibid.: 526–27.

81. Ibid.: 318; see Gauld 1968: 363.

82. Fiske 1876: 43; 1874 v. 2: 379; the latter work is a popularization and emendation of Herbert Spencer's evolutionist "Synthetic Philosophy."

83. Hodgson 1898: 320.

84. Fiske 1879: 86, 97; Wright 1877. The latter work has a biographical sketch of Wright by Charles Eliot Norton. Darwin himself had responded favorably to Wright's work on plants, as well as to Fiske's on infancy.

85. James 1909: 118.

86. Hodgson 1898: 331; see Sidgwick 1915: 43; Tanner 1910: 6.

87. Hodgson 1898: 328.

88. Ibid. As seen (James 1909: 32), James uses very similar language in accounting for the feeling that spirit messages are what they purport to be.

89. Hodgson 1898: 405–6.

90. Morton Prince to William James, December 23, 1905. This letter is taped inside Prince's presentation copy to James of his *Dissociation of a Personality*, a study of the Miss Beauchamp case of multiple personality (for more on which see chapter 4).

CHAPTER FOUR

1. Prince 1906: 233. Karl Miller (1985: 329) points out, as I have noted elsewhere, that "if the literature of the nineteenth century was in love with duality, so was its psychology, and so, at times, was its physiology. Literature and science collaborated in spreading the gospel which enjoined the plurality of the mind. At the start of the century, moreover, they were themselves a duality—aspects of a single knowledge which could still be referred to as 'literature'. But a work of separation was soon to be pursued. They were set apart, and science was declared the domain of rational knowledge, with professions and institutions to secure the protection of standards." Miller (334–35) also gives a general description of the Beauchamp case noting, and I think appositely, that "it might have made a page in a Gothic novel."

2. Hale 1975: 2; Merrill Moore 1938.

3. Prince 1885.

4. See Prince 1903 and 1928. Prince looked back to Bishop Berkeley, who had stated that the only knowledge we have of a thing is our sensation of it; it can therefore never be known "in itself" (1885: 35, 43). Prince thought that the only thing that can be so known is our own personal consciousness. All that can be directly known of another person's consciousness is our perception of its external manifestations: "The parallelism is between your consciousness and my consciousness of your consciousness, or, what is the same thing, between the consciousness in you and the picture in my mind of neural vibrations" (1885: 59). As mentioned in the chapter on George Pellew, one's attitude toward this view could determine how the prospects for survival are regarded. Prince thought the chances for it to be slim: "I can see no escape from what seems to me the logic of 'iron strength' that compels the conclusion that if consciousness is the resultant of an enormously complex organisation of units of that immaterial entity which is the real universe and which manifests itself, but only objectively, to science in an unreal form as 'matter,' that when that particular organisation has become disintegrated by death, the mind itself must cease to exist" (1928: 20).

5. Moore 1938: 708.

6. See Hale (1971) for a detailed examination of this dissatisfaction.

7. Prince 1939: 8.

8. Silas Weir Mitchell 1885: 267. For the general topic of nineteenth-century "lady doctors" and their attitudes, and of Mitchell's in particular, see Wood (1973) and Ehrenreich and English (1979). The former comments: "Mitchell and his peers could indeed afford to pity the fair sex, even perhaps to 'cure' them. Yet the consequent 'cures' bore unmistakable signs of their culturally determined origin, for they made a woman's womb very much a liability. Since her disease was unconsciously viewed as a symptom of a failure in femininity, its remedy was destined both as a punishment and an agent of regeneration, for it forced her to acknowledge her womanhood and made her totally dependent on the professional prowess of her male doctor" (Wood 1973: 37).

9. Beard 1881a: 9.

10. Ibid.: vi. Beard's comments on American women resemble the portrait that can be assembled from Henry James's novels: "In no other country are the daughters pushed forward so rapidly, so early sent to school, so quickly admitted into society; the yoke of social observance . . . must be borne by them much sooner than by their transatlantic sisters—long before marriage they have had much experience in conversation and entertainment" (p. 66).

11. Beard 1881a: 207. The eclectic Dr. Beard was also much interested in phenomena of trance, "which, next to evolution, is the great scientific problem of the century" (p. 332). Americans, again, were found to be more subject to it (p. 88). The cause was found to lie in a redirection of nervous force, suppressing it in one direction, heightening it in another (Beard 1881b: 5).

12. Silas Weir Mitchell 1884.

13. Beard 1880: 5. "Neurasthenia is a chronic, functional disease of the nervous system, the basis of which is the impoverishment of nervous force, waste of nerve-tissue in excess of repair, hence the lack of inhibitory or controlling power—physical or mental—the feebleness and instability of nerve action, and the excessive sensitiveness and irritability, local and general, direct and reflex. . . . Nervousness is really nervelessness" (p. 11). Arthur Kleinman (1980) points out the rather ironic survival of the concept of neurasthenia in Taiwan, the reason as he sees it being a Chinese tendency to "somaticize" rather than psychologize neurotic disorder: "Neurasthenia is the single most commonly used label for sanctioning a medical sick role for minor psychiatric and interpersonal problems in Taiwan" (Kleinman 1980: 128).

14. Prince 1898–99: 81; also see Prince 1910.

15. Prince 1906: 299.

16. Ibid.: 22.

17. Ibid.: 14. "Has never been able to pursue steadily any occupation. . . . Tried three times to do professional nursing and broke down. Is now studying at——College; ambitious; good student; does good work, but always ill; always suffering. Over-conscientious and mentally and morally stubborn. Is very nervous, and different parts of body in constant motion" (p. 14).

18. Silas Weir Mitchell 1986: 5, 13. Mitchell went on at some length in this vein; at least in mind's eye one detects a certain restlessness among his audience when exposed to his testament: "To return to my creed. I am for independence as a human right. I want women to be free and to do what they like. I want no 'paucity of alternatives.' But with this freedom to choose, and this human right to select, I, personally, no more want them to be preachers, lawyers, or platform orators, than I want men to be seamstresses or nurses of children. I want freedom within the noble limitations of sex" (p. 6). "For many women, as for men, the learning won at college goes for nothing. . . . The man goes out into a larger life, yours narrows to home functions. This is what I so much fear. . . . It is this break in home life I dread; for a boy it is natural, for the daughter, no. A woman is *born* to a profession; a man is not" (p. 21).

19. The problem of Miss Beauchamp's true identity has turned out to be rather complex; Gifford (1978: 232) announced that Dr. George Waterman married Mrs. R.E. Forrest (Claire Brenner) in 1912 and that "it was an open secret that the lady was none other than the famous patient of Morton Prince, Sally Beauchamp. Waterman had married a lady whose psychodynamics were in book form!" I accepted this finding myself and repeated it in Kenny (1981: 345n.13). Then upon looking through the Prince papers it proved that Mrs. Forrest's maiden name was not in fact "Claire Brenner" but "Clara Fowler" and I announced this to a psychiatric readership in Kenny (1984) without realizing that it had already been announced in McKellar (1979), though the latter does not indicate his source.

20. Hale 1975: 11.

21. I thank Ann Chesebro of Bradford College for this information.

22. Prince 1906: 12. Ann Lainhart, a registered genealogist of Boston, is responsible for tracing down the vital records pertaining to Clara Fowler's and Nellie Bean's families.

23. Prince 1920: 109.

24. Ibid.: 115. Prince was, shall I say, less than enthusiastic about the emphasis placed by psychoanalysis on the sexual etiology of neurotic complaints: "One school, the so-called psycho-analysts, claims to find in practically all conflicts, a very complicated mechanism involving repression, unconscious processes (generally a sexual wish for the most part from infantile life) a 'censor,' a compromise, conversion and disguisement of the repressed factor in the form of a psycho-neurosis, or other mental and physiological phenomena, substitution, etc. . . . The sole point I wish to make is that, even if so, to find such mechanisms and results to be universal is the reductio ad absurdum just as it would be to find that a conflict between a policeman and a resisting rioter is always carried out by a process which is manifested by a black eye and cracked skull, arrest, trial and conviction of the rioter" (1919: 247–48).

25. Prince 1906: 172–73. In Clara's eyes there seems to have been rivalry between Jones and Prince as well. To the latter she wrote, "I don't believe a word Jones said about what you did last summer. Not a word. But even

if it were true and you did do all sorts of wicked, wicked things (I can't see why they are wicked but if they are) I love you just the same and I shall always love you more than anything in the world" (undated letter signed "C.N.F."). From our perspective it is easy to read into such a letter more than is there; this was a more romantic age, and in any event the letter is evidently Sally's work. Clara's relations with Jones appear to have been ambivalent; Prince reports that he was considerably older than she, that she idealized him, and that her illusions were shattered when he accosted her in Fall River (Prince 1920: 114–15). But, if so shattered, why did they continue, and on what basis? Prince records a comment the Sally persona made about her origins: "I always knew her [that is, the primary personality's] thoughts. . . . She was thinking partly of being penitent and partly of fairy tales, so as not to be conscious of the scholars and teacher, and she was hungry. I was chuckling and thought it amusing. I did not think of anything else except that her fairy tales were silly. She believed in fairies, that they were real. I didn't and don't. At this time she was a little girl. I was there during all the life with J. [presumably Jones] and at [Bradford] College" (Prince 1920: 95). What the phrase "all the life with Jones" means, I have no idea. In 1899 Prince was summoned to Clara's house, where she had fallen into a nervous condition. Prince discovered that yet another personality had entered the scene, when "I arose from my seat and approaching her made a gesture as if to stroke her forehead and eyelids for the purpose of inducing hypnosis. To my surprise she strongly resented this, saying, 'No one shall do that but Dr. Prince'" (Prince 1906: 172). It emerged that she took him for Jones, and he played his part accordingly, discovering that she was reliving the night in Fall River. This new personality was "BIV."

26. Clara Fowler's family history is more complex than one would surmise from reading Prince's reports, and also more obscure. Ann Lainhart found that there was apparently a brother in addition to the one who died in infancy (the latter being "Charles Fowler" who died in 1880 at four days of age of "congenital debility" when Clara was seven). This was "George Fowler," who appears to have been born in 1876, thus being Clara's junior by three years. The Charles Fowler who died seems to have been born the twin-brother of "Mary Fowler"; the latter, who by then was Mary Tooten, proves to have been the executor of John Fowler's will. George Fowler's fate is unknown. Nor is anything known of Clara's relations, if any, with her siblings.

27. Prince 1920: 116; 1906: 12.

28. Prince 1939: 9. Perhaps colored by Prince's later antipathy for psychoanalysis (matched by Freud's antipathy for him) his statement about why the *Dissociation* was published cannot stand as it is. In 1906 psychoanalysis did not yet have much of an international standing; Ernest Jones even was a sub-editor of Prince's *Journal of Abnormal Psychology* until the relationship later went sour.

29. "B.C.A." 1908: 240.

30. William James to Morton Prince, September 28, 1906 (letter in the William James Collection, Houghton Library, Harvard).

31. "Of her own volition she adopted the name *Sally Beauchamp*, taking it, I think, from a character in some book" (Prince 1906: 29). I have been unable to ascertain the source of this name, but there are at least a few indications in Prince's case reports about Clara Fowler's general tastes in literature. For example, in his chapter on "The Birth of Sally," Prince records a conversation in which Miss Beauchamp refers to Henry Rider Haggard's *She*. I can only suppose that Fowler found in this extraordinary and romantic character much to identify with. Haggard's novel was set in Central Africa and "She" is an immortal survivor of classical antiquity gifted with an array of exotic powers, and also a strong will. Elsewhere there is allusion to the novels of Marie Corelli, at the end of the last century the best-selling author in the English language. Corelli's works are potboiling morality plays featuring such characters as women who die from a surfeit of good breeding when betrayed by weak, perfidious men. Fowler's tastes, in short, seem to have been decidedly "popular," and there was much in her reading that could well have been incorporated into Miss Beauchamp's (or rather Sally's) dramatic style.

32. Prince 1906: 16.

33. Ibid.: 25–28. Prince was aware that it is possible to create apparent personalities through hypnosis, a problem that has bedeviled multiple personality research to the present. He disavowed, however, that any such thing occurred in the case of Miss Beauchamp: "As bearing on the question of the possible unconscious education of the subject on the part of the experimenter, I may say here that my experience of this case entirely contradicted the view that I held up to this time. My conviction had been growing that so-called personalities, *when developed through hypnotism*, as distinct from the spontaneous variety, were purely artificial creations —sort of unspoken and unconscious mutual understandings between the experimenter and the subject, by which the subject accepted certain ideas unwittingly suggested by the experimenter. But in opposition to this view the personality known as BIII . . . which first made its appearance during hypnosis, came as a surprise to me; and so far from being the product of suggestion, originated and persisted against my protests and in spite of my scepticism" (p. 26). Of course it should be noted that this personality emerged in hypnosis, which by definition is an alteration in the sense of self, and also that Prince allowed himself to be argued out his of scepticism by the personality that would come to assume the name "Sally." Prince also tried to find out if Miss Beauchamp had any advance knowledge of the concept of alternating personalities, such as to lead her in the hypnotic state "to act out a character after some preconceived theory" (p. 41). Again he could find no evidence of this, but I should point out that Miss Beauchamp can hardly have been ignorant of Jekyll and Hyde, Trilby, et al., if she were as well informed about literature as Prince claimed.

34. Prince 1906: 95.

35. Ibid.: 9.

36. Ibid.: 24.

37. Ibid.: 102.

38. Ibid.: 33–34. Letter from Morton Prince to William James, September 30, 1906, accompanying presentation copy of the *Dissociation;* in William James Collection, Houghton Library.

39. Biographical sketch of Morton Prince by his daughter, Claire Morton Prince; typescript dated May 19, 1944, in the Morton Prince papers, Countway Medical Library, Harvard. Claire Prince reports one of her own encounters with Miss Beauchamp: "Once I took Miss Beauchamp to the Symphony Concert (under protest, I may add, for I hated to be used as a guardian for these disturbed and distraught cases). At the concert all went well until about the middle and "Sally" appeared. I was furious! My father had told me all would be well. I was a little girl, so I went to the telephone and called Papa. I said very succinctly, 'She has changed, Papa, come and get her.' In much haste he said, 'Wait until I get there.' Knowing my dad, and that 'waiting' could mean anything—(hours in fact), I said, 'If you don't come at once, I shall leave her.' I heard a frenzied voice saying, 'Wait, I'll be there.' . . . From then on I was never asked to take a patient out. In fact, I wouldn't have gone."

40. Prince 1906: 233.

41. Ibid.: 120.

42. Ibid.: 137.

43. For more on the relation between "Sally" and the spirit hypothesis see Kenny (1981). Curiously, William McDougall, who would later be a critic of Prince's report, was at the time of its initial publication inclined to seriously entertain the possibility that Sally was a spiritual being; he did so because he could find no place for her in Miss Beauchamp's final unified self, and reasoned that perhaps she did indeed go "elsewhere."

44. Prince 1906: 519.

45. Ibid.: 524.

46. W.S. Taylor 1928: 86–87. Taylor, otherwise quite sympathetic and appreciative of Prince's ideas and clinical practice, expressed mild reservation about the overall impact of the *Dissociation*: "Miss Beauchamp, to be sure, has been very widely heard of. Indeed, the strangeness of her case and the dramatic vividness of its portrayal appear to have caught too forcibly the attention of unaccustomed readers" (p. 3).

47. Undated letter to Morton Prince in the latter's papers, in the Countway Medical Library (as are the other letters to Prince cited henceforth).

48. "B.C.A." 1908: 245.

49. Ibid.: 247.

50. Ibid.: 248.

51. "B" 1908–9: 323.

52. "B.C.A." 1908: 248n.

53. Ibid.: 259.

54. Ibid.: 257.

55. Letter to Morton Prince (Wednesday, undated).

56. Letter to Prince (December 26 or 27, no year).

57. "B.C.A." 1908: 250.

58. Letter to Prince (May 17, 1908).

59. "B" 1908–9: 322.

60. Prince 1919: 237.

61. Manuscript first draft of "B" (1908–9), written November 13, 1907, in Prince's office.

62. "B.C.A." 1908: 244.

63. Undated letters to Prince.

64. Letter to Prince (February 11, 1908).

65. Burnett 1881: 83–84.

66. Ibid.: 131, 87.

67. Undated letter.

68. Letter dated Wednesday, February 19, (no year). "I think I ["B"] *am* the real one, only somewhat changed. In my mind it is like this: go back six years, before Mr. Bean's illness, for that was when the foundation for all this trouble was laid. Say that the original personality had two parts, A and B—not the A and B *you* know, but the two elements in her character —and that B was the stronger, more natural element. She was naturally very lighthearted and happy, buoyant. The day Mr. Bean was taken ill she received a terrible shock. He had a cerebral hemorrhage. Then she began to change, very slowly—she rebelled bitterly, she *could* not have it so and it *was* so. No one knew what his illness was and she bent every energy to conceal his true condition. [Why?!]. She blamed herself for it and after a time she began to have that sense of being double" (to Prince, August 4, 1907).

69. Hopkins's identity unknown.

70. To Prince (Thursday, November 7, 1907).

71. Sunday, January 26, 1908.

72. Prince 1914: xii. In Prince's Preface to this book he expresses his "great obligation to Mrs. William G. Bean for the great assistance she has rendered in many ways to the preparation of this volume. Not the least has been the transcription and typing of my manuscript, for the most part written in a quasi shorthand, reading the printer's proofs, and much other assistance in the preparation of the text for the press. For this her practical and unusually extensive acquaintance with the phenomena has been of great value."

73. I thank Rose Downs Arnold for information pertaining to Waterman's marriage. See also the fifth anniversary report of the Harvard Class of 1895 (1915).

74. Gifford 1978: 227–41.

75. Harvard Class of 1895 (1945): 669–70.

76. I thank Louise Nichols and Stanton Waterman for their recollections.

77. Marx (1970) gives a valuable account, based in part on newspaper cuttings in the Prince papers at the Countway, of the public reception attending publication of the *Dissociation*.

78. Freud was less than enthusiastic about Prince's abilities and his unwill-
ingness to wholeheartedly embrace psychoanalysis. At the time of the
Worcester conference in 1909 Freud wrote Jung that "I received a bitter-
sweet letter from Morton Prince thanking me for something I had sent
him; I must be aware (he says) that he does not agree with me on all points,
the problem of neurosis admits of many sorts (!) of solution, he favours
different ones; he regrets that he has already booked passage . . . so that he
will miss me on both continents, etc. I shall be just as glad not to see him"
(Freud and Jung 1974: 242–43). Later, in 1911, Freud wrote Jung, "I *fully
agree* with your strong criticism of him and the conclusion you draw. He
has no talent at all and is something of a schemer" (p. 398). By this time
Prince and Ernest Jones had gotten into a controversy over the adequacy
of psychoanalytic interpretations. Jones, for his part, would record in his
biography of Freud that Prince "had one serious failing. He was rather
stupid, which to Freud was always the unpardonable sin" (Jones 1955 vol.
2.: 61–62).

79. "I have not always been a psychotherapist [Freud wrote]. Like other
neuropathologists, I was trained to employ local diagnoses and electro-
prognosis, and it still strikes me myself that the case histories I write
should read like short stories and that, as one might say, they lack the
serious stamp of science. I must console myself with the reflection that
the nature of the subject is evidently responsible for this, rather than any
preference of my own. The fact is that the local diagnoses and electrical
reactions lead nowhere in the study of hysteria, whereas a detailed
description of mental processes such as we are accustomed to find in the
works of imaginative writers enables me, with the use of a few psychological formulas, to obtain at least some kind of insight into the course of
that affliction" (Breuer and Freud 1955: 160).

80. Edward Locke 1912a: 48. This play later led to difficulties that suggest
that the theme of multiple personality was in the air more generally. On
May 15, 1913, the *New York Times* reported the following story: "Miss
Amelia Backman began suit yesterday before Judge Mayer in the Federal
District Court, as author of the play 'Estelle,' for alleged infringement of
copyright against David Belasco. . . . She had submitted to Mr. Belasco the
manuscript of her play, and she asserted that in the play 'The Case of
Becky,' the playwright had appropriated her idea of dual personality in
violation of her copyright. . . . Edward Locke, a playwright, took the stand
for the defense. He said he was the author of 'The Case of Becky,' and that
it was in reality the dramatization of a book by Dr. Morton Prince, a nerve
specialist, entitled 'Dissociation of Personality' [*sic*]. In this Dr. Prince
spoke of a female patient with a triple personality, but the witness
explained he had given Becky only a double personality to make it easier
for the actress who was the heroine."

81. DeFoe 1912: 369–70. For another approving review see *The American
Playwright*, November 1912: "The production is as remarkable in the
fitness of the actors as it is in those other details that make the play
remarkable. It is the effective detail that gives the play its unflagging
vitality: and that is art" (p. 355).

82. *Green Book Magazine* vol. 7: 984 (1912).
83. Edward Locke 1912b: 121.
84. Ibid.: 118.

CONCLUSION

1. Sherrill Mulhern, personal communication. Ms. Mulhern, I should add, is involved with a project initiated in France concerning "a comparative, cross-cultural study of religious and pathological dissociative behavior." She requests information relating to this from anthropologists, psychiatrists, and others interested in such matters, her address being:

   Sherrill Mulhern
   Co-directeur. Laboratoire de Récherches sur les Sectes et les Mythes du Futur
   Université de Paris VII
   2 Place Jussieu 75221
   Paris

2. Boor 1982.

3. For general surveys of literature concerning the study of multiple personality see Myers (1903 vol.1: 34–69), James (1981 vol.1: 352–78), Taylor and Martin (1944: 281–300), and Sutcliffe and Jones (1962: 231–69). The latter is the only source at all sensitive to the historical context in which the study and concept of multiple personality arose. The best review of thinking on multiple personality as it now stands is in *Investigations*, the Bulletin of the Institute of Noetic Sciences (1984). Boor and Coons (1983) provide an invaluable comprehensive bibliography of writings on multiple personality. Richard Kluft (n.d.a and n.d.b) provides a summary overview of current thinking concerning the diagnosis and treatment of multiple personality. Another useful compendium focusing on the issue of child abuse is Kluft (1985).

4. American Psychiatric Association 1982: 11.

5. Richard Kluft, being aware of this tendency, warned at the 1985 meetings of the International Society that multiple personality patients are under no obligation to be interesting. Dr. Cornelia Wilbur, on the other hand, states that she has never met a multiple with an IQ of less than 110. Other investigators characterize multiples as having "an excellent working memory, above-average intelligence, and creativity" (Braun and Sachs 1985: 44).

6. Congdon, Hain, and Stevenson 1961.

7. Hawthorn 1983: 23.

8. Rosenbaum 1980. "In the United States, there has been a revival of interest in the multiple personality syndrome. . . .This may reflect the revival of interest in hypnosis, especially as an experimental tool by psychologists, and the disenchantment with the term 'schizophrenia.' Perhaps this new interest will lead to a more disciplined and rigorously 'scientific' approach to the study of multiple personality and dissociated

states, as well as to schizophrenia, which has become an almost meaningless term" (1385).

9. "In 1906 'The Dissociation of a Personality', (his most publicized book), was published in a very dramatic form, to break down the attitude of opposition towards abnormal psychology. The book became so popular that he was called on various occasions to see prominent ladies who thought they had discovered their own multiple personalities" (Claire Morton Prince 1944: 9).

10. *Bowker Annual* 1974: 411–12.

11. American Psychiatric Association (APA) 1980: 257. Other numbered sub-headings include "Psychogenic Amnesia," "Fugue," "Depersonalization Disorder," and the residual "Atypical Dissociative Disorder."

12. APA 1952: 32.

13. APA 1968: 40.

14. APA 1980: 257.

15. Ibid.: 259.

16. Internationally a more conservative tendency is evident, since in the World Health Organization's *Manual of the International Statistical Classification of Diseases, Injuries and Causes of Death* (1977), multiple personality is listed as a subcategory of "hysteria," where it was originally placed in the nineteenth century ("neurasthenia" is retained as well, whereas in *DSMIII* it was abandoned).

17. The author who writes of a multiple personality epidemic asks whether this is due to "an actual increase in the incidence of this disorder, to varying diagnostic inclinations, or to increased tendencies of therapists to report their patients in the literature" (Boor 1982: 302).

18. Greaves 1980: 578. See also Kluft 1984a: 22; Watkins 1984: 73; Bliss 1980: 1388; Coons 1980: 330; Caul 1978a: 5; the list could go on.

19. Greaves 1980: 594.

20. A claim made by Dr. Frank Putnam in workshop at the 1985 meetings. Dr. Putnam is strategically situated at the U.S. National Institute of Mental Health.

21. Bliss 1980: 1393. "It is clear that MPD may not become manifest despite years of clinical observation. Therefore, if exploration of the [diagnostic] indicators and a period of clinical observation does not resolve the matter, hypnosis is used in the diagnostic process" (Kluft 1984a: 23).

22. Bowers et al. 1971: 62; Greaves 1980: 186.

23. Caul 1978a: 1; Watkins 1984: 70.

24. Kluft 1984b: 51; Bliss 1980: 1395.

25. Caul 1978a: 1. "The patient will go through an early denial phase followed by hostility and anger. . . . It is desirable that under hypnotherapy the therapist address all the personalities as much as possible when making such explanations."

26. Kluft 1984b: 55.

27. Gruenewald 1984: 185.

28. Allison 1980. "The Inner Self Helper . . . attempts to guide the patient toward sound mental health. I have had conversations with the ISH aspect of my patients, and I've discovered that they regard themselves as agents of God, with the power to help the main personality. I have encountered as many as six different entities within one individual, each an ISH, and each with a clearly defined rank. The lowest-level ISH is the first to reveal itself during therapy and eventually fuses with the patient. Some of the higher-ranking ISHs never seem truly to fuse; they continue to exist as spiritual teachers of the main personality. They remain dissociated in the mind even after the person becomes whole again" (Allison 1980: 109). Another author who has adopted the concept of the ISH writes that "the ISH can do more and exert more influence than the therapist realizes. As a matter of fact, the therapist will probably be more comfortable once he accepts that the ISH can do more than the therapist in special circumstances" (Caul 1978a: 3). I would recall at this point the relations of Stainton Moses and Mrs. Piper with the Imperator Band—Spiritualist versions of the Inner Self Helper complete with hierarchy of perfection.

29. Smith, Buffington, McCall 1982: 39; Caul 1978a: 4; 1978b: 5; Watkins 1984: 71.

30. Bliss 1980: 1392. "A perceptive, cooperative alter ego [he writes] can be a remarkable guide, keeping the therapist current, while alerting him to resistances or unfinished business" (Ibid.: 1393).

31. Hale 1983: 100.

32. Thigpen and Cleckley 1984: 64.

33. Kluft 1984a: 22.

34. Thigpen and Cleckley 1954: 136; 1957: 211.

35. Schreiber 1973: 65.

36. Ibid.: 67.

37. Ibid.: 63. A somewhat hostile critic of Schreiber's account of Sybil notes that "she [Schreiber] provides us with the details of stylized conversations between the various selves and Dr. Wilbur, but very little sense of the substance of the analytic process. Dr. Wilbur is both one-dimensionally patient and—with her barbiturates and her hypnosis—peculiarly intrusive; and Sybil seems more a shadowy victim than an active participant in her own analysis. . . . Her 16 personalities are displayed like too many pieces of jewelry, like freaks at a circus" (Gordon 1973: 30).

38. Hawksworth 1977.

39. Transcript from Public Broadcasting System program *Frontline* (1984 part II: 13). See Orne et al. (1984).

40. Greaves 1980: 581.

41. *Newsweek*, December 18, 1978: 106; Keyes 1981.

42. 1984: 66. Milligan was treated by Dr. David Caul who himself regards an encounter with a multiple as something of a marvel. "It is some sort of manifestation of ambivalence within us that those who have encountered and/or treated this condition have sometimes found it difficult to separate the intellectual understanding of the notion that such a thing exists

and the emotional impact that such a thing is in fact happening to us and reordering our professional lives. No one treats a multiple and remains the same ever again" (Caul 1978a: 1).

43. Thigpen and Cleckley 1957: 161.

44. Sizemore 1977: 365, 382.

45. Thigpen and Cleckley 1957: 232.

46. "Most of my cases have strong religious beliefs. The ideas of heaven and hell are very real to them. They feel themselves torn between forces of good and evil during their illness. I am convinced that good and evil are very definite, very real forces. I view them as outside influences on the patients' lives. My patients who have related their experiences reinforce this by talking about the devil, Satan or some other specific evil entity fighting against God or His representatives" (Allison 1980: 155). Since Dr. Allison was himself brought up in a strongly religious Presbyterian household and presents himself as a morally tormented individual in his book *Minds in Many Pieces*, this is an interesting observation. Again at the Chicago meetings it was observed that multiples are "99% severely moral masochists." It was also stated that there is "a lot of masochism" among those who choose to work with multiple personality. An entire symposium was devoted to the "effects of therapy on the therapist." It would seem clear that therapist/patient can form a symbiotic system. Perhaps multiples and their therapists are made for each other.

47. Thigpen and Cleckley 1957: 13–15. This is not the first time such a thing has happened. I have already shown how closely multiple personality and the occult were joined in the nineteenth century. In the 1920s Goddard, who described a multiple under the title *Two Souls in One Body* (1927), experienced the same effect when his case became publicly known through the local press. Nonmedical people are sometimes prone to try out the spirit hypothesis themselves, as in the case of a parent who thought his daughter possessed by an "unclean spirit" because she had an affair (R. Douglas Smith 1981: 22). See Wholey (1933) for a similar case.

48. Hawksworth 1977: 116, 126; Peters 1978: 178. Peters commented (see note 5 above) that "we are often highly imaginative individuals for whom fantasy and reality blend into one." She was appreciative that her therapist did not ridicule her belief in possession (Peters 1978: 179).

49. Stevenson 1974: 359.

50. Crabtree 1985: 210.

51. Masson 1985.

52. This story—"Youths Toured Death House"—came from Toronto and was reported in the *Vancouver Sun*, November 1, 1985.

53. See Rosenbaum (1980).

54. APA 1980: 188.

55. Ibid.

56. Ibid.: 321. This possibility received repeated attention in Chicago, and represents a clear vector for the advance of the multiple personality paradigm.

57. Bayer 1981. This source is a radical critique of psychiatry in general, regarding the profession as the policing medical wing of "mainstream" values. Bayer states in his concluding paragraphs that "unlike heterodox tendencies within the profession, the psychiatric mainstream must ultimately affirm the standards of health and disease of the society within which it works. It cannot hold to discordant views regarding the normal and abnormal, the desirable and undesirable, and continue to perform its socially sanctioned function" (p. 194). The trouble psychiatry encountered after the Hinckley verdict indicates the moral and political vulnerability of the discipline.

58. Needham 1981: 76; see also Needham 1973.

59. See Kenny 1978, 1983, and critiques of the foregoing in Simons 1983 and Hahn 1985; also see Simons and Hughes 1985.

60. A reviewer of *Sybil* wrote that "with a schizophrenic mother and both parents adept at 'doublebind,' Sybil found a form of disorder quite other than schizophrenia; clearly more factors are at work, and prediction from form of upbringing to form of breakdown is impossible" (Harding 1973: 26).

References

ARCHIVAL MATERIAL

The chapter on Mary Reynolds is largely based on documentary material in the possession of the Crawford County Historical Society (Meadville, Pennsylvania), supplemented by material held by the College of Physicians of Philadelphia. That in the possession of the former consists of Reynolds family letters and various published and unpublished accounts of the Mary Reynolds case, the latter including a handwritten manuscript by John V. Reynolds, Mary's nephew (cited in note 16 of chapter 1 as John V. Reynolds: n.d.).

The material held by the College of Physicians and entitled "Mitchell Manuscripts, Historical Collections of the Library, College of Physicians of Philadelphia," includes a bound notebook brought together by Silas Weir Mitchell concerning the Reynolds case. The notes to chapter 1 make reference to this collection via the prefix "MM" (Mitchell manuscripts) followed by a number indicating which document in the collection is being cited. The collection includes the following:

MM1: An autobiographical account of Mary's illness addressed to "My Dear Nephew," with a note appended by her nephew that reads as follows: "This manuscript is an exact copy in her own hand writing of a letter written by Miss Mary Reynolds to the undersigned, her nephew, in . . . 1836. It was written to me, at my request, then at Princeton, a student in the Theological Seminary. The deep interest taken in the case by the Rev. Archibald Alexander, D.D., to whom I had given a brief statement of it, was the immediate occasion of my request."

MM2: A cover letter to Silas Weir Mitchell from John V. Reynolds.

MM3: Photocopy of one of Mary's first-state letters (Mary Reynolds to John Reynolds, January 15, 1812).

MM4: Copy of a poetic diatribe against Dr. Blossom, Bemus's assistant.

MM5: An additional copy of MM3.

MM6: Comments by John V. Reynolds on his aunt's letter.

MM7: A newspaper clipping from the *Public Ledger* (apparently inserted by Weir Mitchell out of his own interest) concerning the disappearance of a newspaper editor from Wilkes Barre, Pennsylvania, who turned up in Colorado after losing his memory.

MM8: A manuscript sent to J.K. Mitchell (Silas's father) by Archibald Alexander, and apparently written by John V. Reynolds, Mary's nephew.

MM9: Letter to S.W. Mitchell from William Reynolds, another of Mary's nephews, covering the Alexander manuscript. William Reynolds states that "the first account of the case was given to the Academy of Sciences at Paris by Andrew Ellicot (my grandfather)."

(MM9 is intriguing, and it should be an object of future research to determine just what effect this communication to the Academy of Sciences had on French research concerning multiple personality.)

The rare books section of the Countway Medical Library of the Harvard medical school has papers left by Morton Prince, which include letters to him from Clara Fowler (Miss Beauchamp) and Nellie Bean (B.C.A.). The letters in particular appear to have been assembled by Prince in the course of his writing of case reports. Other material, as Otto Marx has noted, pertains to the public reception of his report of the Beauchamp case (Marx 1970). In addition to this, however, is the biographical memoir of Prince's daughter dated 1944 (cited above as Claire Morton Prince 1944), which she apparently inserted herself, perhaps at the time her father's papers were given over to the Harvard medical school.

PUBLISHED MATERIAL

Abrams, M.H.
 1971 *Natural Supernaturalism.* New York: W.W. Norton.
Addison, Joseph
 1970 *Critical Essays from the Spectator,* edited by D.F. Bond. New York: Oxford.
Alden, Timothy
 1843 Letter quoted in *Historical Collections of the State of Pennsylvania,* edited by S. Day. Philadelphia: George W. Gorton.
Allen, Gay William
 1967 *William James: A Biography.* New York: Viking Press.
Allison, Ralph
 1980 *Minds in Many Pieces.* New York: Rawson, Wade.
American Psychiatric Association
 1952 *Diagnostic and Statistical Manual of Mental Disorders* (DSMI). Washington, D.C.: American Psychiatric Association.
 1968 *DSMII.*
 1980 *DSMIII.*
 1982 *American Psychiatric Association Statement on the Insanity Defense.* Washington, D.C.: American Psychiatric Association.
Augustine, St.
 1927 *The Confessions of St. Augustine,* translated by J.G. Pilkington. New York: Boni & Liveright.
Azam, Eugène
 1887 *Hypnotisme, Double Conscience et Alterations de la Personalité.* Paris: J.B. Bailliere et Fils.
"B" [Nellie Parsons Bean]
 1908–9 "An Introspective Analysis of Co-Conscious Life." *Journal of Abnormal Psychology* 3: 311–60.

"B.C.A" [Nellie Parsons Bean]
1908   "My Life as a Dissociated Personality." *Journal of Abnormal Psychology* 3:240–60.

Baird, Alexander T.
1949   *Richard Hodgson.* London: Psychic Press.

Ballou, Adin
1853   *An Exposition of Views Respecting the Principal Facts, Causes and Peculiarities Involved in Spirit Manifestations.* Boston: Bela Marsh.
1896   *Autobiography of Adin Ballou.* Lowell, Mass.: Vox Populi Press.

Baxter, Norman A.
1954   "History of the Freewill Baptists." Ph.D. diss. (history), Harvard University.

Bayer, Ronald
1981   *Homosexuality and American Psychiatry.* New York: Basic Books.

Bayley, John
1985   "Being Two is Half the Fun." *London Review of Books* 4 July: 13–14.

Beard, George M.
1880   *A Practical Treatise on Nervous Exhaustion (Neurasthenia).* New York: William Wood.
1881a   *American Nervousness: Its Causes and Consequences.* New York: G.P. Putnam's.
1881b   *Nature and Phenomena of Trance.* New York: G.P. Putnam's.
1882   *The Psychology of the Salem Witchcraft Excitement of 1692.* New York: G.P. Putnam's.

Bercovitch, Sacvan
1975   *The Puritan Origins of the American Self.* New Haven: Yale University Press.

Berg, Joseph F.
1856   *Abaddon and Mananain: or Daemons and Guardian Angels.* Philadelphia: Higgins & Perkinpine.

Berger, Peter, and Thomas Luckmann
1967   *The Social Construction of Reality.* Garden City, N.Y.: Anchor Books.

Binger, C.
1966   *Revolutionary Doctor: Benjamin Rush, 1746–1813.* New York: Norton.

Biscop, Paul
1981   "By Spirit Possessed." Master's thesis (anthropology), Simon Fraser University.
1985   "There Is No Death: Belief and the Social Construction of Reality in a Canadian Spiritualist Church." Ph.D. diss. (anthropology), Simon Fraser University.

Bliss, Eugene
   1980   "Multiple Personalities: A Report of 14 Cases with Implications
               for Schizophrenia and Hysteria." *Archives of General
               Psychiatry* 37: 1388–97.

Boor, Myron
   1982   "The Multiple Personality Epidemic." *Journal of Nervous and
               Mental Disease* 170: 302–4.

Boor, Myron, and Philip Coons
   1983   "A Comprehensive Bibliography of Literature Pertaining to
               Multiple Personality." *Psychological Reports* 53: 295–310.

Boorstin, Daniel
   1960   *The Lost World of Thomas Jefferson*. Boston: Beacon Press.

Bowers, M.K., et al.
   1971   "Therapy of Multiple Personality." *International Journal of
               Clinical and Experimental Hypnosis* 19: 57–65.

R.R. Bowker Co.
   1974   *The Bowker Annual of Library and Book Trade Information.*
               New York: R.R. Bowker.

Braun, Bennett, and Roberta Sachs
   1985   "The Development of Multiple Personality Disorder:
               Predisposing, Precipitating, and Perpetuating Factors." In
               Childhood Antecedents of Multiple Personality, edited by
               Richard Kluft. Washington D.C.: American Psychiatric Press.

Breuer, Josef, and Sigmund Freud
   1955   *Studies in Hysteria* (Standard edition of the complete works of
               Sigmund Freud, vol. 2). London: Hogarth Press.

Burnett, Francis Hodgson
   1881   *Through One Administration*. New York: Charles Scribner's.

Byerly, W.W.
   1906   "James Mills Peirce." *Harvard Graduate's Magazine* 14:573–77.

Cady, Edwin H.
   1956   *The Road to Realism*. Syracuse, N.Y.: Syracuse University Press.
   1958   *The Realist at War*. Syracuse, N.Y.: Syracuse University Press.

Capron, E.W.
   1855   *Modern Spiritualism: Its Facts and Fanaticisms, Consistencies
               and Contradictions*. New York: Bela Marsh.

Carlson, Eric T.
   1981   "The History of Multiple Personality in the United States: I. The
               Beginnings." *American Journal of Psychiatry* 138: 666–68.
   1984   "The History of Multiple Personality in the United States: Mary
               Reynolds and Her Subsequent Reputation." *Bulletin of the
               History of Medicine* 58: 72–82.

Caul, David
   1978a   "Treatment Philosophies in the Management of Multiple
               Personality." Paper presented at the American Psychiatric
               Association Conference, Atlanta.

1978b   "Hypnotherapy in the Treatment of Multiple Personalities."
         Paper presented at the American Psychiatric Association
         Conference, Atlanta.

Cerullo, John J.
1982   *The Secularization of the Soul.* Philadelphia: Ishi.

Cleveland, C.C.
1959   *The Great Revival in the West 1797-1805.* N.p., Peter Smith.

Clifford, William Kingdon
1886   "On the Nature of Things in Themselves." In *Lectures and
         Essays.* London: Macmillan.

Coats, R.H.
N.D.   "Birmingham Baptists." (Newspaper clipping in collection
         entitled "Baptist Churches of Birmingham and Surrounding
         Districts" in Birmingham City Library.)

Congdon, M.H., J. Hain, and I. Stevenson
1961   "A Case of Multiple Personality Illustrating the Transition from
         Role-Playing." *Journal of Nervous and Mental Disease* 132:
         497–504.

Couser, G. Thomas
1979   *American Autobiography: The Prophetic Mode.* Amherst:
         University of Massachusetts Press.

Crabtree, Adam
1985   *Multiple Man.* Toronto: Collins.

Cummings, Moses
1858   *Wonderful Works of God.* Irvington: Christian Messenger.

Darnton, Robert
1970   *Mesmerism and the End of the Enlightenment in France.*
         New York: Schocken.

Day, George T.
1853   *The Life of Rev. Martin Cheney.* Providence, R.I.: George H.
         Whitney.

DeFoe, Louis V.
1912   "With the Season Under Way." *Red Book Magazine* 20:369–73.

Denison, Frederic
1878   *Westerly and Its Witnesses.* Providence, R.I.: J.A. & R.A. Reid.

Douglas, Ann
1977   *The Feminization of American Culture.* New York: Knopf.

Doyle, Arthur Conan
1926   *The History of Spiritualism* (2 vols.). London: Cassell.

DuMaurier, George
1894   *Trilby.* London: Osgood, Macilvaine.

Edel, Leon
1975   *Henry James's Letters,* vol. 2 (1875–83). Cambridge: Harvard
         University Press.

Edwards, Jonathan
   1808   *A Treatise Concerning Religious Affections (Works of President Edwards*, vol. 4). Leeds: Edward Baines.
   1817   *The Works of President Edwards*, vol. 1. London: James Black.

Ehrenreich, Barbara, and Deidre English
   1979   *For Her Own Good*. Garden City: Anchor Books.

Ellenberger, Henri F.
   1956   "Fechner and Freud." *Bulletin of the Menninger Clinic* 20: 201–14.
   1970   *The Discovery of the Unconscious*. New York: Basic Books.

Feinstein, Howard M.
   1984   *Becoming William James*. Ithaca, N.Y.: Cornell University Press.

Fellman, Anita, and Michael Fellman
   1981   *Making Sense of Self*. Philadelphia: University of Pennsylvania Press.

Fiske, John
   1874   *Outlines of Cosmic Philosophy* (2 vols.) London: Macmillan.
   1876   "The Unseen World." In *The Unseen World and Other Essays*. Boston: Houghton Mifflin.
   1879   "Chauncey Wright." In *Darwinism and Other Essays*. Boston: Houghton Mifflin.
   1896   "A Universe of Mind-Stuff." In *Excursions of an Evolutionist*. Boston: Houghton Mifflin.

Free-Will Baptist General Conference
   1848   *A Treatise on the Faith of the Free-Will Baptists*. Dover, N.H.: Free-Will Baptist Printing Establishment.

Freud, Sigmund
   1955   *The Future of an Illusion*. London: Hogarth Press.
   1959   "An Autobiographical Study." *Standard Edition* vol. 20. London: Hogarth Press.
   1961a   "The Ego and the Id." *Standard Edition* vol. 19. London: Hogarth Press.
   1961b   "A Seventeenth Century Demonological Neurosis." *Standard Edition* vol. 19. London: Hogarth Press.
   1966   "Pre Psycho Analytic Publication." *Standard Edition* vol. 1. London: Hogarth Press.

Freud, Sigmund, and Carl Jung
   1974   *The Freud-Jung Letters*. Princeton: Princeton University Press.

Fuller, Robert C.
   1982   *Mesmerism and the American Cure of Souls*. Philadelphia: University of Pennsylvania Press.

Gauld, Alan
   1968   *The Founders of Psychical Research*. New York: Schocken.

Gifford, George
  1978   "George Arthur Waterman 1872–1960, and Office Psychiatry."
            In *Psychoanalysis, Psychotherapy and the New England
            Medical Scene, 1894–1944*, edited by George Gifford. New York:
            Science History Publishers.

Goddard, Henry
  1927   *Two Souls in One Body?* New York: Dodd, Mead.

Goodrich-Freer, Ada
  1907   "A Case of Double Personality." *Occult Review* 5, no. 1:
            95–104; no 2: 96–101.

Gordon, James S.
  1973   "Sybil." *New York Times Review of Books.* 17 June.

Greaves, G.B.
  1980   "Multiple Personality 165 Years after Mary Reynolds." *Journal
            of Nervous and Mental Disease* 168: 577–96.

Gregory, O.
  1833   *Memoirs and Private Correspondence of the Rev. Robert Hall.*
            London: Griffin & Co.

Gruenewald, Doris
  1984   "On the Nature of Multiple Personality: Comparisons with
            Hypnosis." *International Journal of Clinical and Experimental
            Hypnosis*, 32: 170–90.

Hahn, Robert
  1985   "Culture-Bound Syndromes Unbound." *Social Science and
            Medicine* 21: 165–71.

Halbwachs, Maurice
  1980   *The Collective Memory.* New York: Harper Colophon.

Hale, Ellen
  1983   "Inside the Divided Mind." *New York Times Magazine*,
            17 April.

Hale, Nathan G.
  1971   *Freud and the Americans.* New York: Oxford.
  1975   "Introduction," to Morton Prince, *Psychotherapy and Multiple
            Personality.* Cambridge: Harvard University Press.

Hall, G. Stanley
  1918   "A Medium in the Bud." *American Journal of Psychology* 29:
            144–58.

Hammond, C.
  1852   *The Pilgrimage of Thomas Paine.* Rochester: D.M. Dewey.

Harding, D.W.
  1973   "Crazy Mixed Up Kids." *New York Review of Books* vol. 20,
            no. 10; 14 June.

Hardinge, Emma
  1870   *Modern American Spiritualism.* New York: American News
            Company.

Harlow, Virginia
1949   "William Dean Howells and Thomas Sergeant Perry." *Boston Public Library Quarterly* 1: 135–50.
1950   *Thomas Sergeant Perry: A Biography.* Durham, N.C.: Duke University Press.

Harvard College Class of 1895
1915   *Fifth Report.* Cambridge: Crimson Printing Co.
1945   *Fiftieth Report:* Cambridge.

Hatch, Nathan O.
1980   "The Christian Movement and the Demand for a Theology of the People." *Journal of American History* 67: 545–67.

Hawksworth, Henry
1977   *The Five of Me.* New York: Pocket Books.

Hawthorn, Jeremy
1983   *Multiple Personality and the Disintegration of Literary Character.* New York: St. Martin's Press.

Heelas, Paul
1981   "Introduction: Indigenous Psychologies." In *Indigenous Psychologies: The Anthropology of the Self,* edited by Paul Heelas and Andrew Lock. New York: Academic Press.

Hilgard, Ernest
1977   *Divided Consciousness: Multiple Controls in Human Thought and Action.* New York: Wiley-Interscience.

(no author)
n.d.   *History of Crawford County, Pennsylvania.* N.p., Warner, Beers & Co.

Hodgson, Richard
1891–92   "A Case of Double Consciousness." *Proceedings of the Society for Psychical Research* 7: 221-55.
1898   "A Further Record of Further Phenomena of Trance." *Proceedings of the Society for Psychical Research* 13: 284–582.

Honorable Society of Cymmrodorion
1959   *The Dictionary of Welsh Biography Down to 1940.*

Horton, Robin
1961   "Destiny and the Unconscious in West Africa." *Africa* 31: 110–16.
1983   "Social Psychologies: African and Western." In Myer Fortes, *Oedipus and Job in West African Religion.* Cambridge: Cambridge University Press.

Howe, M.A. DeWolfe
1906   *A Memoir of Richard Hodgson.* Boston: Tavern Club.
1924   *Barrett Wendell and His Letters.* Boston: Atlantic Monthly Press.
1934   *Semi-Centennial History of the Tavern Club 1884–1934.* Cambridge, Mass.: Riverside Press.
1941   *A Venture in Remembrance.* Boston: Little, Brown.

Howells, Mildred
1928   *Life in Letters of William Dean Howells*. Garden City, N.Y.: Doubleday, Doran.

Howells, William Dean
1880   *The Undiscovered Country*. Boston: Houghton, Mifflin.
1888   Review of George Pellew's *In Castle and Cabin, Harper's Weekly* October.
1890   Review of George Pellew's *John Jay. Harper's*, September.
1892a "Introduction," to George Pellew, *The Poems of George Pellew*. Boston: W.B. Clarke.
1892b "George Pellew." *Cosmopolitan* 13: 527–30.
1903   *Questionable Shapes*. New York: Harper.
1907   *Between the Dark and the Daylight*. New York: Harper.

Hyslop, James H.
1907   "Dr. Richard Hodgson." *Journal of the American Society for Psychical Research* 1: 2–15.

Institute of Noetic Sciences
1984   *Investigations* 1: 1–23.

International Society for the Study of Multiple Personality
1985   *Newsletter* 3.

James, Alice
1964   *The Diary of Alice James*, edited by Leon Edel. New York: Dodd, Mead.

James, William
1890   "The Hidden Self." *Scribner's Magazine* 7: 361–73.
1897   *The Will to Believe*. New York: Longmans, Green.
1909   "Report on Mrs. Piper's Hodgson Control." *Proceedings of the Society for Psychical Research* 23: 2–121.
1914   *The Varieties of Religious Experience*. New York: Longmans, Green.
1920   *The Letters of William James* (2 vols.). Boston. Atlantic Monthly Press.
1976   *Essays in Radical Empiricism*. Cambridge: Harvard University Press.
1977   *A Pluralistic Universe*. Cambridge: Harvard University Press.
1981   *Principles of Psychology* (3 vols.). Cambridge: Harvard University Press.

Janet, Pierre
1929   *The Major Symptoms of Hysteria*. New York: Macmillan.

Jones, A.D.
1842   *Memoir of Elder Abner Jones*. Boston: William Crosby.

Jones, Ernest
1955   *The Life and Work of Sigmund Freud* (vol. 2). New York: Basic Books. (vol. 3, 1957)

Kenny, Michael G.
1978   "*Latah:* The Symbolism of a Putative Mental Disorder." *Culture, Medicine, and Psychiatry* 2: 209–23.

1981   "Multiple Personality and Spirit Possession." *Psychiatry* 44: 337–58.
1983   "Paradox Lost: The Latah Problem Revisited." *Journal of Nervous and Mental Disease* 171: 159–67.
1984   "Miss Beauchamp's True Identity." *Journal of the American Psychiatric Association* 141:920.

Kenny, Michael G. (ed.)
1985   "New Approaches to Culture-Bound Mental Disorders." *Social Science and Medicine* 21: 163–228.

Kerr, Howard
1972   *Mediums, and Spirit Rappers, and Roaring Radicals*. Urbana: University of Illinois Press.

Keyes, Daniel
1981   *The Minds of Billy Milligan*. New York: Random House.

Kleinman, Arthur
1980   *Patients and Healers in the Context of Culture*. Berkeley: University of California Press.

Kluft, Richard
1984a   "An Introduction to Multiple Personality Disorder." *Psychiatric Annals* 14: 19–24.
1984b   "Aspects of the Treatment of Multiple Personality Disorder." *Psychiatric Annals* 14: 51–55.
1984c   "Treatment of Multiple Personality Disorder: A Study of 33 Cases." *Psychiatric Clinics of North America* 7: 9–29.
n.d.a.   "Making the Diagnosis of Multiple Personality Disorder (MPD)." *Directions in Psychiatry* vol. 5, Lesson 23.
n.d.b.   "The Treatment of Multiple Personality Disorder (MPD): Current Concepts." *Directions in Psychiatry* vol. 5, Lesson 24.

Kluft, Richard (ed.)
1985   *Childhood Antecedents of Multiple Personality*. Washington D.C.: American Psychiatric Press.

Langley, A.S.
1939   *Birmingham Baptists Past and Present*. Birmingham, England: Kingsgate Press.

Langness, L.L.
1965   "Hysterical Psychosis in the New Guinea Highlands: A Bena Bena Example." *Psychiatry* 28: 258–77.

Lewis, I.M.
1971   *Ecstatic Religion*. Harmondsworth, England: Penguin Books.

Lienhardt, Godfrey
1961   *Divinity and Experience*. Oxford: Clarendon Press.

Locke, Edward
1912a   "How I Made Belasco Produce My Play." *McClure's Magazine* 39: 44–53.
1912b   "The Case of Becky." *Hearst's Magazine* 22: 113–28.

Locke, John
1959   *An Essay Concerning Human Understanding*. New York: Dover.
McKellar, Peter
1979   *Mindsplit*. London: Dent.
McLoughlin, William G.
1971   *New England Dissent, 1630-1833* (2 vols.) Cambridge: Harvard
            University Press.
Macklin, June
1977   "A Connecticut Yankee in Summer Land." In *Case Studies in
            Spirit Possession*, edited by V. Crapanzano and V. Garrison.
            New York: Wiley.
Macnish, Robert
1854   *The Philosophy of Sleep*. Hartford: Silus Andrus.
Malone, Dumas (ed.)
1934   "Pellew, Henry Edward." In *Dictionary of American Biography*,
            vol. 8: 409–10.
Marini, Stephen A.
1982   *Radical Sects of Revolutionary New England*. Cambridge:
            Harvard University Press.
Marx, Otto
1970   "Morton Prince and the Dissociation of a Personality." *Journal
            of the History of the Behavioral Sciences* 6: 120–30.
Masson, Jeffrey
1985   *The Assault on Truth*. New York: Penguin.
Mead, George Herbert
1934   *Mind, Self and Society*. Chicago: University of Chicago Press.
Miller, Karl
1985   *Doubles: Studies in Literary History*. London: Oxford
            University Press.
Miller, Perry
1939   *The New England Mind: The Seventeenth Century*. Cambridge:
            Harvard University Press.
Mitchell, John Kearsley
1859   *Five Essays*, edited by S.W. Mitchell. Philadelphia: J.B.
            Lippincott.
Mitchell, S.L.
1816   "A Double Conciousness, or a Duality of Person in the Same
            Individual." *Medical Repository* 3: 185–86.
Mitchell, Silas Weir
1884   *Fat and Blood*. Philadelphia: J.B. Lippincott.
1885   *Lectures on Diseases of the Nervous System*. Philadelphia: Lea
            Brothers.
1889   *Mary Reynolds: A Case of Double Consciousness*. Philadelphia:
            Wm. J. Dorman.
1896   *Address to the Students of Radcliffe College*: Cambridge.

Miyoshi, Masao
    1969   *The Divided Self*. New York: New York University Press.
Moore, Merrill
    1938   "Morton Prince, M.D., 1854-1929." *Journal of Nervous and Mental Disease* 87: 701-10.
Moore, R. Lawrence
    1972   "Spiritualism and Science: Reflections on the First Decade of the Spirit Rappings." *American Quarterly* 24: 474-500.
    1977   *In Search of White Crows*. New York: Oxford.
Morison, Elting E.
    1951   *The Letters of Theodore Roosevelt*, vol. 1. Cambridge: Harvard University Press.
Morrison, A.B.
    1873   *Spiritualism and Necromancy*. Cincinnati, Ohio: Hitchcock & Walden.
Moses, William Stainton ["M.A. (Oxon)."]
    1879   *Spirit Identity*. London: W.H. Harrison.
    1880   *Higher Aspects of Spiritualism*. London: E.W. Allen.
    1894   *Spirit Teachings*. London: London Spiritualist Alliance.
Myers, Frederic W.H.
    1903   *Human Personality and its Survival of Bodily Death* (2 vols.) London: Longmans, Green.
Needham, Rodney
    1973   *Belief, Language and Experience*. Oxford: Blackwell.
    1981   "Inner States as Universals: Sceptical Reflections on Human Nature." In *Indigenous Psychologies: The Anthropology of the Self*, edited by Paul Heelas and Andrew Lock. London and New York: Academic Press.
Neisser, Ulric (ed.)
    1982   *Memory Observed: Remembering in Natural Contexts*. San Francisco: W.H. Freeman.
Nelson, G.K.
    1969   *Spiritualism in Society*. London: Routledge and Kegan Paul.
Newman, Philip
    1964   "'Wild Man' Behavior in a New Guinea Highlands Community." *American Anthropologist* 66: 1-19.
Nicolson, M.H.
    1946   *Newton Demands the Muse*. Princeton: Princeton University Press.
Orne, Martin, David Dinges, and Emily Orne
    1984   "On the Differential Diagnosis of Multiple Personality in the Forensic Context." *International Journal of Clinical and Experimental Hypnosis* 32: 118-69.
Pellew, George
    1888a   *Woman and the Commonwealth*. Boston: Houghton, Mifflin.
    1888b   "The New Battle of the Books." *The Forum* 5: 564-73.

1888c	*In Castle and Cabin.* New York: G.P. Putnam's.
1890	*John Jay.* Boston: Houghton, Mifflin.
1892	*Poems of George Pellew.* Boston: W.B. Clarke.

Perry, Ralph Barton
1936   *The Thought and Character of William James.* Boston: Little, Brown.

Perry, Thomas Sergeant
1906   *John Fiske.* Boston: Small, Maynard.

Peters, Christina
1978   *Tell Me Who I Am Before I Die.* New York: Rawson Associates.

Piper, Alta
1929   *The Life and Work of Mrs. Piper.* London: Kegan Paul, Trench, Trubner.

Plumer, W.S.
1860   "Mary Reynolds: A Case of Double Consciousness." *Harper's Magazine* 20: 807–12.

Podmore, Frank
1902   *Modern Spiritualism,* London: Methuen.
1908   *The Naturalisation of the Supernatural.* New York: G.P. Putnam's.
1910   *The Newer Spiritualism.* London: Unwin.

Priestley, Joseph
1806   *Memoirs of Dr. Joseph Priestley.* Northhampton, Pa.: John Binns.

Prince, Morton
1885   *The Nature of Mind and Human Automatism.* Philadelphia: J.B. Lippincott.
1898–99   "A Contribution to the Study of Hysteria and Hypnosis." *Proceedings of the Society for Psychical Research* 14: 79–97.
1903   "Professor Strong on the Relation Between the Mind and the Body." *The Psychological Review* 10: 650–58.
1906   *The Dissociation of a Personality.* New York: Longmans, Green.
1910   "Cerebral Localization from the Point of View of Function and Symptoms." *Journal of Nervous and Mental Disease* 37: 337–54.
1914   *The Unconscious.* New York: Macmillan.
1919   "The Psychogenesis of Multiple Personality." *Journal of Abnormal Psychology* 14: 225–80.
1920   "Miss Beauchamp: the Theory of the Psychogenesis of Multiple Personality." *Journal of Abnormal Psychology* 15: 67–135.
1928   "Why the Body Has a Mind and the Survival of Consciousness after Death." *Mind* 37: 1–20.
1939   *Clinical and Experimental Studies in Personality.* New York: Sci-Art Publishers.
1971   *Psychotherapy and Multiple Personality,* edited by Nathan G. Hale. Cambridge: Harvard University Press.

1975   *Psychotherapy and Multiple Personality: Selected Essays,* edited
            by Nathan G. Hale. Cambridge: Harvard University Press.

Raupert, J. Godfrey
1914   *The Dangers of Spiritualism.* St. Louis: B. Herder.
1919   *The New Black Magic.* New York: Devin-Adair.

Reise, Walther, and Ebbe Hoff
1950–51   "A History of the Doctrine of Cerebral Localization." *Journal of
            the History of Medicine and Allied Sciences* 5: 50–71; 6:
            439–70.

Reynolds, John
1870   *Autobiography of John Reynolds* (privately printed on the
            occasion of his 88th Birthday).

Reynolds, John Earle
1938   *In French Creek Valley.* Meadville, Pa.: Crawford County
            Historical Society.

Ribot, Théodule
1882   *Diseases of Memory,* translated by W.H Smith, New York: D.
            Appleton.
1887   *Diseases of Personality,* translated by J. Fitzgerald. New York:
            Fitzgerald.

Rider, Fremont
1909   *Are the Dead Alive?* New York: B.W. Dodge.

Robbins, Anne Manning
1911   *Both Sides of the Veil.* Boston: Sherman, French.

Rose, R.B.
1960   "The Priestley Riots of 1791." *Past and Present* 18: 68-75.
1964   "Protestant Nonconformity." In *A History of the County of
            Warwick,* edited by W.B. Stephens, vol. 7. London.

Rosenbaum, Milton
1980   "The Role of the Term Schizophrenia in the Decline of
            Diagnoses of Multiple Personality." *Archives of General
            Psychiatry* 37: 1383–85.

Rush, Benjamin
1835   *Medical Inquiries and Observations upon the Diseases of the
            Mind.* Philadelphia: Grigg & Elliot.

Schofield, R.W.
1963   *The Lunar Society of Birmingham.* London: Oxford.

Schreiber, Flora Rheta
1973   *Sybil.* New York: Warner Communications.

Sidgwick, Mrs. Henry
1905–7   "Richard Hodgson: In Memoriam." *Proceedings of the Society
            for Psychical Research* 19: 356–67.
1915   "A Contribution to the Study of the Psychology of Mrs. Piper's
            Trance Phenomena." *Proceedings of the Society for Psychical
            Research* 28: i–652.

Simons, Ronald C.
1980   "The Resolution of the Latah Paradox." *Journal of Nervous and Mental Disease* 168: 195–206.
1983   "Latah II: Problems with a Purely Symbolic Interpretation." *Journal of Nervous and Mental Disease* 171: 168–75.

Simons, Ronald C., and Charles C. Hughes (eds.)
1985   *The Culture-Bound Syndromes.* Dordrecht: Reidel.

Sizemore, Chris Costner
1977   *I'm Eve.* New York: Jove/HBJ.

Smith, Elias
1840   *The Life, Conversion, Preaching, Travels and Sufferings of Elias Smith.* Boston.

Smith, G.D.
1977   "Religion and the Development of American Culture: Western Pennsylvania 1760-1820." Ph.D. diss. (history), Harvard University.

Smith, R. Douglas
1981   "Hypnosis, Multiple Personality, and Magic: A Case Study." *Voices: The Art and Science of Psychotherapy* 17: 20-23.

Smith, R. Douglas, Perry Buffington, and Ray McCall
1982   *Multiple Personality: Theory, Diagnosis, and Treatment.* New York: Irvington.

Smith, Timothy L.
1957   *Revivalism and Social Reform.* New York and Nashville: Abingdon Press.

Starr, Paul
1982   *The Social Transformation of American Medicine.* New York: Basic Books.

Stevenson, Ian
1974   *Twenty Cases Suggestive of Reincarnation.* Charlottesville: University of Virginia Press.

Stevenson, Robert Louis
1886   *The Strange Case of Dr. Jekyll and Mr. Hyde.* London: Longmans, Green.

Stock, R.D.
1982   *The Holy and the Daemonic from Sir Thomas Browne to William Blake.* Princeton: Princeton University Press.

Strouse, Jean
1982   *Alice James.* Boston: Houghton, Mifflin.

Sutcliffe, J.P., and J. Jones
1962   "Personal Identity, Multiple Personality, and Hypnosis." *International Journal of Clinical and Experimental Hypnosis* 10: 231-69.

Tanner, Amy
1910   *Studies in Spiritism.* New York: Appleton.

Taylor, Besse
1927 "Elder John Taylor." Records and Papers. Westerly Historical Society: 61–70.

Taylor, Eugene
1983 William James on Exceptional Mental States. New York: Scribners.

Taylor, W.S.
1928 Morton Prince and Abnormal Psychology. New York: Appleton.

Taylor, W.S., and M.F. Martin
1944 "Multiple Personality." Journal of Abnormal and Social Psychology 39: 281–300.

Thigpen, Corbett, and Hervey Cleckley
1954 "A Case of Multiple Personality." Journal of Abnormal and Social Psychology 49: 135–51.
1957 The Three Faces of Eve. New York: Popular Library.
1984 "On the Incidence of Multiple Personality Disorder." International Journal of Clinical and Experimental Hypnosis 32: 63–66.

Thomas, D.
1970 Travels Through the Western Country in the Summer of 1816. N.p., Hafner.

Townend, Peter (ed.)
1967 Burke's Peerage. London: Burke's Peerage Ltd.

Turner, Victor
1974 Dramas, Fields, and Metaphors. Ithaca, N.Y.: Cornell University Press.

Watkins, John
1984 "The Bianchi (L.A. Hillside Strangler) Case: Sociopath or Multiple Personality." International Journal of Clinical and Experimental Hypnosis 32: 67–101.

Wayland, Francis
1854 The Elements of Intellectual Philosophy. N.p., Phillips, Sampson.

Wendell, Barrett
1891 Cotton Mather: The Puritan Priest. New York: Dodd, Mead.

WGBH Educational Foundation
1984 Transcripts of Frontline documentary, The Mind of a Murderer (2 parts). Boston.

Whittemore, J.K.
1906 "James Mills Peirce." Science 24: 40–48.

Wholey, C.C.
1933 "A Case of Multiple Personality." American Journal of Psychiatry 12: 653–88.

Wiener, Philip
1965 Evolution and the Founders of Pragmatism. New York: Harper & Row.

Wills, Gary
  1979   *Inventing America.* New York: Vintage.

Wood, Ann Douglas
  1973   "The Fashionable Diseases: Women's Complaints and Their Treatment in Nineteenth-Century America." *Journal of Interdisciplinary History* 4: 25–52.

World Health Organization
  1977   *Manual of the International Statistical Classification of Diseases, Injuries and Causes of Death.* Geneva.

Wright, Chauncey
  1877   *Philosophical Discussions.* New York: H. Holt.

Young, Robert Maxwell
  1970   *Mind, Brain and Adaptation in the Nineteenth Century.* Oxford: Clarendon.

Index

Abuse: childhood sexual, in "Sybil" case, 16, 176; etiology of multiple personality, role in, 15, 176; and Masson's critique of Freud, 176–77. *See also* Freud, Sigmund; Trauma

Addison, Joseph: on light and landscape, 193n.35; Mary Reynolds and prose of, 44; *Spectator*, and concept of transmigration, 46. *See also* Reynolds, Mary; Transmigration

American Psychiatric Association: and Benjamin Rush, 41; on causation of mental disorder, 162–63; *Diagnostic and Statistical Manual* of, 165–67; and the insanity defense, 162–63. *See also Diagnostic and Statistical Manual*; Insanity defense

Amnesia: in Ansel Bourne, case of, 67; Benjamin Rush, description by, 192n.26; and hypnosis, 17–18; in Mary Reynolds, case of, 27; multiple personality, importance in diagnosis of, 14–15, 28, 180; in Nellie Bean, case of, 149; situational factors affecting, 17–18. *See also* Bean, Nellie Parsons; Bourne, Ansel; Hypnosis; Memory; Multiple Personality; Reynolds, Mary

Anthropology: and cultural relativism, 185; and psychiatry, 182; and spirit possession, 1, 2, 189n.1

Augustine, Saint: on divided self, 6; and Puritan culture, 6. *See also* Puritanism

"B" (pseudonym). *See* Bean, Mrs. Nellie Parsons

"B.C.A." (pseudonym). *See* Bean, Mrs. Nellie Parsons

Bali: multiple personality and similarity to trance on, 187

Ballou, Adin: reflections on life and the spirit world, 103; Universalist, utopian socialist, and Spiritualist, 99–100. *See also* Spiritualism; Universalist Church

Baptist Church: and Calvinism, 29, 73; conversion as criterion for membership, 37; and Elias Smith, 73; "Free-Will" Baptists, 23, 74–75; and Mary Reynolds, family of, 29, 38; Robert Hall and Robert Robinson, 191n.20. *See also* Bourne, Ansel; Calvinism; Conversion; Reynolds, Mary; Smith, Elias

Bean, Mrs. Nellie Parsons ("B" and "B.C.A.," pseudonyms): amnesia, mutual, of personalities, 149; as "Bertha Amory," 153; chapter concerning, synopsis of, 20–21; family of, 140; literature, role of in self-knowledge, 153; as Morton Prince's research assistant, 155, 210n.72; *My Life as a Dissociated Personality*, 152; neurasthenia, initial diagnosis of, 132, 141; personalities, characteristics of, 149; remarriage, problem of, 154; sexual factors in case, Morton Prince on, 151; spirit possession, imagery of in case, 150; trauma, apparent absence in early history, 140; true identity discovery of, 140; widowhood, effects on, 152. *See also* Amnesia; Burnett, Frances Hodgson; Literature; Neurasthenia; Prince, Morton; Spirit possession; Trauma

Beard, Dr. George Miller: *American Nervousness*, 133; on Jamesian quality in American women,

Alice; Myers, Frederic, W.H.;
Piper, Mrs. Lenora; Prince,
Morton; Protestantism; Society
for Psychical Research;
Spiritualism

Janet, Pierre: American researchers,
influence on, 87; on "Félida X,"
case of, 87; on multiple personality, its unusual incidence in
America, 197n.34. *See also*
James, William; Prince, Morton

Jefferson, Thomas, 25, 59; and Benjamin Rush, 40

Jekyll and Hyde (*Dr. Jekyll and Mr.
Hyde*): Christian themes in tale
of, 4; current incarnations of,
181; and multiple personality,
4; in play derived from case of
Clara Norton Fowler, 158; as
Romantic theme, 83. *See also*
Fowler, Clara Norton; Nature
and culture; Romanticism; Stevenson, Robert Louis

Jones, Rev. Abner: and Elias Smith,
founders of "Christian"
Church, 75. *See also* "Christian" Church

Jones, Ernest: biographer of Freud,
92; and Clark University con-
ference on psychology, 92; with
Morton Prince on the *Journal of
Abnormal Psychology*, 207n.28;
Morton Prince, recollections of,
131. *See also* Freud, Sigmund;
Prince, Morton

Jung, Carl: and Clark University
conference on psychology, 92,
109; and G. Stanley Hall, 109;
spirit medium, encounter with,
109

Kuhn, Thomas: on paradigm formation and "normal science," 180

Lévi-Strauss, Claude: on nature and
culture, 5. *See also* Nature and
culture

Lewis, I.M.: on spirit possession,
189n.1. *See also* Spirit
possession

Literature: Clara Norton Fowler,
role in case of, 208n.31; Mary
Reynolds, literary influences on,
43–49, 95; and multiple personality, 4; Nellie Parsons Bean,
importance in case of, 153; self-
knowledge, importance to
acquisition of, 18. *See also*
Bean, Nellie Parsons; Fowler,
Clara Norton; Self-knowledge

Locke, Edward: and "The Case of
Becky," play based on experiences of Clara Norton Fowler,
157–58, 211n.81

Locke, John: and empiricism, 81;
Mary Reynolds, relevance to
case of, 27–28, 81; personal
identity, and relation to memory, 28, 190n. 2; and *tabula
rasa*, 27; William James, on
Locke and multiple selves,
198n.36. *See also* Amnesia;
Empiricism; Multiple personality; Reynolds, Mary

"M.A. (Oxon.)" (pseudonym). *See*
Moses, Rev. William Stainton

"MacLeod, Fiona" (pseudonym). *See*
Sharp, William

Macnish, Robert: Mary Reynolds,
and case of, 56, 197n.32; on
multiple personality and mesmerism, relation between,
194n.47; and multiple personality, French understanding of,
86, 197n.32. *See also* Mesmerism; Reynolds, Mary

Masson, Jeffrey: *The Assault on
Truth*, critique of Freud, 176.
See also Abuse; Freud, Sigmund

Mead, George Herbert, on multiple
personality, 22

Meadville (Pa.): description of, in
1816, 191n.11; location, 31;